Edited and with an introduction by
Alan Williams

Film and
Nationalism

Rutgers
University
Press
New Brunswick,
New Jersey,
and London

Library of Congress Cataloging-in-Publication Data

Film and nationalism / edited and with an introduction by Alan Williams.
    p.   cm. — (Rutgers depth of field series)
  Includes bibliographical references and index.
  ISBN 0-8135-3039-3 (cloth : alk. paper) — ISBN 0-8135-3040-7 (pbk. :
alk. paper)
  1. Motion pictures.   I. Williams, Alan, 1947–   II. Series.

PN1994.F43817   2002
791.43—dc21   2001041685

British Cataloging-in-Publication data for this book is available from the British
Library.

This collection copyright © 2002 by Rutgers, The State University
For copyrights to individual pieces please see first page of each essay.

Manufactured in the United States of America

Contents

A "Global" (Postnational) Future?

Film and Nationalism

Alan Williams

Introduction

The cinema, the nation: both are comparatively recent phenomena in the grand scheme of history, and both seem poised for radical change—though of what sort one cannot say. Yet we would be mistaken to assume that the recent, intense debate about "globalization" (both in mass media, and in economic and cultural relations in general) means that the relations between cinema and nationalism have only recently become destabilized. To the contrary, cinema and nation have always had shifting, problematic functions with regard to one another and to the larger arena of world culture.

Nationalism (and Cinema)

In the beginning, the cinema appeared to many observers to be the first truly global, transnational medium, for this simple reason: it had no, or very little, language. Later, during its first decade, it acquired language (intertitles) but still had no speech. Modern scholars of film and nationalism almost invariably take Benedict Anderson's seminal book *Imagined Communities: Reflections on the Origin and Spread of Nationalism* as their point of departure, and particularly his definition of the modern nation: "It is an imagined political community—and imagined as both inherently limited and sovereign."[1] But we might do well to worry about other of Anderson's arguments when we think about cinema and nations, particularly his idea that "print-language is what [originally] invents nationalism" (134). For the odd fact—in Andersonian terms—is that when cinema had only print-language, that is to say written titles, it was comparatively untouched by nationalism—at least, by self-conscious and potentially aggressive nationalism. It was still an inherently international medium: to make a "foreign" version of a film, you had only to put in new intertitles in the new target language.[2] National barriers would definitively arrive only with (recorded) *speech*. It seems likely that the technology is what is crucial here; one could argue that sound recording preserves, objectifies and opens speech to cultural manipulation and examination in some of the same ways that print once did.

Anderson's book is ritually invoked by almost all film scholars who deal with questions of film and nationhood—invoked for the catch phrase "imagined community," and then, most often, abandoned. Future film scholars might do well to study Anderson, and other, recent and innovative works in the field, more closely—if only to confront the extent to which *any* study of nationalism, in any area (and even the fiction film) must be profoundly *historical*. For Anderson, the origin of true nationalism requires two sets of circumstances: an absence and a presence. The absence is the relative decline of the great cultural systems of the *religious community* and the *dynastic realm*. The "nation" does not exactly replace these things, but they must be in retreat for true nationalism to come into being. The necessary new presence is of two systems: print language, which creates inclusive, extendable communities, and a new way of thinking of history—as taking place in "homogenous, empty time" (26). This is the time of the modern calendar, in which the nation can be

> conceived as a solid community moving steadily down (or up) history. An American will never meet, or even know the names of more than a handful of his 240,000-odd [*sic*] fellow Americans. He has no idea of what they are up to at any one time. But he has complete confidence in their steady, anonymous, simultaneous activity (26).

Note that, although Anderson doesn't make the point forcefully (he corrects this to some extent in the book's second edition), a homogeneous, empty *space* is a necessary correlate for his "empty" time. Note, also, that both empty time and empty space are not only characteristic of the novel, as he argues, but even more so of the "classical" narrative cinema.

In Anderson's analysis, nationalism has gone through a series of relatively distinct stages, from the "anti-metropolitan resistance" of European colonists in the Western hemisphere (roughly 1760–1830), to the consolidation of more recent, complex nationalisms which can exist in spite of combining multiple languages, thanks to modern audiovisual mass media (for example, Mozambique or Switzerland). The crucial element in this progression—for which print-language is absolutely necessary—is the creation of "a 'model' of 'the' independent national state [which became] available for pirating."[3] From about the second decade of the nineteenth century on, this model imposed a rigorous standard of inclusiveness (a "nation" includes all the members of a particular linguistic community within a historically coherent, "empty" space), which resulted in pressures to abolish serfdom and slavery, to promote popular education, to expand suffrage, and so on. This would be so even in the "official nationalisms" that later arose in countries such as Russia to defend entrenched power-groups ("primarily, but not exclusively, dynastic and aristocratic [ones that were] threatened with exclusion from, or marginalization in, popular imagined communities" [109–10]).

According to Anderson, print-language was crucial in the early development of nationalism. It was print-language that allowed the dissemination of nationalist documents such as dictionaries and grammars of "native" languages, as well as adaptably nationalist genres such as novels. And it was print-language that assured the preservation and dissemination of the very concept of the nation, that made it "available for pirating." In other words, Anderson considers nationalism a "modular" phenomenon— though a more familiar synonym (in cinema studies at least) would be *generic*. And therein may lie a serious problem for film scholars who rely on Anderson's book. In a bracing critique in his book *Film/Genre*, Rick Altman argues that "Anderson concentrates on the moment when a nation was formed and stops there, failing to acknowledge the ongoing nature of the process he has described."[4] Nationhood, in other words, is not merely established, it must be *maintained*; its definition, therefore, will inevitably shift over time.

Furthermore, modern mass media would play an absolutely crucial role in this ongoing process of sustaining and (in the process) redefining nationalism(s). Rather than simply being *related to* the nation, the cinema would be an essential part of a *process* of defining nations—and not solely in Anderson's last, multilingual phase of nation formation. The cinema and other mass media would be essential arenas for conflicting interest groups to quarrel over the definition of the "nation." We have seen such conflicts enacted most overtly in the state of Israel and its recently reactivated quarrel over the definition of Jewishness. But all nations enact such quarrels: France, for example, has lately engaged in a debate over the representation of Marianne, symbol of Liberty. As Altman points out, national anthems and other symbols of nationhood are perpetual points of conflict, and such conflicts are routinely carried out in the mass media, with cinema having a place of pride on the cultural and technological battleground.

National Cinemas

At the core of any discussion of film and nationalism lies the question: What is a national cinema? In arguably the most influential single recent article about the subject, Andrew Higson points out that the idea of a national cinema "has been appropriated in a variety of ways, for a variety of reasons: there is not a single universally accepted discourse."[5] Higson's highly condensed, at times elliptical, argument offers one way of conceptualizing the dominent approaches to the topic. Of crucial importance is his observation that most scholars simply equate "national cinema" with the body of films produced in or by a given country, while patterns of film *consumption* (which invariably involve an international range of product) are neglected. In concentrating on production at the expense of viewing practices, most scholars concerned with the topic assume that a "national" cinema assumes different aspects as it is examined from different perspectives, and/or that it may be broken down into conceptually different sectors of production. Stephen Crofts offers one typology of ideal sorts of national cinemas. In

Crofts's view, national cinemas may produce several forms of cinema: "art films" that target a specialized, upscale market; or "third cinema," which confronts the question of competing with "Hollywood" head on, by articulating a critique of commercial mainstream cinema; or a purely commercial mainstream cinema that differs from "Hollywood" mainly by its use of the nation's particular language and cultural themes; and so on, with most "national cinemas" being combinations of the various categories. This sort of typology is extremely useful, but we should be wary of letting it lead us to conclude that there is such a thing as a "national cinema." We might do better to think about national cinemas in the way that Rick Altman proposes that we study film genres—as sites of conflict among different interest groups (and film scholars are simply one interest group among many).

Evidence of such conflicts abounds: in France, a virtual war has recently broken out between French filmmakers and the film critics for the other mass media (principally newspapers). The filmmakers accuse the critics of seeking to kill the French film industry by means of their hurtful reviews of domestic productions and their loving attention to American works. The critics reply that the filmmakers are spoiled children, only making films thanks to state support; that the Americans make "better" films, and it is the critics' job to tell this unpleasant truth. Lost in the shuffle is the fact that the French cinema industry, almost uniquely in Europe, produces a small but fairly regular number of mainstream "hit" productions (Stephen Crofts's third category), chiefly in the two great genres of postwar French filmmaking—comedy and historical costume drama.

Interestingly, neither side in the current dispute has much interest in such works, and for the purpose of this particular public debate they simply do not exist as part of French "national" cinema. Nor do these works have much weight in books written by foreigners (including my own) about "French" cinema. So what is French national cinema? In a sense, it is whatever you need it to be to make a point in the ongoing struggle to conceptualize France, and the cinema. Typologies of the various perspectives from which one may participate in the struggle, such as those offered in this collection and elsewhere, are helpful as long as we do not forget that the underlying process is *dynamic* and perpetually *unfinished*. We must also remember that such typologies tend to make "national cinemas" seem things-in-themselves, and not part of a complex dynamic in which they do things *to* and *for* nations.

National cinemas can, as we will see, function as economic weapons in the competitive arena of world capitalism. The American cinema, though not as big an engine of capital importation as sometimes thought, brings in dollars to the United States, year after year. Other governments want to resist this, first of all, for economic reasons—to keep "their" money at home. But the example of France is there to demonstrate that cinema can function also as a weapon of (state supported) *cultural* nationalism—it can promote "national values" in the face of other, putatively inferior national values. Governments can support films they deem worthy, and withhold support from unworthy ones, as part of an international politics of culture. This does not necessarily mean only films that show the nation in a flattering light: the French government, for example, has promoted certain "suburb films" (*banlieu-films*) that offer grim portrayals of the life led by members of minority groups in the housing projects that surround most major French cities.[6] These films are presumably supported as examples of the great liberty available to French filmmakers, and of the innovations they can make in form and subject matter thanks to their superior cultural climate.

Earlier state-sponsored uses of cinema were more direct in their nationalism. Lenin is said to have considered the Soviet cinema "the most important art" because of its supposed power to mold mass opinion, and other governments once demonstrated similar attitudes toward the medium. The propaganda film is, for many readers, the first thing that comes to mind when one considers the topic of "film and nationalism." Here it is crucial to distinguish between fiction and nonfiction modes, for not all types of films are equally suited for mobilizing and reinforcing the idea of the Nation. We know now what filmmakers and bureaucrats alike did not know when the great early works of nationalistic cinema were made: that there is virtually no evidence that the fiction film is an effective medium for changing audience attitudes. Fiction films can, probably (though even this is open to debate), change *behaviors*—make people more violent, more inclined to go shopping, more sexually active—more effectively than they can change *ideas*. Nonfiction films, or "documentaries," might be somewhat more effective at this (though probably not as effective as face-to-face interaction, as in a lecture, an argument with a peer, or a religious service). But even here, there is no clear-cut evidence of easy influence.

And evidence has, in fact, been sought. Critics, theoreticians, and historians of cinema have too often assumed the truth of the "most important art" formulation and remained either ignorant of, or hostile to, the large body of empirical research conducted by American scholars in the field of mass communications, since the end of World War II.[7] More than two decades of careful studies of cinema and, more often, television were devoted to the search for effects of mass media on audience "attitudes." Researchers took for granted that such effects existed, and were perplexed to find them so difficult to prove. Wilbur Schramm and D. F. Roberts somewhat mockingly called this orientation the "bullet theory," in which mass media aimed messages at passive audience members, conveying fixed messages and provoking comparatively uniform changes in attitudes. But no evidence was found to substantiate the bullet theory, and it was largely abandoned—in mass communication research, though not in cinema studies—by the 1970s.[8]

Prior to modern mass communications research, the modern politician who best understood the ideological limitations of the fiction film was Nazi propaganda master Joseph Goebbels. As Eric Rentschler and others have shown, the Nazis made comparatively few propagandistic fiction films; the small number of "homefront films" analyzed by Manuela von Papen in a very useful study are, with strikingly few exceptions, the farthest that Nazi cinema would go in this vein.[9] (The almost unique exception is *Jew Süss* [1940], which was not a Goebbels-generated project and not, arguably, very effective as propaganda—except, presumably, for the already committed anti-Semite.) On the other hand, the German industry specialized in short "culture films" created to be shown *with* the fiction films.[10] (Many of these could perhaps better be characterized as advertisements for fascism, rather than as hard-core propaganda.) Most of the Nazi nonfiction film production reeks of "preaching to the converted"; even the supposedly hyper-influential *Triumph of the Will* is, if one accepts Brian Winston's bracing analysis, less impressive in fact than it is in reputation.[11] One should not, however, dismiss this production, or the feature films that perhaps reinforced the same messages: sometimes, preaching to the converted is a very, very useful thing to do. If *Triumph of the Will* in fact only confirmed a small number of young Nazis in their beliefs, that would have potentially been a very important thing.[12]

Does this mean that fiction films play little or no role in the (re)creation and maintenance of nationalism? Obviously not. If films are not terribly effective tools of nationalist (or any) propaganda, they appear to be capable of doing other things. If they cannot by themselves mobilize nations and give them a new direction, they can, apparently, *reflect* and *keep in circulation* values and behaviors associated with a particular nation. This process appears to work best when not the product of conscious policy-making. No United States government thought to encourage the production of Westerns, for example, yet this genre functioned for many decades as a kind of public forum where different conceptions of America were played out. The work on fiction film by the cultural anthropologists who studied and collaborated with Margaret Mead has been largely forgotten today; nonetheless it offers some stunning examples of how films can be seen as reflecting "national character" and also, presumably, helping to keep that "character" relatively uncontaminated by exotic influences.

What is missing, however, from the film analyses of Mead, Gregory Bateson, Rhoda Métraux, Martha Wolfenstein, and their colleagues, is a sense that the configurations they study can change over time, and can signal stresses in the national body politic. Coming some four decades later to some of the very same phenomena studied by Mead's circle, Noël Burch and Geneviève Sellier argue that figures like the French cinema's ubiquitous "suffering father" come and go and have changing contexts depending on the historical moment, reflecting an ongoing, collective coming-to-grips with national traumas (the German occupation of France, for example).

More studies of national cinemas from this perspective would be extremely helpful. They would probably reveal, as Burch and Sellier assert, that "popular" national cinema is much more responsive to its changing social climate than is generally believed. (The prejudice of so many writers is to assume that only Great Artists can "reflect" Great Events.)

One quite specific subset of (implicitly or explicitly) nationalistic films has drawn the particular attention of recent scholars: works that depict the major national *other*(s)—Jews for Nazi cinema; North Africans for the French; Native Americans, Latin Americans, and African Americans in "classical Hollywood cinema." One would think, to read some denunciations of mainstream commercial cinema, that it is always uniquely and perniciously racist, at all times and everywhere in the world. But Jean-Michel Frodon has argued that even the most effectively nationalistic cinema is rarely successful at inciting racial, ethnic, or national enmity (with the partial exception, doubtless, of the demonizing of wartime enemies—but isn't this also a case of "preaching to the converted"?).[13] Frodon argues that fiction films can serve as a *projection nationale,* or "projection of the nation," but only in a positive, inclusive sense. (One classic experiment in social psychology might be cited to support Frodon: it was found that "fear arousing" communications tended to decrease receptivity to their message—the more fear aroused, the less influence on the audience.)[14]

One should begin any approach to the limitations of a *projection nationale* by noting that films that are overwhelmingly negative in their portrayal of the Other, like *Jew Süss* and *The Birth of a Nation,* are comparatively—but only comparatively—rare. The Other is more typically an ambiguous figure; some of Them are like Us, and some are different. Some of Us are actually rather like Them (for example, the character of Ethan Edwards in John Ford's *The Searchers*). The figure of the Other can provide a splendid occasion for the mise-en-scène of arguments between conflicting interest groups about what constitutes the Nation. The entire question is, obviously, subject to potentially emotional disputes. What looks "positive" to a middle-class French critic like Frodon will look rather different to a French man or woman of Arab origins, or to a Native

American confronted with a film like *The Searchers*. But the debate is well worth the heated emotions it can raise.

This area of study—images of the ("foreign" or domestic) Other—is merely the most prominent part of a larger, comparatively underdeveloped area of investigation, which we might call the study of cinematic "international relations." If we grant that national cinemas exist, no matter how problematic it is to define them or specify what they "do" for a nation, then they will necessarily not be defined, or act, in isolation. Here, perhaps more than in any other area, we must keep in mind Andrew Higson's advice to consider what audiences actually *see* at least as much as what their film industry *makes*. Even in the United States, at least some films that appear on movie screens are "foreign"; in much of the rest of the world, the majority of films are. Who decides what films get distributed, receive heavy marketing, and so on? Who does the subtitling or dubbing and—much more important—according to what principles are these done (and this is anything but a simple matter)?[15] Who plays the crucial role of cultural *gatekeeper*—such as those mass media film critics in France who now find American movies to be "better" than the domestic production, or the highbrow critics who presume to tell American and other anglophone audiences what are the best Hong Kong martial arts films?

The ways of studying the cinema's international relations are multiple and fragmented. One promising method is the study of the international remake; for it is not only Hollywood that has plundered the cinemas of other countries for raw material. Other media, as well as cinema, can provide an international source of product: one of the most striking recent examples of an international cross-generic hybrid is Jorge Fons and Vincente Leñero's *Midaq Alley* (1995), a Mexican adaptation (and narrative transposition, from Cairo to Mexico City) of a celebrated Egyptian novel by Naghib Mafouz. This film is not a mere footnote to the otherwise "pure" history of a national cinema, but rather is one of the top grossing and most critically acclaimed Mexican films ever made. (But what did they think of it in Egypt? And how many Latin American spectators had read, or even heard of, the original novel? This area can be complicated indeed.)

Economic Imperialism

Without doubt, the most important aspect of cinematic international relations is in the area of economics. It is conventional, however, to assume that state and nation are two different things: the former an ensemble of laws and institutions, the latter a kind of cultural glue that helps everything to cohere. This anthology will accept the distinction and devote comparatively little space to questions of tariffs, quotas, and international industrial espionage; but these are nonetheless vitally important. We must at least situate the question of cinema and nationalism in the context of economic relations among states in order to get very far. For the cinema industry has never had a "level playing field" on which all nations can compete equally. The exact tilt of the playing field and the rules of the game have changed dramatically over time; this has never been simply a matter of state action, nor merely a question of the relative strengths of different international business communities, but a complicated and shifting mix of both. Part of the problem, in fact, is the widespread if tacit notion that the State and "free enterprise" are conceptually distinct under capitalism; in terms of cinema, quite specifically, they never are.

To see the larger forces at work, we must always keep some sense, however schematic, of historical context. The international economic condition of the cinema was one thing before World War I, quite another during the "golden age" of the American studio system (roughly from World War I until the late 1950s), and more recently has entered a new, confusing configuration in which American dominance has gotten both more virulent than it was previously, and less culturally "American." To talk sensibly of films or issues from these different periods one must always remain aware of how different they are at the level of their international "economic base."

Before World War I (or more accurately, until a few years before the war; but the change was only widely noted at the time of that conflict), the great power in world cinema was France. The so-called "studio system" was born there, later to be reborn in the United States. Its major features were: (1) cinema production following the principle of the division of labor (scriptwriters only write scripts, directors only direct, art directors only design sets, etc.); (2) vertical integration of production, distribution, and sales; and (3) modern capitalist financing (via stock and bond markets). That this "system" was in place in France before it could develop in the United States is not, perhaps, as surprising as might first seem. France at that time had more sophisticated capital markets than the United States, a more urban population, and more stability and established networks of commerce in rural areas.

One thing France did *not* have, however, was an interventionist state apparatus. French cinema before World War I was a free market ideologue's dream world—the government had little to do with the movies, except for taxing them (mainly at the level of exhibition) and very occasionally dithering about whether, and how, to censor them. The French government's hands-off approach to industrial development was, in the beginning, a great advantage to the French major studios, but it did not remain so. Mature industries typically need some form of state support and regulation. The dramatic loss of French control over the world film market that took place in the years 1912–1916 was more a failure of government than a failure of capitalist zeal. (The French capitalists survived: they simply retreated from full-scale "studio system" operations to being domestic distributors and exhibitors of films made by others). In the years that followed, the United States government would not make the same mistake.

Today, virtually all treatments of the question of national cinemas begin by acknowleging the fact that the American audiovisual industry is the 800-pound gorilla of world media. It is there, all but totally dominant, and if not everyone is afraid of it, all act in relation to it. It is amusing to note that before World War I, France was in the same position in the world market. And agitation to do something about this situation was plentiful—from film producers in the "colonized" countries, though not from most exhibitors. In the United States, the trade press of the day, as Richard Abel has demonstrated, was full of nationalist rhetoric: Americans should watch *American* movies; kick the foreigners out; and so on.[16] And, as is the case today, the bulk of the moviegoing public was indifferent to the struggle. They *liked* the "foreign" product. The State, too, was indifferent; when French control of the American market collapsed, this was not due to any action by the government of the United States. In France, however, two disastrous policies hastened the fall of an ambitious and perhaps overextended cinema industry: a law against "export of capital," which meant that profits from American operations had to be "repatriated" rather than being plowed back into new films and facilities aboad; and the total mobilization of fit male citizens at the very outset of World War I—which essentially shut down domestic French production. Producers in the United States, and elsewhere in the world, then moved in to fill the vacuum.

No doubt, government bureaucrats throughout the world learned a lesson from sudden withdrawal of France from its export markets—which affected not only cinema, but other industries as well (automobiles, aircraft, and so on). The period that follows is characterized by interventionist state practices in the film industries of a number of countries: Germany, the Soviet Union and—most successfully and influentially—the United States. Shortly after the consolidation of the first vertically integrated American "majors" (the major players in the "studio system"), there began a campaign of covert, international industrial espionage, by government and film industry working together. The goal was to assure continued American dominance in the world cinema market. Cinema historians, with a few exceptions, have chosen to ignore this phenomenon. Some have assumed that American cinema dominated the world market after 1915 because of intrinsic advantages held by the big American companies—economies of scale, a large domestic market, and so on. Other observers have assumed that the American film industry dominated the world either because it made "better" films (generally, the view taken by right-wing critics) or because it made films that spread the subtle, addictive poisons of capitalist consumerism (generally the view of left-wing critics). But there is a third possibility: that the integrated majors were substantially aided by a series of mercantilist-minded American governments that considered films to be a major export item to be promoted abroad in all ways possible, fair and foul.

The dividing line between government and industry interests in what Jens Ulf-Moller has called the American "film wars" was anything but clear.[17] From the industry side, liaison was assured by the Motion Picture Producers and Distributors of America (MPPDA), under the direction of Will Hays—best known to most students of cinema as Hollywood's chief censor. But before coming to Hollywood, Hays had been a nationally prominent Republican politician, and his position in Hollywood was, in a sense, quasi-governmental. He and a succession of American government administrations worked in happy collaboration for over two decades, not coincidentally the high-water mark of the American "studio system." This semi-secret trade war involved extensive industrial espionage and even direct "covert action," enlisting the help of selected individuals and organizations in foreign film industries. These efforts continued during the first two terms of the Roosevelt administration, which certainly saw the cinema as an economically and socially important component of American "national projection." But soon enough, other matters would take precedence in Washington, D.C., and break up the cozy alliance of movie moguls and politicians.

The Tilt of the (Post)Modern "Playing Field"

State support of the American industry began to waver with recovery from the Great Depression; after World War II, United States concerns for economic recovery in the devastated overseas economies seems to have led to a deliberate slackening in the conduct of the cinema trade wars. Government relations with the American film industry had definitely altered by the end of the war, though the signs of change were present well before: one odd, symptomatic byproduct of the new circumstances was the movies' implementation of the revived "good neighbor policy" toward Latin America. As one learns in the curious story told by Ana López in this volume, the American cinema set out to be a kind of cultural ambassador below the Rio Grande; this policy entailed not only the production of propaganda films for export, but also the softening of ethnic images of Latin Americans in mainstream film fare in the United States.

This was, to say the least, an entirely different sort of cooperation between industry and government than previous efforts to dominate foreign film markets by whatever means necessary. A similarly benign policy would later be implemented, though less systematically, toward Europe after World War II. Some aspects of this policy indirectly influenced the course of academic film studies: the film and cultural studies work of Margaret Mead, Martha Wolfenstein, and their colleagues received financial support from various government agencies, presumably in the interest of creating greater acceptance of European cultural norms in the United States—with the side effect of helping to create a scholarly literature on "foreign" cinemas.

At the same time but on another front of relations between the United States government and the film industry, antitrust efforts that had been suspended during the Depression began to weaken the major integrated film companies, culminating in the consent decree in 1948 requiring the movie theater chains to divest themselves of their production facilities.[18] The studio "system" was long to die; conventionally, its demise is said to have occurred by the late 1950s. Largely as a result of the breakup of the industry, during some periods of the 1960s, almost ten percent of films shown in the United States were not made there.[19] Though this proportion might seem almost laughably small, it was big enough: this was the golden age of the "foreign film" in the American market.

It is all but certain that the French and the various other "new waves" and "new cinemas" would not have been as successful as they were (economically) without this sudden porosity of the American exhibition market. But it did not last. Antitrust efforts often have the odd effect of strengthening the industries or companies that are broken up by government decree. And the breakup of the old, genteel studios unleashed long suppressed forces of a new phase of American capitalism beginning in the early 1970s. Thus began the era of the "blockbuster" feature (which is probably what makes so many historians and cinephiles nostalgic about the bad old days of the "studio system").

The importance for international markets of this new style of producing and marketing films cannot be underestimated. Without state action, and initially without vertical monopolies, the American cinema began, with works like *Jaws* and other "high concept" films, to reassert dominance, not only in its own market but in the world market as well. This was the first blow of a one-two punch: the second was the partial reconstitution of the old studio system in a new form. Beginning in 1980, the justice department under President Reagan began to depart dramatically from previous antitrust policies, and ceased, effectively, to enforce rules against vertical media monopolies. The new "system," however, did not reintegrate movie theaters into its structure, but chose the new dominant audiovisual medium for its exhibition component: television.

Capitalism, combined with enlightened antitrust action, works wonders. The new studio system is far more subtly structured and varied than the old. It is also more aggressive in the world market. Film producers in other countries could justifiably be nostalgic for the tender attentions of Will Hays and studio heads like Louis B. Mayer. The new media lords feel no need to leave even token national industries in place in foreign markets. This is now done in the name of "free trade," and it is anything but a coincidence that the one exception to the abolition of trade barriers in the General Agreement on Tariffs and Trade is for audiovisual media. But can protectionism really save national film and television industries? Even in France—the source of the greatest resistance to American "free trade" hegemony—American products are gaining in market share, even as state-protected feature films continue to be produced but make less and less money every year. In response, major European producers have taken to making "Europudding" features: American-style films, made in English and with a mix of European and American players, and coproduced with a United States–based (though not necessarily "American") media giant.

This situation is beginning to raise the question: at least on the level of big-budget, star-driven cinema, is there going to be any "national" film production left (even, as Jonathan Rosenbaum argues in this collection, in the United States)? Maybe the whole question of "film and nationalism" will one day be a kind of historical curiosity. But not yet. André Bazin once wrote of the postwar threat to French cinema by the newly available American products, that the foreign films were dangerous precisely because they were more organically *national* than were the domestic products (the "Tradition of Quality").[20] Bazin may well have been limited in his focus (the American cinema had its own "Tradition of Quality" with many of the same faults, and virtues, as the French), but he did emphasize a crucial fact: in the rest of the world, in the 1940s and 1950s, American cinema was most certainly received as a "national cinema," albeit a particularly powerful one. This is worth remembering because, today, the label "national cinema" is typically opposed to "Hollywood cinema"—as if "Hollywood" were not situated in a national context. And, indeed, the big question today is whether Hollywood cinema is still viably "American." Economic control of several media giants in the United States has effectively migrated overseas—though not always with financially rewarding results—to Japan and, most recently, France.

And if Hollywood cinema is no longer organically "American," can the rest of the world be far behind? Perhaps a Gresham's law of cinema might operate, with "bad" (global) films driving out "good" (national) ones. This alarmist scenario, however satisfying intellectually, seems far-fetched when considered empirically. But one thing that does seem to have happened is that the American cinema industry has now reached a situation similar to that of France in the postwar era, as analyzed by Bazin. It is split between a big-budget, export-driven cinema that seems, zombielike, to live on outdated conventions, and a smaller-budget, relatively "independent" sector which seems more vital (if not always more artful).

The Global, the National, and the International

The "global" cinema made in Hollywood is largely the domain of so-called "action films"—tales of good versus evil featuring spectacular sensory experience and spare dialogue. This is one genre (or perhaps a set of related genres—neo-disaster films, action sci-fi, high-voltage espionage thrillers, and so on) that is more salient than the rest of world cinema to most mainstream critics, but it is not all of filmmaking, even in the United States. It has long been a transnational genre, as long ago as the nineteenth century, in its precinematic, theatrical form as stage melodrama. But other genres remain persistently "national," even in the United States—most notably, perhaps, comedy. (Whatever one thinks of "gross-out" comedies, they are, doubtless, typically "American.") But there are also (to speak only of the United States) horror films, lower-budget, character-driven crime dramas, and satire. And in Bombay film-makers continue to make musicals; and in Hong Kong, martial-arts films—even if the glory days of these two film capitals are perhaps past.

In terms of the landscape of nationalism, today's commercial narrative cinema might perhaps best be thought of as a continuum, the most salient feature of which is budget. On one end, there is the capital-intensive, increasingly faceless "global" cinema of the related "action film" genres. On the other end, there is the low-budget, film festival–oriented "art," "independent," or *auteur* cinema; this sector may properly be termed "international." The difference between global and international is crucial in today's marketplace: on the film festival and the art house/independent cable channel circuit, a visible national origin is *de rigeur*, almost as important as a visible author/director. These films function, in part, as armchair travel experiences for the global couch-potato class. In the middle of the financial continuum, finally, we have the medium-budget "national" production, designed for a home audience (and closely related audiences—Canada for the United States, Belgium for France, and so on) with comparatively little ambition for the export market.

It is worth pondering the differences, at the level of "national-ism," between these mid-budget home-audience films and the inter-national art house films. The international art cinema, too, involves markers of national origin, but in different ways. The art-house work is usually *self-consciously* national. The ideal film festival success, to judge by recent history, is a work which goes against the grain of its "own" national cinema or national state apparatus: the most strik-ing examples would be films banned, denounced, or commercially discouraged in their domestic markets. The international *auteur* comes from a national tradition, but defines himself as much against it as within it. The films themselves will often involve "foreigners" or "foreign" locations, as in Wong Kar-wai's *Happy Together* (1997), a "Hong Kong" film with Chinese characters in which most of the action takes place in South America. (One could also cite Jim Jarmusch's *Stranger Than Paradise* [1984] as an earlier, American example of the other strategy: a foreign woman comes to the United States, defamiliarizing it for the film audience, and for her American friends and relatives.)

This internationalism also characterizes, though in a denatured, relatively unproblematic way, the big-budget "global" cinema, where international casts and multiple national locations are, if not the rule, at least quite common. But in the mid-level, "national" production, very little of this obtains. It is in this type of production that national differences are to be observed on various levels—most obviously, of film genre. But more interesting is that it is here that one may find the national differences, as analyzed convincingly by Michel Chion, of a *formal* sort. Chion argues that whereas image track conventions are relatively standardized throughout the world, *sound* practices reveal notable national differences:

> Is there a "European" sound [practice]? Everything I know shows the contrary. The differences between Italy and France . . . are as large as those between France and the United States. . . . Young French filmmakers fresh out of film school continue to think that the French way of doing things is the only way in the world, or is the only way to "resist" the aesthetic Americanization of their cinema. . . .[21]

Thus, according to Chion, most French filmmakers (but not, we should note, "Europudding" directors such as Luc Besson) do not use the resources of Dolby multichannel sound, considering it a kind of Trojan horse for American sound practices. Yet they would not, presumably, be prejudiced (or as prejudiced) against a certain sort of lens or color process for the same reason. The differences between national cinemas at the level of sound practices are well known and worthy of more study than they have received, from the Italian cinema's apparent fondness for dubbed voices speaking "nonregional" accents (a kind of "general Italian" like the "general American" that dominated American cinema until quite recently) to the French de-emphasis of sound effects of everyday life (such as light switches and footsteps, typically lower in volume on French soundtracks than on American ones).

One way to see, or rather hear, such differences, is to compare different national release versions of the "same" film—for example, the Australian and American versions of *Mad Max,* where a distinct, more layered style of sound mixing in the original work is at least as important a difference as the toned down, less "Australian" accents in the sound track of the American version. Chion is probably right that the most striking "national" differences of film style are to be heard rather than seen. Still, it seems likely that his notion of a universal visual style needs refining. Film editing and the rhythm of filmic action may well still have a "national" character. David Bordwell argues that a "pause/burst/pause structure," though originating in combat sequences from martial arts films, is "deeply characteristic of Hong Kong cinema."[22] And the ever popular "canned theater" that still satisfies domestic audiences in France (but rarely exports well) often retains the slow, stately editing and acting rhythms of the first widescreen films of the 1950s. Obviously, these two examples are genre-related, and at this level the most obvious differences between mid-budget "national" film productions may perhaps best be approached through the notion of genre. But genre is no more simple an idea than nationalism, and Rick Altman's seminal book on the subject is there to warn us that any generic approach to national filmmaking will be anything but easy.[23] Differences in sound style, on the other hand, arguably go beyond most (though not all) generic distinctions; perhaps, as the history of the cinema seems to suggest, they bear more directly on issues of "national character."

At any rate, study of the formal characteristics of national cinemas is for the moment comparatively underdeveloped, with the exception of the many analyses of "classical Hollywood cinema" (most of them not oriented toward American cinema as a national cinema, but useful in that context nonetheless).[24] The relations between this "classical American" cinema and the new global action cinema deserve careful study. The challenge to contemporary cinema studies in this area, as in others, is that the objects of study are mutating while we examine them. The selection of articles in this anthology can only indicate a few of the worthwhile paths of investigation in a field that is in complex, fascinating play on the stage of world culture.

NOTES

1. Benedict Anderson, *Imagined Communities: Reflections on the Origin and Spread of Nationalism*, (2d ed. (London & New York: Verso, 1991).

2. And this did not merely apply to American features abroad. Kristin Thompson has given a fascinating chronicle of an early, silent era precursor of the modern "europudding" tendency in "National or International films? The European Debate during the 1920s" (*Film History* 8:3 (1996): 281–96).

3. This model is said to be "a complex composite of French and American elements" (p. 81n34), though France does not fit in at all well to the various stages of nationalism. Anderson's revisionist account minimizes the importance of the French Revolution in the creation of a "modular" idea of nationhood. One often has to look for it in the footnotes.

4. Rick Altman, *Film/Genre* (London: British Film Institute, 1999), 198.

5. Andrew Higson, "The Concept of National Cinema," on p. 52 of this volume.

6. The most telling example here is Richet's *Ma 6-té va crack-er* (*My City Is Cracking Up*, 1998), which was promoted abroad by Unifrance and other governmental entities, and was screened (with new subtitles) by TV5, the international French-language satellite service—while at the same time other sectors of the government were working to limit its viewership within France.

7. Those who have been hostile, rather than ignorant, have preferred theory to empirical verification, thanks to systems of thought—most notably, psychoanalysis, but also various schools of Marxism—that make certain empirical findings literally unthinkable. Another complication is that few "mass com" studies since the late 1940s have involved the cinema—the medium being displaced by television as the audiovisual medium preferred by investigators. But much of the literature on television is sufficiently general to apply with little or no modification to the older medium of film.

8. Schramm and Roberts are summarized, and the trend of mass communications research characterized, in George Comstock et. al., *Television and Human Behavior* (New York: Columbia University Press, 1978), 313–14.

9. Manuela von Papen, "Keeping the Home Fires Burning?—Women and the German Homefront Film 1940–1943," *Film History* 8:3 (1996): 44–63.

10. To call these works "nonfiction" today is of course to make that word stretch a bit. But they were intended to be taken as such. The Nazis imposed a similar pattern of production in occupied France, where almost none of the fiction films were anti-semitic (for example), but large numbers of the documentary short subjects were.

11. Brian Winston, "Was Hitler There? Reconsidering *Triumph of the Will*," *Sight and Sound* 50:2 (1980/81): 102–107.

12. For example, its showings at the Paris World's Fair in 1937 were, reportedly, life-changing experiences for young French right-wingers such as Robert Brassilach (who would be executed after the war, in essence, for the very fervor of his commitment to his cause).

13. Jean-Michel Frodon, *La Projection nationale: Cinéma et Nation* (Paris: Editions Odile Jacob, 1998), 33–38 (on the "positivité naturelle" of the fiction film).

14. The research, *and* a study with a different method that gave different findings, is cited in Melvin L. De Fleur and Sandra Ball-Rokeach, *Theories of Mass Communications*, 3d ed. (New York: David McKay, 1975), 241–42. The original experiment is reported in Irving Janis and Seyman Feshback, "The Effects of Fear-Arousing Communications," *Journal of Abnormal and Social Psychology* 48 (1953): 78–132. The study was of strategies for convincing audiences of the necessity of good dental hygiene.

15. For a wonderful introduction to some of the problems here, see Abé Mark Nornes, "For an Abusive Subtitling," *Film Quarterly* 52:3 (Spring 1999): 17–34.

16. Richard Abel, "The Perils of Pathé, or the Americanization of the American Cinema," in Leo Charney and Vanessa R. Schwartz (eds.), *Cinema and the Invention of Modern Life* (Berkeley & Los Angeles: University of California Press, 1995), 183–226.

17. Jens Ulf-Moller, *The "Film Wars" Between France and the United States: Film-Trade Diplomacy, and the Emergence of the Film Quota System in France, 1920–1939* (Unpublished Ph.D. dissertation, Brandeis University, 1998).

18. It is more often said that the "studios" had to divest themselves of their theaters—but the latter represented up to 90 percent of the book value of the corporations. Production was a handy thing to have, but the theaters were where the real money was made.

19. Estimates provided by representatives of Unifrance U.S.A. during "French Cinema in the 1990s" (conference at Baruch College, New York City, April 17, 1999). A personal recollection may give some sense of the degree of market penetration: I saw European anthology films, such as *Spirits of the Dead* and *Casanova '70*—dubbed in English and on the lower half of double bills—on a fairly regular basis at the Liberty Theater in Ellensburg, Wash. (pop. 8,750 at that time) during the early 1960s.

20. André Bazin (trans. Stanley Hochman), "Reflections for a Vigil of Arms," in *French Cinema of the Occupation and Resistance: The Birth of a Critical Esthetic* (New York: Ungar, 1981), 99–100.

21. Michel Chion, "Problèmes et solutions pour développer l'étude du son, en Europe et dans le monde." *Iris* 27 (Spring 1999): 21–22 (my translation).

22. David Bordwell, *Planet Hong Kong: Popular Cinema and the Art of Entertainment* (Cambridge, Mass. and London: Harvard University Press, 2000), 229.

23. Altman, op. cit.

24. The most important, unrivaled despite its age, is David Bordwell, Kristin Thompson, and Janet Staiger, *The Classical Hollywood Cinema: Film Style & Mode of Production to 1960* (London: Routledge & Kegan Paul, 1985).

Theoretical
Perspectives

Stephen Crofts

Reconceptualizing
National Cinema/s

Part I. Introduction

1992: quincentenary of Europe's invasion of the Americas, year of
Europe's anticipated economic union, year of fierce ethnic-religious
conflicts in what were Yugoslavia and the Soviet "Union," and the
year of Afro-American outrage at its abuse by a white American judi-
cial system. A year, then, which exposes the exploitation of indigenous peoples, the perceived importance of supra-national trading
blocs, the imposition of nationalisms on sub-national populations,
and the violence inflicted on such groups in the name of "national
unity." As a post-Enlightenment organizer of populations, the nation
has recently been seriously frayed at its edges under the pressure of
ethnic, religious, democratic and other forms of dissent, in particular consequent upon the disintegration of Soviet Communism and
Pax Americana.

Analysis of national cinemas is the more urgent in the face of
other major changes which have recently affected world cinema: the
global spread of corporate capital, the consolidation of global markets, the speed and range of electronic communications (Hebdige
1990: v–vi). This essay seeks to theorize the global range of national
cinemas in terms of the multiple politics of their production, distribution, and reception, their textuality, their relations with the
state and with multiculturalism. These terms and their interactions
constitute the basis of a project of disaggregating the term "national

From *Quarterly Review of Film and Video* 14:3 (1993), pp. 49–67. Copyright ©
OPA (Overseas Publishers Association) N.V. with permission granted by Taylor &
Francis Ltd.

cinema" (the "national" especially should perhaps carry mental quotation marks throughout what follows). The essay limits itself to the feature film, and historically goes back to 1945, focusing in particular on recent years. This reconceptualization takes as axiomatic the issues set out by Andrew Higson as requiring address in considering national cinemas: the range of films in circulation within a nation-state, the range of sociologically specific audiences for different types of film, and the range of discourses circulating about film (1989: 44–45). while recognizing that the second of these is amenable only to micro-analyses inappropriate to a synoptic essay such as this.[1]

Part II. Varieties of National Cinema Production

Especially in the West, national cinema production is usually defined against Hollywood. This extends to such a point that in Western discussions, Hollywood is hardly ever spoken of as a national cinema, perhaps indicating its transnational reach. That Hollywood has dominated most world film markets since as early as 1919 is well known (Thompson 1985; Guback 1976; Sklar 1975). Whereas in 1914 90 percent of films shown worldwide were French, by 1928, 85 percent were American (Moussinac 1967 [1925]: 238). And for all the formal disinvestiture secured domestically by the 1948 Paramount Decree, transnationally Hollywood still operates effectively as a vertically integrated business organization.

Throughout most film-viewing countries outside South and Southeast Asia, Hollywood has successfully exported and naturalized its construction of the cinema as fictional entertainment customarily requiring narrative closure and assuming a strong individual—usually male—hero as the necessary agent of that closure. In anglophone markets especially, Hollywood interests have often substantially taken control of the distribution and exhibition arms of the domestic industry. Elsaesser can thus comment: "Hollywood can hardly be conceived . . . as totally other, since so much of any nation's film culture is implicitly 'Hollywood'" (1987: 166).

In the context of such unequal cultural and economic exchange, most national cinema producers have to operate in terms of an agenda set by Hollywood though, as indicated by the fourth variety of national cinema listed below, some Asian cinemas significantly maintain their own terrain. The political, economic, and cultural regimes of different nation-states license some seven varieties of "national cinema" sequenced in rough order of decreasing familiarity to the present readership: (1) cinemas that differ from Hollywood, but do not compete directly, by targeting a distinct, specialist market sector; (2) those that differ, do not compete directly *but* do directly *critique* Hollywood; (3) European and Third World entertainment cinemas that struggle against Hollywood with limited or no success; (4) cinemas that ignore Hollywood, an accomplishment managed by few; (5) anglophone cinemas that try to beat Hollywood at its own game; (6) cinemas that work within a wholly state-controlled and often substantially state-subsidized industry; and (7) regional or national cinemas whose culture and/or language take their distance from the nation-states which enclose them.

It should be noted at the outset that, as in most taxonomies, these categories are highly permeable. Not only do individual films cross-breed from between different groups, but a given national cinema, operating different production sectors, will often straddle these groupings. Thus French cinema operates in the first and third fields, with exceptional forays into the second, and Australian in the fifth and first with yet rarer excursions into the second, while Indian produces in the fourth, the first and the second. Moreover, the export of a given text may shift its category, most commonly recycling films of the second and sixth groupings as the first, as art cinema. In such cases, distribution and reception criteria supplant production and textual criteria. Part Three below will amplify the frequently depoliticizing effects of this shift.

A. European-Model Art Cinemas

This is, to most of the present readership, the best-known form of national cinema. Indeed, it constitutes the limits of some accounts of national cinema that collapse national cinema into the European art film flourishing in the 1960s and 1970s (Neale 1981). This model aims to differentiate itself textually from Hollywood, to assert explicitly or implicitly an indigenous product, and to reach domestic and export markets through those specialist distribution channels and exhibition venues usually called "arthouse." Outside Europe, the model includes, for example, the art cinema of India exemplified by Satyajit Ray, as well as the Australian period film.

Insofar as the discourses supporting such a model of national cinema are typically bourgeois-nationalist, they also subtend the European popular cinemas considered below. Those of the former are more elitist and more targeted at export markets for financial and cultural reasons. (This is not to say, of course, that popular cinemas do not seek out foreign markets.) National pride and the assertion at home and abroad of national cultural identity have been vital in arguing for art cinemas. Central, too, have been arguments about national cultural and literary traditions and quality as well as their consolidation and extension through a national cinema; hence the frequent literary sources and tendencies in this European model of national cinema (Elsaesser 1989: 108, 333).

Such arguments have issued in and maintained legislation for European cinemas of quality as well as European popular cinemas. The most meaningful legislation has been that for state subvention, directly via grants, loans, prizes and awards, or indirectly through taxation (the state in the post–World War II period replaces the private patronage which outside Russia substantially supported the art/avant-garde cinema of the 1920s). State legislation has also been used to govern quotas and tariffs on imported films. These various legislative and financial arrangements allow for the establishment of what Elsaesser calls a "cultural mode of production" (1989: 41–43) as distinct from the industrial mode of Hollywood. Though it depends on state subsidies—increasingly via television—this production mode is successful because of a meshing, often developed over decades, between economic and cultural interests in the country concerned. Such a mesh is less common in other modes of national cinemas considered below. Significantly, as elucidated by Colin Crisp, the French cinema—that most successfully nationalist of national cinemas—became so in the post-1945 era by virtue of its cinema workers' vigorous campaign against the post-Vichy influx of Hollywood films which obliged the government to impose a quota on Hollywood imports as well as box-office taxes to subsidize indigenous feature film production (Crisp 1993: ch. 2). A key variant affecting the success of an art cinema is the cultural status of cinema relative to other artistic practices in the country concerned. France rates cinema more highly than West Germany, for instance, with Britain in between, and Australia, adopting a European funding model, hovers near the bottom.

Textually, European-model art cinema has been typified by features such as the psychologized characterization, narrational ambiguity and objective verisimilitude noted by David Bordwell (1979 and 1985). And in defiance of claims that art cinema died with Tarkovsky, such textual features survive, with the metaphysics and the high-cultural address, in the work of Resnais, Rivette, Rohmer, and newcomers like Kieslowski and Greenaway. But Bordwell's schema is modified by two factors. The supersession of early 1960s existentialism by later 1960s political radicalism and subsequent apoliticisms is one, pursued later. The other is Hollywood's development of its own art cinema. This has contributed to a blurring of boundaries between specialist and entertainment market sectors in its own market and abroad, and has weakened the assertions of independence made by other art cinemas. The generic mixing of Hollywood from, say, the early 1960s has been complicated by its interchange with European art cinema developments. Hollywood has developed its own art cinema after and alongside the spaghetti Western, Nouvelle Vague *hommages* to Hollywood genres and directors, Fassbinder's recasting of Hollywood melodrama and gangster genres and the adoption by such directors as Schlondorff, Hauff and Jodrell of Hollywood genres and modes of character identification to deal with nationally specific, West German and Australian issues. Penn, Altman, Schrader and Allen in the first wave all had their own favorite European influences, while a later star such as Lynch arrives with a more postmodernist pedigree; and Soderberg, Hartley and Stilman have more modest projects. A principal upshot has been a blurring of national cinema differences. Coupled with the aging market demographics of the European art film—the babyboomers forsake the cinema for their families—this blurring leaves these production sectors less able to differentiate their product from Hollywood's. Such insecurity is compounded by substantial American successes at recent Cannes festivals, long the preserve of European films.

While a politicized art cinema diverges from the metaphysical orientation of the textual norms cited above, state subsidy does impose limitations. Elsaesser neatly pinpoints the contradictions ensuing from state subsidy of a cultural mode of film production: it encourages aesthetic difference from the dominant (Hollywood) product, but discourages biting the hand that feeds it (1989: 44). In the West German instance, this tension explains the adoption of political allegory as a mode of self-censorship, as variously seen in *Artists at the Top of the Big Top: Disoriented* (as regards state funding of film), *The American Friend* (American cultural influences in West Germany) and *Germany, Pale Mother* (recent German history and feminist readings of it). Left political films found their way through the liberal pluralist interstices of such cultural funding arrangements: for example, the critical realism of a Rosi or a Rossellini and the critical anti-realism of Kluge and Straub-Huillet. Godard, in the heady affluent days of turn-of-the-70s New Leftism, constituted a limit-case: on the basis of his cultural prestige as renowned art film director, he persuaded four television stations to finance ultra-leftist films, only one of which was then screened (Crofts 1972: 37). Such explicit leftism partly borrows its discourses from, and marks a border zone between, a European art cinema and the second mode of national cinema.

B. Third Cinema

1960s–1970s Third Cinema opposed the United States and Europe in its anti-imperialist insistence on national liberation, and in its insistence on the development of aesthetic models distinct from those of Hollywood and European art cinema. As Getino and Solanas proclaimed in their famous 1969 manifesto, "Towards a Third Cinema":

> While, during the early history . . . of the cinema, it was possible to speak of a German, an Italian or a Swedish cinema clearly dif-

ferentiated from, and corresponding to, specific national characteristics, today such differences have disappeared. The borders were wiped out along with the expansion of US imperialism
and the film model that it imposed: Hollywood movies. . . . The
first alternative to this type of cinema . . . arose with the so-
called "author's cinema" . . . the second cinema. This alternative
signified a step forward inasmuch as it demanded that the filmmaker be free to express him/herself in non-standard language.
. . . But such attempts have already reached, or are about to reach,
the outer limits of what the system permits. . . . In our times it
is hard to find a film within the field of commercial cinema . . .
in both the capitalist and socialist countries, that manages to
avoid the models of Hollywood pictures. (1969: 20–21)

From the perspective of revolutionary, national liberation movements in Latin American, African and Asian nations, such an identification of "first" with "second" cinemas has an understandable
basis in a critique of bourgeois individualism. For the existentialist-
influenced "universal" humanism of much 1960s art cinema (canonically Bergman, Antonioni, Resnais) shares a Western individualism
with the achieving heroes of Hollywood who resolve plots within
the global-capitalist terms of a United States world view.

Third Cinema has proven to be one of the more elastic signi-
fiers in the cinematic lexicon. Some writers have tried to homog-
enize the enormously diverse range of Third World film production
under its rubric (see Burton 1985: 6–10 and Willemen 1987:
21–23 discussing Gabriel 1982), while others have sought to build
on the 1960s liberationist political moment of Getino and
Solanas's manifesto, a moment extending well into the 1980s in
ex-Portuguese colonies in Africa. Insofar as Third Cinema distinguishes itself politically and largely aesthetically from Hollywood
and European art cinema models, its history has been a fitful one.
In its concern with "a historically analytic yet culturally specific
mode of cinematic discourse" (Willemen 1987: 8), its radical edge
distinguished it also from the bulk of Third World production, primarily devoted to comedies, action genres, musicals and varieties
of melodrama/romance/titillation. Especially in the 1960s, such
radicalism rendered Third Cinema liable to ferocious censorship.

More recently, Third Cinema abuts and overlaps with art film's textual norms and, its militant underground audience lost, seeks out art cinema's international distribution-exhibition channels. Names such as those of Solanas, Mrinal Sen, Tahimik, Sembène and Cissé serve notice of the ongoing importance of Third Cinema as a cinema of political and aesthetic opposition.

It follows from its political oppositionality and Third World "national [cultural] powerlessness" (Stam, 1991: 227) that funding for such cinema is highly unreliable. In the instance of films from impoverished, black African one-party states with few cinemas and minimal film culture, film subsidy is easier found in France, in Switzerland, or from the United Kingdom's Channel 4 and BBC2. Such production conditions give Third Cinema a more urgent intensity than the political allegories of West German cinema and raise vital questions about the cultural role played by First World financing of Third World cinemas. Rod Stoneman of Channel 4 sounds an appropriate warning note on international co-productions: "Vital though the input of hard currency from European television may be, it is important that it does not distort the direction of African cinema" (quoted in Leahy 1991: 65).

Discourses on Third Cinema undo many First World notions of national cinema, perhaps most strikingly the notion of national cultural sovereignty. As polemically adopted by the 1986 Edinburgh Film Festival Special Event on the topic, Third Cinema offered a particular reconceptualization of national cinema. It became a means of disaggregating the congealed stolidity of a British film culture unwilling to recognize in its midst a plethora of ethnic, gender, class and regional differences (Pines and Willemen 1999). The Event extended the definition of Third Cinema to take in, for instance, black British cinema. Another conceptual dividend of Third Cinema is its decisive refutation of the easy Western assumption of the coincidence of ethnic background and home. Pinochet's military dictatorship in Chile, for example, produced a diasporic cinema. As Zuzana Pick notes: "The dispersal of filmmakers [. . .] made problematic their identification within the Chilean national and cultural formation" (1987: 41). Similarly exiled have been such erstwhile Fifth Generation Chinese filmmakers as Wu Tianming,

Chen Kiage, Huang Jianxin and Zhang Yimou, whose *Ju Dou,* co-produced with a Japanese company, is still banned in China, probably for its allegorical resonances of the 1960s–1989 period as well as for the expressed concern that it is a "foreign exposé" of a "backward China." And within their "own" countries filmmakers such as Paradjanov and Yilmaz Guney have been exiled and/or imprisoned. Such troublings of First World homogenizing concepts of rotion will be pursued later.

C. Third World and European Commercial Cinemas

Art cinema and Third Cinema, the two best-known reactions to Hollywood, do not exhaust the field. Both Europe and the Third World produce commercial cinemas that compete, with varying degrees of success, with Hollywood product in domestic markets. These cinemas, and all those considered henceforth, are less well-known than the first two because they are less exported to the European and anglophone film cultures which largely define the critical terms of national cinemas.

Much Third World production, as distinct from Third Cinema, aims, like European art cinema, to compete with Hollywood in indigenous markets—or, in Africa, with Indian cinema too—but it differs from European art cinema in being populist. This may be explained, in part, by lesser degrees of American cultural influence (that is, there is more screen space) and by the fact that local cultural elites outside Latin America are weaker and little concerned with cinema, thus encouraging lesser art cinemas. (Third World cinema here excludes China and Russia, considered later.)

European commercial cinema, however, should be treated here. It targets a market sector somewhat distinct from European-model art cinema, and thus vies more directly with Hollywood for box-office. Its most successful country has been France, where until 1986 indigenous cinema won out over Hollywood at the local box-office. French production, it might be noted, has partly dissolved the industrial/cultural distinction by successfully promoting *auteurs* within an industrial context. Other European commercial/art cinemas such as Holland's and Ireland's, based on small language communities, have a much more parlous existence, with production levels often tailing off to zero per year and with few exports. Typical genres of a European commercial cinema include the thriller, comedy, and, especially in the 1960s, soft-core.

Excluding the booming economies of East Asia, the dependent capitalist status of most Third World countries, with stop-go economies and vulnerability to military dictatorships with short cultural briefs, rarely provides the continuous infrastructural support which nurtures indigenous cinemas. Economic dependency and hesitant cultural commitment typically promote private over public forms of investment which further weaken indigenous film production. John King notes the common failure in Latin America to bite the bullet for import quotas:

> [I]n general the state has been more successful in stimulating production than in altering distribution and exhibition circuits. The transnational and local monopolies have strongly resisted any awasures to restrict the free entry of foreign films and have grudgingly obeyed, or even ignored, laws which purport to guarantee screen time to national products. . . . The logic of state investment was largely economic: to protect the profits of dominantly private investors. There are fewer examples of what Thomas Elsaesser calls a "cultural mode of production."
>
> (1990: 248–49)

Throughout the Third World, with exceptions noted below, foreign (mainly Hollywood) films dominate local screens. Even in Turkey, where "film production was [. . .] neither dominated by foreign companies nor supported or tightly controlled by the state [. . .] the market was still dominated by the four or five hundred imported films (mostly Hollywood movies)" (Armes 1987: 195–96). Uruguay represents an extreme instance, insofar as it has a dynamic film culture and almost no local production (King 1990: 94). Yet that same film culture afforded more admissions to Solanas's *Tangos: El Exilio de Gardel* than to *Rambo* (Solanas 1990: 115). Slightly differently, Tunisia has since 1966 hosted the significant Carthage Film Festival while having only some seventy film theaters, insufficient to sustain regular local production. In francophone black Africa, only recently has the French distribution duopoly been displaced, allowing the screening of more African films on African screens (Armes 1987: 212, 223).

Countries of the East Asian economic boom clearly differ. While Japan is Hollywood's largest overseas market, in 1988 domestic product retained 49.7 percent of box-office (Lent 1990: 47), specializing largely in softcore and adolescent melodramas (Yoïchi 1990: 110). And South Korea in the same year battled the MPEAA to reduce Hollywood imports to roughly five per year (Lent 1990: 122–23). As such, it broaches the category of "Ignoring Hollywood."

D. Ignoring Hollywood

In Paul Willemen's gloss, "some countries (especially in Asia) have managed to prevent Hollywood from destroying their local film industry" (1987: 25). This option is open only to nation-states with large domestic markets and/or effective trade barriers, such as India and Hong Kong (there are some similarities between these countries and totalitarian cinemas considered below). In these Asian countries, culturally specific cinemas can arise and flourish. In Hong Kong, the national cinema outsells Hollywood by a factor of four to one. And in India the national cinema sells four times as many tickets per year as does Hollywood in the United States. In 1968, a typical year, the Indian industry produced 773 films, 262 more than Hollywood. That Indian features are produced in some 20 languages for local consumption protects Indian films very ably from foreign competition (Lent 1991: 230–31). And in the Hollywood vein—if less expansively—Bombay exports its product to Indian communities worldwide, just as Hong Kong exports through East Asia, dominating the Taiwan market, for instance, and to Chinatowns throughout the Western world. Furthermore, Indian cinema long colonized Ceylon (now Sri Lanka). All Sinhalese films prior to 1956 were made in South India, and "local actors were decked out as Indian hewn and heroines who mouthed Sinhalese" (Coorey and Jayatilaka 1974: 303).

E. Imitating Hollywood

Some sectors of some national cinemas have sought to beat Hollywood at its own game—and overwhelmingly failed. Such aspirations have emanated largely from anglophone countries: Britain, Canada, Australia. In the memorable dictum of British producer, Leon Clore, "If the United States spoke Spanish, we would have a film industry" (quoted by Roddick 1985: 5). State investment in the countries' film industries has secured relatively stable production levels, but has not guaranteed a culturally nationalist product. Anglophony has encouraged these nations to target the West's largest, most lucrative—and well-protected—market, that of the United States. But these national cinemas have already had their indigenous cultural bases modified, if not undercut, by the substantial inroads made into domestic distribution and exhibition by Hollywood interests and product. Geoffrey Nowell-Smith's provocative remarks on British cinema are yet more pertinent to Canada and Australia: "British cinema is in the invidious position of having to compete with an American cinema which, paradoxical as this may seem, is by now far more deeply rooted in British cultural life than is the native product" (1985: 152). Already weaker than those of major European countries, the local film cultures of these anglophone nations have been further weakened through the 1980s by the unequal economic exchanges which have locked British, Canadian and Australian film production increasingly into dependence on the United States market through pre-sales and distribution guarantees. For each success story like *A Fish Called Wanda* and *Crocodile Dundee* that have drawn on some local cultural values, there have been hundreds of films made in these lesser-player countries which, in trying to second-guess the desires of the United States market, have produced pallid imitations. An index of the price exacted for the American/world distribution of *Crocodile Dundee* can be seen in the re-editing required by Paramount, which quickened the narrative pace and made the film took more like a wholesome family entertainment (Crofts 1990). A fantasy of a foreign market can, then, exercise an inordinate influence over "national" product.

The logic of such blithe bleaching-out of domestic cultural specificity can have two further consequences: the country may become
an offshore production base for Hollywood—witness Britain,
Canada, and Australia's branch of Warner Brothers' "Hollywood on
the Gold Coast"—or Hollywood may exercise its longstanding vam-
pirism of foreign talent (Prédal 1990). In the Australian case, all the
major name directors of the 1980s have now moved to Hollywood,
most without returning to Australia: the two George Millers, Peter
Weir, Gillian Armstrong, Fred Schepisi, Bruce Beresford, Phil Noyce,
Carl Schultz, Simon Wincer. Four leading Australian actors have
now made the Hollywood grade: Mel Gibson, Judy Davis, Bryan
Brown, Colin Freils. Even that stalwart of Australian cultural
nationalism, playwright and scriptwriter David Williamson, has
been writing a script in Hollywood. Similarly Bangladeshi and
Indian talent.

F. Totalitarian Cinemas

Sixth, there is the national cinema of the totalitarian state: Fascist
Germany and Italy, Chinese cinema between 1949 and the mid-
1980s, and, of course, the Stalinist regimes of the Soviet bloc. By far
the predominant mode of the Communist brand of such national
cinemas has been socialist realism, which sought to convince viewers of the virtues of the existing political order (Crofts 1976). Peripheral to this core production has been the often political art cinema of
Tarkovsky, Jancsó, Makaveyev, Wajda, various proponents of the
Cuban and Czech New Waves, and Chinese Fifth Generation cinema. Such peripheral production has been conditional upon the lib-
eralism or otherwise of national policies at the time, both as regards
cultural production and the cultural diplomacy of products exported.
A further aspect of any analysis of this mode of national cinema
might seek to disentangle cultural specificities from the homogenizing fictions of nationalism. As Chris Berry notes in surveying
Fifth Generation departures from the Han Chinese norm, there are
"56 races in the People's Republic" (Berry 1992: 44). The undoubted
popularity of such Communist and also fascist cinemas might need
to be mapped against the discursive regimes and the range of other

entertainment, within and outside the home, offered by such nation-states.

G. Regional/Ethnic Cinemas

Given the historical recency of the disintegration of the nation-state and its forcefully homogenizing discourses and political sanctions, it is not surprising that ethnic and linguistic minorities have generally lacked the funds and infrastructure to support regional cinemas or national cinemas distinct from the nation-states which enclose them. Marvin D'Lugo has written of Catalan cinema as "something like a national cinema" (1991: 131), but perhaps the best-known regional cinema, the Québecois, has benefitted from cultural and political support strong enough to propel its major naional director, Denys Arcand, into international fame. Cinemas such as the Welsh have not achieved such prominence nor, within settler societies, have Aboriginal, Maori or Native American cinemas, nor indeed, within an immigrant society, has Chicano cinema, though Afro-American cinema reaches back to Oscar Micheaux and has broken into the mainstream with Spike Lee and others.

Part III. Marketing Options for National Cinemas

I separate out this topic from production to counter the still wide-spread tendency of film histories and theories to gloss over what for almost all cinema producers is a vital, if not the paramount factor in their calculations: namely, markets. While some sectors of national cinema production do not seek export—witness the German *arbeiterfilm,* most Chinese film and most "poor cinema"—a great deal of national cinema is produced for export as well as domestic consumption. National cinemas thus compete in export markets with each other and with the big other of Hollywood.

A. Exporting National Cinemas

Whereas Hollywood markets itself through well-established trans-national networks and with relatively standardized market pitches of star, genre and production values, the export operations of (other) national cinemas are far more hit-and-miss affairs. Their three principal modes of marketing or product differentiation are by the nation of production, with different national labels serving a sub-generic function; by authorship; and for portions of art cinema, by less censored representations of sexuality, especially in the Bardot days of the 1950s and 1960s, but still now, as witness Almodóvar. All three modes of differentiation were, and remain, defined against Hollywood, promising varieties of authenticity and frisson which Hollywood rarely offered. As Hollywood sets the terms of national cinemas' self-marketing, so too does its market power and pervasive ideology of entertainment limit the circulation of national cinemas. In foreign, if not also in their domestic markets, national cinemas are limited to specialist exhibition circuits traditionally distinct from those of Hollywood product. These comprise arthouse cinemas—themselves recently increasingly blurred with mainstream outlets—film festivals, specialist television slots addressing middle- to high-brow viewers, and minority video and laser-disc product, not to mention other, rarer exhibition modes such as community, workplace and campus screenings.

Even for as grand a player as Hollywood, export markets can impose some limitations. Roger Ebert reports that Hollywood's persisting reluctance to figure non-white heroes is attributed within the business to the fact that export markets—despite often being less white than the domestic one—lag behind the temper of the United States market (1990). So much the worse, then, for the export aspirations of culturally specific national cinema product. Few states substantially underwrite their export market operations. (The operations of, say, SavExportFilm until 1989 would repay detailed attention.) Distributor take-up of foreign film material for arthouse circulation frequently excludes the culturally specific. Thus New German Cinema is exported largely without Schroeter or Kluge, and Australian cinema almost entirely without the social realist film. Such exclusions can enable the resultant cultural constructions of the exporting country in terms of the sun-tinted spectacles of armchair tourism. At film festivals, a major meeting point of national cinema product and potential foreign buyers, the dominant film-critical discourse is the depoliticizing one of an essentialist humanism ("the human condition") complemented by a tokenist culturalism ("very French") and an aestheticizing of the culturally specific ("a poetic account of local life") (Boehringer and Crofts 198). With its emphasis on "originality" and "creativity," it is this discourse of art cinema which can facilitate the representation of political film in the tamer terms of art cinema (Crofts and Ros 1977: 52–54). As indicated above in "Imitating Hollywood," national cinema producers often cautiously bank on their foreign markets' imputed uninterest in the culturally specific. Without cross-cultural contextualization—a broadly educational project—foreign distribution of national cinemas, then, will tend to erase the culturally specific. One shrewd and successful strategy has been the combination of cultural universals (family madness, artistic ambition, rape) with specific local inflections effected by several Australian films of the last few years—*Sweetie, Shame, High Tide,* and *Celia*—that successfully target European film and TV markets.

B. Reading Foreign National Cinemas

The foregoing comments on the cultural selectivity of distributors' choices of films to import point to various possibilities of cross-cultural reception. Three features will be noted here: blank incomprehension; misreadings, usually projected appropriations; and the responses of producing countries to foreign praise.

Firstly, some local cultures can remain impervious to outside readings because producer and consumer share few or no cultural knowledges. A striking instance is the films made by the Navajo Indians with the anthropologists Sol Worth and John Adair (Worth and Adair 1960). Unexposed to film and television, the Navajos' innocence of close-ups gave non-indigenous American viewers no understanding of the need to focus on, say, a saddle blanket in the middle distance of a long-shot, while non-indigenous viewers' ignorance of the blanket's cultural significance gave them no purchase on the scene's Navajo meaning. Other examples include the rich cultural mythology of Latin American or Chinese films, religious emblems in Algerian or Iranian Muslim cinema, dance customs in

Indonesian cinema, the cultural density of local reference in Kluge, or indeed the knowledge of African colonial French which enables one to know that the title of the film, *Chocolat,* is slang for both "black" and "screwing."

The second feature has been well characterized in Elsaesser's and Rentschler's analyses of the United States appropriation of the New German Cinema (Elsaesser 1980: 80; Rentschler 1982). Rentschler, for example, remarks on the tripartite process of United States reviewers' ignoring both the cultural specificities and the production processes of the texts concerned, together with their corollary elevation of the author as prime source of meaning. As I have noted elsewhere, *Crocodile Dundee* offered its United States viewers a new set on which to inscribe American frontier myths and to rediscover an age of innocence (Crofts 1992).

Finally, the third feature can be illustrated by two samples of producing countries' responses to foreign praise of their product. When a 1980 Cannes Prize for Supporting Actor was awarded to Jack Thompson for his role in *Breaker Morant,* the film was re-released, after an indifferent run in Australia, to unanimous critical praise, and went on to scoop eleven of fifteen Australian Film Institute Awards that year (Crofts 1980). *Red Sorghum'*s winning of the 1988 Berlin Film Festival's Golden Bear gave a fillip to its wide popularity with Chinese students and youth (Tian 1989).

Foreign constructions of nations will be crucially affected by national cinematic representations—alongside those of cuisines, football teams and so on. In line with Benedict Anderson, Philip Rosen has observed that "identifying the . . . coherences [of] a 'national cinema' [and] of a nation . . . will always require sensitivity to the countervailing, dispersive forces underlying them" (Rosen 1984: 71). The nation can subsume into a fictional identity all manner of differences, across axes of class, gender, sexual preference, ethnicity, cultural capital, religion, and so on. Discourses of national cinema reception tend to effect similar homogenizations, if only insofar as each film is seen as representative of the producing nation (desolate sunburnt landscape as a prime marker of Australianness, melancholic engagement with a traumatic history as index of German-ness, etc.). Such reductive national-cultural symbolizations crowd out more complex articulations of national identity. This tendency is challenged only at limit-case points where a politicized cinema explores differences of class, gender, ethnicity, region, etc., within say, the "United" Kingdom.

Part IV. Conclusions

Several film-historiographical and film-theoretical conclusions can be developed from the foregoing. In general, this essay seeks to enable a consideration of national cinemas in non–First World terms. This firstly requires acknowledging a wider range of national cinemas than is regularly treated under that rubric. Film scholars' mental maps of world film production are often less than global. Even as assiduously encyclopedic an historian as Georges Sadoul devotes more pages of his *Histoire du Cinéma* to the Brighton School and the beginnings of Pathé than he does to the whole of Latin American cinema between 1900 and 1962 (1962: 43–64, 421–37). As Edward Said magisterially demonstrates with reference to "Orientalism" as academic discipline and world-view, so the world-views of different national film cultures are substantially informed by their country's relations—military, economic, diplomatic, cultural, ethnic—with other parts of the globe (1985). Thus Sadoul, informed by French colonialism, knows more of African cinema than of Latin American, while an American scholar, informed by the United States imperium and substantial Hispanic immigration, knows more of Latin American than African cinema, and a British scholar, informed by European and American cultural influences, may not see much outside that transatlantic axis. At the other end of the East-West axis, a hybrid, non-Eurocentric film culture such as the Thai—even if it does not as yet support substantial film scholarship—draws substantially on both Hong Kong and Hollywood sources as well as local production. Annette Hamilton thus remarks that "the average viewer in Thailand or Singapore has been exposed to a much wider range of visual material in style, genre, and cultural code that is the case for any 'average Western viewer'" (1992: 91).

Such skewed world views will demonstrably influence canon formation in the country concerned. And given that Third World production—for that is the prime excluded category—is more plentiful than European and North American by a factor of more than two to one (Sadoul 1962: 530–31). Luis Buñuel's trenchant comments on the canon of world literature could justly apply to that of world cinema:

> It seems clear to me that without the enormous influence of the canon of American culture, Steinbeck would be an unknown, as would Dos Passos and Hemingway. If they'd been born in Paraguay or Turkey, no one would ever have read them, which suggests the alarming fact that the greatness of a writer is in direct proportion to the power of his other country. Galdós, for instance, is often as remarkable as Dostoevski, but who outside Spain ever reads him? (1984 [1962]: 222)

To pursue the question of canon formation in relation to national cinemas demands examination not only of historically changing international relations of the kinds set out above, and of the force of such institutions as SavExportFilm and the European Film Development Office in cultural diplomacy, but also of the taste-brokering functions of film festivals and film criticism.

The ongoing critical tendency to hypostatize the "national" of national cinema must also be questioned in non–First World terms. Not only do regional and diasporic cinema production challenge notions of national cinemas as would-be autonomous cultural businesses. So, too, Hollywood's domination of world film markets renders most national cinemas profoundly unstable market entities, marginalized in most domestic and all export markets, and thus readily susceptible, *inter alia*, to projected appropriations of their indigenous cultural meanings. Witness the discursive (re)constructions of national cinemas in the process of their being exported. Ahead of India and Hong Kong Hollywood remains the big(est) other, the world's only film producer to have anything like transnational vertical integration of its industry. Study of any national cinema should include distribution and exhibition as well as production within the nation-state.

The nation-state itself has for a while been manifestly losing its sovereignty. It has been pressured both by transnational forces—canonically American in economic and cultural spheres, and Japanese in economic, and more recently cultural spheres—and simultaneously by the sub-national, sometimes called the local. The multiculturalism, the cultural hybridity of the nation-state has increasingly to be recognized. Recent instances of assertion of ethnicity, for instance, center on linguistic rights and cultural protection: from the Spanish regular in public notices in American cities to people from the Iberian Peninsula who describe themselves as Basque or Catalan rather than Spanish; from the nationalism of Québecois cinema and Welsh programs for S4C in the United Kingdom to the substantial Greek video markets throughout Australia, especially in Melbourne, the third largest Greek city in the world. Minorities or majorities defined by political dissent, class, ethnicity, gender, religion, or region are the everyday stuff of many people's lives: witness the five nations, three religions, four languages and two alphabets which went to constitute the "nation" Yugoslavia. Recall, also, from a 1962 essay by Leroi Jones (later Amira Baraka) called "'Black' is a Country": "[T]he Africans, Asians, and Latin Americans who are news today because of their nationalism [. . .] are exactly the examples the black man [*sic*] in this country should use in his struggle for *independence.*" (1968 [1962]: 84). Alongside such sub- and supra-national emphases, however, it is vital to recognize the political significance in other contexts, especially in developing countries, of rhetorics of nation and nationalism as means of fighting for independence from imperialist powers. Recall here the dominant genre of Vietnamese cinema, anti-imperialist propaganda.

Politics, in other words, is a matter of unequal distributions of power across axes of nation as well as of class, gender, ethnicity, etc. The political engagements that people do (or do not) make will vary with their social and political contexts, and their readings of those contexts. In considering national cinemas, this implies the importance of a political flexibility able, in some contexts, to challenge the fictional homogenizations of much discourse on national cinema, and in others to support them. And it would be foolhardy to underestimate the continuing power of the nation-state. To acknowledge these powers, by the same token, is not to disavow the cultural hybridity of nation-states; nor to unconditionally promote national identities over those of ethnicity, class, gender, religion, and the other axes of social division which contribute to those identities; nor, finally, to buy into originary fantasies of irrecoverable cultural roots, or into the unitary, teleological and usually masculinist fantasies in which nationalisms display themselves. That said, the struggle of many national cinemas has been one for cultural, if not also economic, self-definition against Hollywood or Indian product.

While cultural specificity, then, is by no means defined exclusively by the boundaries of that recent Western political construct, the nation-state, at certain historical moments—often moments when nationalism connects closely with genuinely populist movements, often nation-building moments (Hinde 1981)—national developments can occasion specifically national filmic manifestations which can claim a cultural authenticity or rootedness. Examples include some of the best known cinema "movements." Italian Neo-Realism, Latin American Third Cinema and Fifth Generation Chinese Cinema all arose on the crest of waves of national-popular resurgence. The French Nouvelle Vague marked a national intellectual-cultural recovery in the making since the late 1940s, whereas the events of May 1968 were more nationally divisive, leaving a clear political imprint in the works of Marker, Karmitz and Godard and Gorin markedly absent from the films of Rohmer or Malle. New German Cinema drew much of its strength, as Elsaesser has shown, from a 1960–1970s student audience and an allied concern to make sense of the traumas of recent German history (1989). The Australian feature film revival took off on a surge of cultural nationalism developing through the 1960s (Crofts forthcoming). Interestingly, such cinema movements occupy a key position in conventional histories of world cinema, whose historiography is not only nationalist but also elitist in its search for the "best" films, themselves often the product of such vital politico-cultural moments. As such, these are the films most frequently exported, and thus often occlude critical attention to films which may well be more popular.

In the context of the relations of unequal economic and cultural exchange obtaining between Hollywood and (other) national cinemas, the generation and/or survival of indigenous genres is a gauge of the strength and dynamism of a national cinema. Outstanding instances in non-Hollywood post-1945 cinema would be the Hong Kong martial arts film, the French (stylish) thriller of Chabrol, Beneix, and others, and in Britain, the Gothic horror film and the Ealing comedy. Less stable indigenous genres include the *Heimat* film in West Germany and the period film and social-realist film in Australia. A vital research area concerns the intersections between given genres and the national. A range of questions present themselves. For example: Under what conditions do culturally specific genres arise? How do imported (usually Hollywood) genres affect the generic range of a given national production sector? Does Chinese production even have genres?

The production category which most obviously confounds any attempts at a neat parcelling of "national" cinemas is of course the international co-production. This is more likely than not—and regularly so at the upper end of the budget range—to encourage the culturally bland. Nowell-Smith cites *Last Tango in Paris* as one of "a number of recent major films [that] have had no nationality in a meaningful sense at all" (1985: 154). And Rentschler develops a pointed comparison between *The Tin Drum*'s easy generalities and the more demanding cultural specificities of *The Patriot* (1984: 58–59).

Gloomy prognostications for a "Europudding" future of European co-production may well be exaggerated. For alongside directors such as Annaud, Besson, and Wenders, who, in *Variety*-speak are "a chosen few Euro helmers able to finesse international pics" (Williams 1992: 31), there are to be reckoned the strong successes of such culturally specific product (co-produced or not) as *Toto le Héros* and *The Commitments*. While countries with smaller local markets will often use co-production agreements to recoup costs, in the lower and middle budget ranges this need not necessarily work against culturally specific interests. Co-productions are actively encouraged by the European Film Development Office's promotional support for films financed from three or more member countries, and the Office argues its respect for national cultural specificities (Schneider 1992). And international co-productions do positively facilitate the treatment of such supra-national ethnic/religious issues as are dealt with in *Europa, Europa.* The mesh, or conflict, between economic and culturally specific interests will vary with the interests concerned at a given point in time.

Latent in preceding sections of this essay have been some key theoretical assumptions, and this is the third respect in which cinemas need to be thought of less in First World terms. Gabriel and Stam have both critiqued the imperialist *données* of center/periphery theories as applied to film theory (Gabriel 1986; Stam 1991)— though it has to be said that, provided multiple centers be recognized, such theories are still crucial to understanding global economic *Realpolitik.*

Underpinning First World approaches to national cinemas is the master antinomy of self/other (the linguistic sexism, as will be seen, is adopted advisedly). This essay suggests the inappropriateness, in theorizing differences of nations and national cinemas, of what Homi Bhabha calls the "exclusionary imperialist ideologies of self and other" (1989: 111). National cinematic self-definition, like *national* self-definition, likes to pride itself on its distinctiveness, on its standing apart from other(s). Such a transcendental concept of an ego repressing its other(s) urges abandonment of the self/other model as an adequate means of thinking national cinemas. For this dualist model authorizes only two political stances: imperial aggression and defiant national chauvinism. It can account neither for Third Cinema's move beyond what Solanas calls its "experimental" phase, nor for the existence of such projects as those of "Imitating Hollywood." Still less can it make sense of the hybridity of national cultures, including those of the notionally most pristine imperial centers. Trinh T. Minh-ha well characterizes the fluid, labile, hybrid nature of cultural identities:

> [D]ifference in this context undermines opposition as well as separatism. Neither a claim for special treatment, nor a return to an authentic core (the "unspoiled" Real Other), it acknowledges in each of its moves, the coming together and drifting

apart both within and between iderdity/identities. What is at
stake is not only the hegemony of Western cultures, but also
their identities a unified cultures; in other words, the realization
that there is a Third World in every First World, and vice-versa.
The master is made to recognize that His Culture is not as
homogeneous, not as monolithic as He once believed it to be; He
discovers, often with much reluctance, that He is just an other
among others.   (1987: 3)

With the recognition of ethnic-cultural hybridity, Bhabha notes,
"the threat of cultural difference is no longer a problem of other
people. It becomes a question of the otherness of the people-as-
one." (1990: 301).

Along these lines, Rey Chow has made explicit the feminization
of the oriental other which was implicit in Said (Chow 1991; Said
1985: 6, 309). And from her work around *Yellow Earth* it is possible
to elaborate a kind of hierarchy of othering processes which affect a
Western reading of this film's Chinese 1930s female peasant protagonist: Western over Chinese, male over female, urban over peasant, present over past (1990: 84). Such work offers sophisticated
methodological counters to the projected appropriateness of most
taste-brokers of foreign cinemas, who usually promote individual
artistic creativity, and at a different discursive level, of Fredric Jameson's blithe determination that "all third world texts are necessarily . . . to be read as . . . national allegories," which elides not only
individual creativity but also almost all local cultural specificities
(1966: 69).

NOTE

1. As regards the advisability of placing film within the "mediascape" of audiovisual provision in given countries, it should be said that the variety of such provision
is enormous. While it may be relatively straightforward to map the cinema/
television/video nexus in Western Europe—television being increasingly the primary
producer and exhibitor of European-model art cinema, with video as supplementary
to theatrical screenings of a range of types of other films—other countries operate
within quite different and less stable coordinates. Witness the rarity of broadcast television in poorer Asian, Pacific, and African countries, or the flourishing videotheques
in Pakistan, Taiwan, Burma, Kampuchea and Vietnam which screen black market
videos of films smuggled out of Thailand. These and subsequent examples point to
very considerable national "mediascape" variations, but the scholarship which would

support a fuller questionting here of the "cinemas" in "national cinemas" is both too massive and too dispersed for the present project. I would like to acknowledge Thomas Elsaesser's raising of this issue when I presented an earlier version of this essay at his kind invitation at the University of Amsterdam, January 16, 1992.

WORKS CITED

Anderson, Benedict. *Imagined Communities* (London: Verso, 1993).

Armes, Roy. *Third World Film Making and the West* (Berkeley and London: University of California Press, 1987).

Berry, Chris. "Ram, Chinese Film and the Politics of Nationalism," *Cinema Journal* 31:2 (Winter 1992).

Bhabha, Homi. "The Commitment to Theory." In *Questions of Third Cinema*, ed. Jim Pines and Paul Willemen (London: British Film Institute, 1989).

———. "DissemiNation." In *Notion and Narration*, ed. Homi Bhabha (London and New York: Routledge, 1990).

Bothringer, Kathe and Stephen Crofts. "The Triumph of Taste," *Australian Journal of Screen Theory* 8 (1980).

Bordwell, David. "Art Film as a Mode of Film Practice," *Film Criticism* 4:1 (1979).

———. *Narration in the Fiction Film* (London: Methuen, 1985).

Buñuel, Luis. *My Last Sigh* (1982; reprint, London: Jonathan Cape, 1984).

Burton, Julianne. "Marginal Cinemas and Mainstream Critical Theory" *Screen* 26:3–4 (May–August 1985).

Chow, Rey. "Silent is the Ancient Plain: Music, Filmmaking and the Conception of Reform in Chinese New Cinema," *Discourse* 12:2 (Spring–Summcr 1990).

———. *Women and Chinese Modernity* (Minneapolis: University of Minnesota Press, 1991).

Coorey, Philip and Amarnath Jayatilaka. 1974. "Sri Lanka (Ceylon)." In *International Film Guide*, ed. Peter Cowie (London: Tantivy Press, 1974).

Crisp, Colin. *Classic French Cinema, 1930–1960* (Bloomington: Indiana University Press, forthcoming).

Crofts, Stephen. *Australian Cinema as National Cinema* (New York: Columbia University Press, 1993).

———. "Breaker Morant Rethought," *Cinema Papers* 30 (December 1990).

———. "Crocodile Dundee Overseas." *Cinema Papers* 77 (January 1990).

———. "Cross-Cultural Reception Studies: Culturally Variant Readings of *Crocodile Dundee*," *Continuum* 6:1 (1992).

———. "Ideology and Form: Soviet. Socialist Realism and Chapayev," *Film Form* 1 (1976).

———. *Jean-Luc Godard* (London: British Film Institute, 1972).

———. "Shifting Paradigms in the Australian Historical Film," *East–West Film Journal* 5:2 (July 1991).

D'Lugo, Marvin. "Catalan Cinema: Historical Experience and Cinematic Practice," *Quarterly Review of Film and Video* 13:1–3 (1991).

Ebert, Roger. Public Lecture, University of Honolulu, Hawaii, November 28, 1990.

Elsaesser, Thomas. "Chronicle of a Death Retold," *Monthly Film Bulletin* 54:641 (June 1987).

———. "Colonialism and 'Law and Order Critictsm,'" *Screen* 27:3–4 (May–August 1986).

———. "Primary Identificaton and the Historical Subject: Fassbinder and Germany," *Cine-Tracts* 11 (Fall 1980).

————. *New German Cinema: A History* (London: Macmillan, 1989).

Gabriel, Teshome. *Third Cinema in the Third World* (Ann Arbor, Mich.: UMI Research Press, 1982).

Getino, Octavio and Fernando Solanas. "Towards a Third Cinema," *Afterimage* 3 (1969).

Guback, Thomas. "Hollywood's International Market." In *The American Film Industry*, ed. Tino Balio (Madison: University of Wisconsin Press, 1976).

Hamilton, Annette. "The Mediascape of Modern Southeast Asia," *Screen* 33:1 (Spring 1992).

Hebdige, Dick. "Subjects in Space," *New Formations* 11 (Summer 1990).

Higson, Andrew. "The Concept of National Cinema," *Screen* 30:4 (Autumn 1989).

Hinde, John. *Other People's Pictures* (Sydney: Australian Broadcasting Commission, 1961).

Jameson, Fredric. "Third World Literature in the Era of Multinational Capital," *Social Text* 15 (Fall 1986).

Jones, Leroi. "'Black' is a Country." In *Home: Social Essays* (1962; reprint, London: MacGibbon and Kee, 1968).

King, John. *Magical Reels: A History of Cinema in Latin America* (London: Verso, 1990).

Leahy, James. "Beyond the Frontiers," *Monthly Film Bulletin* 58:686 (March 1991).

Lent, John. *The Asian Film Industry* (Austin, Tex.: University of Texas Press, 1990).

Moussinac, Leon. *L'Age Ingrat du Cinéma* (1925; reprint, Paris: EFT, 1967).

Neale, Steve. "Art Cinema as Institution," *Screen* 22:1 (Spring 1981).

Nowell-Smith, Geoffrey. "But Do We Need It?" In *British Cinema Now*, ed. Martin Auty and Nick Roddick (London: British Film Institute, 1985).

Pick, Zuzana. "Chilean Cinema in Exile," *Framework* 34 (1987).

Pines, Jim and Paul Willemen. *Questions of Third Cinema* (London: British Film Institute, 1999).

Prédal, René. "Un rassemblement mondial de talents." In *L'amour du cinéma Américain*, ed. Francis Bordat (Paris: Cinémaction/Corlet/Télérama, 1990).

Rentschler, Eric. "American Friends and the New German Cinema," *New German Critique* 2:4–5 (Fall–Winter 1982).

————. *New German Cinema in the Course of Time* (Bedford Hills, New York: Redgrave, 1984).

Roddick, Nick. "If the United States Spoke Spanish We Would Have a Film Industry." In *British Cinema Now*, ed. Martin Auty and Nick Roddick (London: British Film Institute, 1985).

Rosen, Philip. "History Textuality, Nation: Kracauer, Burch, and Some Problems in the Study of National Cinemas," *Iris* 2:2 (1984).

Sadoul, Georges. *Histoire du Cinéma* (Paris: Flammarion, 1962).

Said, Edward. *Orientalism* (1978; reprint, London: Penguin, 1985).

Schneider, Ute. Seminar, Sydney Film Festival, June 9, 1992.

Sklar, Robert. *Movie-Made America* (New York: Random House, 1975).

Solanas, Fernando. "Amérique Latine: le point de vue d'un cinéaste." In *L'amour du cinéma Americain*, ed. Francis Bordat (Paris: Cinémaction/Corlet/Télérama, 1990).

Stam, Robert. "Eurocentrism, Afrocentrism, Polycentrism," *Quarterly Review of Film and Video* 13:1–3 (1991).

Thompson, Kristin. *Exporting Entertainment America in the World Film Market 1907–34* (London: British Film Institute, 1985).

Tian Zhuangzhuang. Seminar, Brisbane, June 7, 1985.

Trinh T. Minh-ha. "Introduction," *Discourse* 8 (Fall–Winter 1987).

Willemen, Paul. "The Third Cinema Question: Notes and Reflections," *Framework* 34 (1997).

Williams, Michael. "Films without Frontiers?" *Variety* (February 10, 1992).

Worth, Sol, and John Adair. *Through Navajo Eyes* (Bloomington: Indiana University Press, 1972).

Yoichi, Umemoto. "Quelles images pour le Japan?" In *L'amour du cinéma Americain,* ed. Francis Bordat (Paris: Cinémaction/Corlet/Télérama, 1990).

Andrew Higson

The Concept
of National Cinema

Although the term "national cinema" is often used to describe simply the films produced within a particular nation-state, this is neither the only way in which the term bas been used, nor is it, I want to argue, the most appropriate way of using the term. This article is not, however, intended as an examination of any historically concrete national cinema. It is intended instead as an'exploration of some of the implications of using the term "national" in discourse about cinema (the film industry, film culture), moving towards an argument that the parameters of a national cinema should be drawn at the site of consumption as much as at the site of production of films; an argument, in other words, that focuses on the activity of national audiences and the conditions under which they make sense of and use the films they watch. In so far as reference is made to historically specific national cinemas, most of my examples will relate to British cinema (and, of course, Hollywood), but I would hope that much of what I have to say is generalizable to other national cinemas—at least those of Western Europe—as well.[1]

The concept of national cinema has been appropriated in a variety of ways, for a variety of reasons: there is not a single universally accepted discourse of national cinema. In general terms, one can summarize these various mobilizations of the concept as follows. First, there is the possibility of defining national cinema in economic terms, establishing a conceptual correspondence between the terms "national cinema" and "the domestic film industry," and therefore being concerned with such questions as: Where are these films made,

and by whom? Who owns and controls the industrial infrastructures, the production companies, the distributors and the exhibition circuits? Second, there is the possibility of a text-based approach
to national cinema. Here the key questions become: What are these
films about? Do they share a common style or world view? What
sort of projections of the national character do they offer? To what
extent are they engaged in "exploring, questioning and constructing a notion of nationhood in the films themselves and in the consciousness of the viewer"?[2]

Third, there is the possibility of an exhibition-led, or consumption-
based, approach to national cinema. Here the major concern has
always been to do with the question of which films audiences are
watching, and particularly the number of foreign, and usually American films which have high-profile distribution within a particular
nation-state—a concern which is generally formulated in terms of an
anxiety about cultural imperialism. Fourth, there is what may be
called a criticism-led approach to national cinema, which tends to
reduce national cinema to the terms of a quality art cinema, a culturally worthy cinema steeped in the high-cultural and/or modernist
heritage of a particular nation-state, rather than one that appeals to
the desires and fantasies of the popular audiences.

In other words, very often the concept of national cinema is used
prescriptively rather than descriptively, citing what *ought* to be the
national cinema, rather than describing the actual cinematic experience of popular audiences. As Geoffrey Nowell-Smith has noted, it
has always been something of a struggle to enable "the recognition
of popular forms a a legitimate part of national cultural life."[3]

If these are some of the ways in which the term national cinema
has been used, what are the processes by which, or what are the conditions under which, a particular mode of film practice, or a specific
range of textual practices, or a particular set of industrial practices
comes to be named a national cinema? Indeed, what is involved in
calling forth the idea of a national anything, cultural or otherwise?
In other words, what is involved in positing the idea of nationhood
or national identity?

To identify a national cinema is first of all to specify a coherence
and a unity; it is to proclaim a unique identity and a stable set of

meanings. The process of identification is thus invariably a hege-monizing, mythologising process, involving both the production and assignation of a particular set of meanings, and the attempt to con-tain, or prevent the potential proliferation of other meanings. At the same time, the concept of a national cinema has almost invariably been mobilised as a strategy of cultural (and economic) resistance: a means of asserting national autonomy in the face of (usually) Holly-wood's international domination.

The process of nationalist mythmaking is not simply an insid-ious (or celebratory) work of ideological production, but is also at the same time a means of setting one body of images and values against another, which will very often threaten to overwhelm the first. The search for a unique and stable identity, the assertion of national specificity does then have some meaning, some useful-ness. It is not just an ideological sleight of hand although it must always also be recognised as that. Histories of national cinema can only therefore really be understood as histories of crisis and conflict, of resistance and negotiation. But also, in another way, they are histories of a business seeking a secure footing in the mar-ketplace, enabling the maximisation of an industry's profits while at the same time bolstering a nation's cultural standing. At this level, the politics of national cinema can be reduced to a market-ing strategy, an attempt to market the diverse as, in fact, offering a coherent and singular experience. As Thomas Elsaesser has sug-gested, "internationally, national cinemas used to have a generic function: a French, Italian or a Swedish film sets different hori-zons of expectation for the general audience—a prerequisite for marketing purposes,"[4] and it is this attempt to establish a generic narrative image, a particular horizon of expectation, which is at stake.

There are perhaps two central methods, conceptually, of estab-lishing or identifying the imaginary coherence, the specificity, of a national cinema. First, there is the method of comparing and con-trasting one cinema to another, thereby establishing varying degrees of otherness. Second, there is what might be termed a more inward-looking process, exploring the cinema of a nation in relation to other already-existing economies and cultures of that nation-state.

The first of these means of defining a national cinema is premised upon the semiotic principle of the production of meaning and identity through difference. The task is to try to establish the identity of one national cinema by its relationship to and differentiation from other national cinemas: British cinema is what it is by virtue of what it is not—American cinema, or French cinema, or German cinema, etc. . . . . Elsaesser again: "Other countries try to maintain themselves on a terrain staked out by the competition. West Germany is one example, but the implications affect all developed countries whose wase of cultural identity is based on a need to maintain markers—and markets—of difference vis-à-vis the products of the international entertainment business."[5] To some extent, then, the process of defining a national cinema, and thereby establishing some sort of unique and self-contained identity, takes meaning in the context of a conceptual play of differences and identities. And, as Benedict Anderson has argued, "nations . . . cannot be imagined except in the midst of an irremediable plurality of other nations."[6]

Within this discourse cinema itself is almost taken for granted, and the task becomes one of differentiating between a variety of apparently nationally constituted modes of cinematic practice and filmically produced signs and meanings. Such an operation becomes increasingly problematic as cinema develops in an economy characterised by the international ownership and circulation of images and sounds. It is therefore necessary to examine the overdetermination of Hollywood in the international arena. By Hollywood, I mean the international institutionalization of certain standards and values of cinema, in terms of both audience expectations, professional ideologies and practices and the establishment of infrastructures of production, distribution, exhibition, and marketing, to accommodate, regulate, and reproduce these standards and values. While Hollywood's classical period and its studio system may have disappeared, whatever the prophecies about the end of cinema in the late 1970s and early 1980s, cinema—and Hollywood—are, in the late 1980s, still very much alive and key components in the international mass entertainment business. This is the era of the multiplex, the package deal, the blockbuster, but also the revival of genre cinema and the serial film, even if the site and system of delivery are no longer primarily theatrical.

Hollywood never functions as simply one term within a system of equally weighted differences. Hollywood is not only the most internationally powerful cinema—it has also, of course, for many years been an integral and naturalised part of the national culture, or the popular imagination, of most countries in which cinema is an established entertainment form. In other words, Hollywood has become one of those cultural traditions which feed into the so-called national cinemas of, for instance, the western European nations. "Hollywood can hardly be conceived . . . as totally other, since so much of any nation's film culture is implicitly 'Hollywood.'"[7] Being both a naturalised part of national culture, and also, visibly different, even exotic,[8] Hollywood thus functions as a doubled mode of popular fantasy, hence its propensity to be dismissed as escapism.

Geoffrey Nowell-Smith has attempted to account for the appeal of American films in the British market as follows—and his account would seem at least to be partially applicable to other national cinemas as well:

> The hidden history of cinema in British culture, and in popular culture in particular, has been the history of American films popular with the British public. The strength of American cinema was never just economic . . . [and] the basic reason for Hollywood's dominance was artistic and cultural. The American cinema set out in the first place to be popular in America where it served an extremely diverse and largely immigrant public. What made it popular at home also helped make it popular abroad. The ideology of American cinema has tended to be far more democratic than that of the cinema of other countries. This in part reflects the actual openness of American society, but it is above all a rhetorical strategy to convince the audiences of the virtues and pleasures of being American. Translated into the export arena, this meant a projection of America as intensely— if distantly—appealing. When matched against American films of the same period, their British counterparts came across all too often as restricting and stifling, subservient to middle class artistic models and to middle- and upper-class values.[9]

At times, Nowell-Smith's claims seem overstated.[10] To suggest, for instance, that "British cinema . . . has never been truly popular in Britain"[11] is to ignore the box-office success over the years of numerous British stars, film, genres and cycles of film. And to argue in terms of a generalised, monolithic "British public" is to ignore class, race, gender and regional differences. Even so, Nowell-Smith's revaluation of American films in terms of the appeal of apparently democratic aspirations seems useful. For a start, it displaces the idea that American box-office success in foreign markets is due solely to manipulative marketing and aggressive economic control. Furthermore, it challenges the conventional attacks, both conservative and radical, on American culture by noting the way in which its integration into the British cultural formation broadens the cultural repertoire available to audiences. As Tony Bennett has suggested, the argument that America is involved in a form of cultural imperialism "although not without point . . . misses much of the essential ambivalence of the impact of American popular culture in Britain which, in many respects, has been more positive, particularly in making avaliable a repertoire of cultural styles and resources . . . which, in various ways, have undercut and been consciously mobilised against the cultural hegemony of Britain's traditional élites."[12]

The rhetoric of democracy and populism is built into the formal organization of the American film, with its classically strong and dynamic narrative drive towards individual achievement—although this also points to the limitations of the rhetoric, since problems and their resolutions are invariably articulated only in relation to the *individual* within a substantially unchanged capitalist patriarchy. Further, classical Hollywood cinema conventionally ties this narrative structure of achievement to the romantic appeal of the formation of the heterosexual couple, and situates the narrative both within a visual form whose mise-en-scène and organisation of spectacle and spectating has proved intensely pleasurable, and within a physical context of film-watching which emphasises the process of fantasising. Overall, this form has a propensity to engage the spectator thoroughly in a complex series of identifications, with an almost ruthless disregard of the nationality (as well as class and gender) of the spectator, and it is often the figure of the star which holds together these various formal strategies, narrative, visual and identificatory.

This is not to suggest that many British films, for instance, do not also work within the same formal system. But it is generally accepted that American filmmakers innovated, applied, and exploited this form of filmmaking much earlier and more consistently than their British counterparts who operated with a much more mixed, and so-called "primitive," variety of modes of representation, compared to Hollywood where this mode of representation had become institutionalised by 1917. It is also generally accepted that Hollywood has had the resources, which British film producers have lacked, to exploit the potential appeals of the institutional mode of representation.[13] Thus, for instance, British cinema has never been able to sustain a star system on the same glamorous scale as Hollywood for long periods of time—not least since Hollywood tends to consume British stars for its own films, thereby increasing the stake that British audiences have in those films.

If we confine discussion to film production, it makes sense in this context to speak of national cinemas as nonstandard and marginal activities. Part of the problem, of course, is the paradox that for a cinema to be nationally popular it must also be international in scope. That is to say, it must achieve the international (Hollywood) standard. For, by and large, it is the films of the major American distributors which achieve national box-office success, so that filmmakers who aspire to this same level of box-office popularity must attempt to reproduce the standard, which in practice means colluding with Hollywood's systems of funding, production control, distribution and marketing. Any alternative means of achieving national *popular* success must, if it is to be economically viable, be conceived on an international scale, which is virtually impossible for a national film industry, unless it has a particularly large domestic market, as in the case of the Bombay film industry. The difficulty is to establish some sort of balance between the "apparently incompatible objectives of a national cinema—to be economically viable but culturally motivated," "to be 'national' in what is essentially an international industry."[14]

Historically, at least within the Western European countries, there has been one major solution to this problem, one central strategy for attempting to reconcile the irreconcilable and maintain both some form of national cultural specificity and achieve a relative degree of international visibility and economic viability: the production of an art cinema, a nationally-based (and in various ways state-subsidised) cinema of quality. As Steve Neale has argued, art cinema has played a central role "in the attempts made by a number of European countries both to counter American domination of their indigenous markets in film and also to foster a film industry and a film culture of their own."[15] The discourses of "art," "culture," and "quality," and of "national identity" and "nationhood," have historically been mobilised against Hollywood's mass entertainment film, and used to justify various nationally specific economic systems of support and protection. But there are two further points to note here. First, that this is yet another instance of "the peculiarity of a national film production within an international marketplace,"[16] since the market for art cinema is indeed decidedly international, as is the network of film festivals and reviewing practices, and other means of achieving a critical reputation and both a national and an international cultural space for such films.[17] And second, that perhaps the situation isn't quite so peculiar after all, given the increasing tendency for international co-productions (invariably with the involvement of one or other of the still-extant national television networks), and the development of transnational forms of industry support and protection within the European Community.

However, the various international art cinemas have rarely achieved a national popular success, partly because of their modes of address, and partly because of the international hegemony of Hollywood at the level of distribution, exhibition and marketing. Indeed, in the case of the British film industry at least, the distribution and exhibition arms of that industry have primarily been organized to foster, extend, and consolidate the domination of the British market by American popular film. Thus for some time the major American studios have had their own distribution companies operating in Britain, while the major British companies have built up close relationships with American producers and distributors, who often also have substantial financial interests in British companies. British companies have found this sort of cooperation necessary, since, in capitalist terms, the American film industry was much better organised before the British film industry, and was able to pursue imperialist policies with some vigour, undercutting the charges of local distributors, since they could go into the British market in the knowledge that costs had already been recovered from the huge American domestic market.[18]

In other words, the influence of Hollywood on domestic markets is always much more than simply a question of the poverty or élitism of domestic filmmaking. This suggests that national cinema needs to be explored not only in relation to production, but also in relation to the questions of distribution and exhibition, audiences, and consumption, within each nation-state. The idea that Hollywood—and now, of course, television—has become a part of the popular imagination of British cinema audiences needs to be taken seriously.

As such, it becomes insufficient to define national cinema solely by contrasting one national cinema to another, and we need also to take into account the other key way of defining a national cinema—what I have suggested is a more *inward-looking* means, constituting a national cinema not so much in terms of its difference from other cinemas, but in terms of its relationship to an already existing national political, economic and cultural identity (in so far as a single coherent identity can be established) and set of traditions. In this way, British cinema would be defined in terms of already established discourses of Britishness, by turning in on itself, on its own history and cultural formation, and the defining ideologies of national identity and nationhood, rather than by reference to other national cinemas—bearing in mind always that Hollywood may itself be an integral part of that cultural formation.

At one level, in terms of political economy, a national cinema is a particular industrial structure; a particular pattern of ownership and control of plant, real estate, human resources and capital, and a system of state legislation which circumscribes the nationality of that ownership—primarily in relation to production. The relative economic power of a notional film industry will depend upon the degree to which production, distribution, and exhibition are integrated, regulated, technically equipped, and capitalised; the size of the home market and the degree of penetration of overseas markets. At the level of production, we need to take into account both the means and modes of production employed (the organisation of work, in terms of systems of management, division of labour, professional organisations and ideologies, availability of technology, etc.) and the access that producers have to both domestic and overseas markets. It is important to recognise also that even the domestic market is not homogeneous, and that production companies often deliberately limit themselves to specific areas of exploitation, especially when faced with the mainstream box-office supremacy of the major American distributors overseas. These limited areas of exploitation will, in many cases, be areas considered marginal (that is, marginally profitable) by Hollywood (low-budget films, B movies, films made primarily for the domestic market rather than for export, art cinema, and so on).

It is worth underlining again the role of the state, and the terms of its intervention in the practices of a film industry, in determining the parameters and possibilities of a national cinema (as both an economically viable and a culturally motivated institution)—at least since the mid 1910s, when governments began to recognise the potential ideological power of cinema, and cinema itself could seem to be something like a national cultural form, an institution with a nationalising function. But it is also important to recognise that the state intervenes only when there is a felt fear of the potential power of a foreign cinema, and particularly when the products—and therefore the ideologies and values—of a foreign cinema are widely circulated within a nation-state, and assumed to be having also a detrimental effect on that nation-state's economy. In other words, while it is conceptually useful to isolate a single national cinema, it is necessary also that it is seen in relation to other cinemas.

The same of course is true when we come to examine the cultural identity of a particular national cinema. The areas that need to be examined here are, first, the content or subject matter of a particular body of films—that which is represented (and particularly the construction of "the national character"), the dominant narrative discourses and dramatic themes, and the narrative traditions and other source material on which they draw (and particularly the degree to which they draw on what has been constructed as the national heritage, literary, theatrical or otherwise)—in other words, the ways in which cinema inserts itself alongside other cultural practices, and the ways in which it draws on the existing cultural histories and cultural traditions of the producing nation, reformulating them in cinematic terms, appropriating them to build up its own generic conventions. Second, there is the question of the sensibility, or structure of feeling, or world-view expressed in those films. And third, there is the area of the style of those films, their formal systems of representation (the forms of narration and motivation which they employ, their construction of space and staging of action, the ways which they structure narrative and time, the modes of performance they employ and the types of visual pleasure, spectacle and display with which they engage), and their modes of address and constructions of subjectivity (and particularly the degree to which they engage in the construction of fantasy and the regulation of audience knowledge).

In considering cinema in terms of cultural identity, it is necessary also to pay attention to the processes by which cultural hegemony is achieved within each nation-state; to examine the internal relations of diversification and unification, and the power to institute one particular aspect of a pluralistic cultural formation as politically dominant and to standardise or naturalise it. Historical accounts of national cinemas have too often been premised on unproblematised notions of nationhood and its production. The search for a stable and coherent national identity can only be successful at the expense of repressing internal differences, tensions and contradictions—differences of class, race, gender, region, etc. It is important also to pay attention to historical shifts in the construction of nationhood and national identity: nationhood is always an image constructed under particular conditions, and indeed nationalism itself, as a concept in the modern sense, can only be traced back to the late eighteenth century.[19] "History," as Benedict Anderson puts it, "is the necessary basis of the national narrative."[20]

As Stephen Heath has suggested, "nationhood is not a given, it is always something to be gained"[21]—and cinema needs to be understood as one of the means by which it is "gained." Thus, definitions of British cinema, for instance, almost always involve, on the one hand, the construction of an imaginary homogeneity of identity and culture, an already achieved national identity, apparently shared by all British subjects; and on the other hand, the valorisation of a very particular conception of "British cinema," which involves ignoring whole areas of British cinema history. In each case, a process of inclusion and exclusion is enacted, a process whereby one thing is centralised, at the same time necessarily marginalising another, a process wherein the interests of one particular social group are represented as in the collective or national interest, producing what Anderson has called "the imagined community of the nation."[22]

Proclamations of national cinema are thus in part one form of "internal cultural colonialism": it is, of course, the function of institutions—and in this case national cinemas—to pull together diverse and contradictory discourses, to articulate a contradictory unity, to play a part in the hegemonic process of achieving consensus, and containing difference and contradiction.[23] It is this state of contradictoriness which must always be borne in mind in any discussion of national cinema. Cinema never simply reflects or expresses an already fully-formed and homogeneous national culture and identity, as if it were the undeniable property of all national subjects; certainly, it privileges only a limited range of subject positions which thereby become naturalised or reproduced as the only legitimate positions of the national subject. But it needs also to be seen as actively working to construct subjectivity as well as simply expressing a pre-given identity.

National cinema is, then, a complex issue, and I would argue that it is inadequate to reduce the study of national cinema only to consideration of the films produced by and within a particular nation-state. It is important to take into account the film culture as a whole, and the overall institution of cinema and to address the following issues:

- the range of films in circulation within a nation-state—including American and other foreign film—and how they are taken up at the level of exhibition; in the present as, of course, film art "in circulation" and "exhibited" or on display in a variety of ways, and not just to be physically pcojected at cinemas (multiplexes, city-centre cinemas, art-house cinemas, etc.): they are available on video and via the various forms of broadcast and cable television as *films,* but they are also present and recycled in popular culture *intertextually,* as icons, reference points, standards and pastiches;

- the range of sociologically specific audiences for different types of film, and how these audiences use these films in particular exhibition circumstances; that is to say, we need to take into account not only the historically constituted reading practices and modes of spectatorship and subjectivity, the mental machinery and relative cultural power or readerly competences of different audiences—but also the experience of cinema(s) in a more general cultural semse: the role of marketing and audience expectation, the reasons why particular audiences go to the cinema, the pleasures they derive from this activity, the specific nature of the shared social and communal experience of cinema-going, differentiated according to class, race, gender, age, etc., the role of television (and video) in mediating and transforming the experience of cinema, the different experiences offered by the various types of theatrical exhibition spaces. It is worth remembering that, from the point of view of economic historians such as Douglas Gomery, film industries marked by a high degree of horizontal and vertical integration can be seen as no more nor less than highly diversified cinema circuits, where production is a necessary high-risk service industry, and where cinemas are as much luxurious sites for the consumption of or advertising for commodities other than films, as they are sites for the fantasy experience of watching fitms;[24]

- the range of and relation between discourses about film circulating within that cultural and social formation, and their relative accessibility to different audiences. Crucial among these discourses is the tension between, on the one hand, those intellectual discourses which insist that a proper national cinema must be one which aspires to the status of art (and therefore adheres to the current dominant definitions of cinema as an art form), discourses which, from a particular class perspective, dismiss Hollywood's popular cinema as culturally debilitating; and on the other hand, those more populist discourses where, in effect, the idea of "good entertainment" overrides questions of "art" or "nationality." This latter discourse suggests that a cinema can only be national, and command a national-popular audience if it is a mass-production genre cinema, capable of constructing, reproducing, and recycling popular myths on a broad scale, with an elaborate, well capitalised and well resourced system of market exploitation. Again, the role of television must be taken into account as one of agents which generates, sustains and regulates film cultures and renders discourses about the cinema more or less accessible.

To explore national cinema in these terms means laying much greater stress on the point of consumption, and on the *use* of film (sounds, images, narratives, fantasies), than on the point of production. It involves a shift in emphasis away from the analysis of film texts as vehicles for the articulation of nationalist sentiment and the interpellation of the implied national spectator, to an analysis of how actual audiences construct their cultural identity in relation to the various products of the national and international film and television industries, and the conditions under which this is achieved.

The current state of film studies is characterised by a tension between those who are working on the political economics of cinema and those who analyse and investigate textuality and the putative spectator, and by the corresponding absence of much work on actual audiences, beyond the examination of critical discourses. Bordwell, Staiger and Thompson have proposed the most acceptable form of relationship or mediation between political economy and textuality in terms of a sort of sociology of organisations and professional ideologies.[25] Clearly, this is something that could be fruitfully explored in relation to other national cinemas. But it doesn't at present help to bridge the gap between textual analysis, the analysis of critical discourses in print-form, and the vast continent of the popular audiences for film—and the question of audiences has to be crucial for the study of national cinemas. For what is a national cinema if it doesn't have a national audience?

NOTES

1. This article is based on a chapter from a PhD thesis which I am currently preparing. I would like to acknowledge the work of Thomas Elsaesser in enabling me to develop some of the arguments advanced here.

2. Susan Barrowclough, "Introduction: The Dilemmas of a National Cinema," in Barrowclough, ed., *Jean-Pierre Lefebere: The Quebec Connection* (BFI Dossier no. 13, 1981), 3.

3. "Popular culture," *New Formations* 2 (Summer 1987): 80.

4. "Chronicle of a Death Retold: Hyper, Retro or Counter-Cinema," *Monthly Film Bulletin* 54:641 (June 1987): 167.

5. *New German Cinema: A History* (London, BFI/Macmillan, 1989), 6–7.

6. "Narrating the Nation," *Times Literary Supplement,* June 13, 1986, 659; see also Benedict Anderson, *Imagined Communities: Reflections on the Origin and Spread of Nationalism* (London: Verso, 1983).

7. Elsaesser, "Chronicle of a Death Retold," 166.

8. See Nowell-Smith, *New Formations*, op. cit., 81.

9. "But Do We Need It?" in Martin Autry and Nick Roddick, eds., *British Cinema Now* (London: BFI, 1985), 152. For other writers advancing a similar argument, see also Paul Swann, *The Hollywood Feature Film in Post-War Britain* (London: Croom Helm, 1987); Paul Willemen, "In Search of an Alternative Perspective: An Interview with Armand and Michelle Mattelait," *Framework* 26–27 (1985): 56; Geoffrey Nowell-Smith, "Gramsci and the National-Popular," *Screen Education* 22 (Spring 1977); Don MacPherson, "The Labour Movement and Oppositional Cinema: Introduction," in *Traditions of Independence* (London: BFI, 1990), 127–28; Peter Miles and Malcolm Smith, *Cinema, Literature, and Society: Élite and Mass Culture in Inter-War Britain* (London: Croom Helm, 1987), 170–78; Robert Murphy, "A Rival to Hollywood? The British Film Industry in the Thirties," *Screen* 24:4–5 (July–October 1983).

10. See Tony Aldgate, "Comedy, Class and Containment: The British Domestic Cinema of the 1930s," in James Curran and Vincent Porter, eds., *British Cinema History* (London: Weidenfeld and Nicholson, 1983). See also my "Saturday Night or Sunday Morning? British Cinema in the Fifties," in *Ideas and Production* IX–X (1989): 146–49.

11. Nowell-Smith, "But Do We Need It?" 152.

12. "Popular Culture and Hegemony in Post-War Britain," in *Politics, Ideology and Popular Culture,* Unit 18 of Open University Popular Culture course (U203), 13.

13. See, e.g., David Bordwell, Janet Staiger and Kristin Thompson, *The Classical Hollywood Cinema* (London: RKP, 1985); Barry Salt, *Film Style and Technology: History and Analysis* (London: Starwood, 1983); Kristin Thompson, *Exporting Entertainment* (London: BFI, 1986); Charles Barr, ed., *All Our Yesterdays: 90 Years of British Cinema* (London: BFI, 1986); Roy Armes, *A Critical History of British Cinema* (London: Secker and Warburg, 1978).

14. Elsaesser, *New German Cinema*, 3 and 39.

15. "Art Cinema as Institution," *Screen* 22:1 (1981): 11.

16. Elsaesser, *New German Cinema*, 49.

17. See Neale, op. cit., 34–35.

18. See chapters on the film industry in Curran and Porter, eds., op. cit., and Barr, ed., op. cit.; and Margaret Dickinson and Sarah Street, *Cinema and State* (London: BFI, 1985).

19. See Eugene Kamenka, "Political Nationalism: The Evolution of the Idea," in Kamenka, ed., *Nationalism* (London: Edward Arnold, 1976), 3–20; and Tom Nairn, *The Break-up of Britain* (London: Verso, 1981), 329–41.

20. Op. cit., 659.

21. "Questions of Property: Film and Nationhood," *Cine-tracts* 1:4 (Spring/Summer 1978): 10.

22. Op. cit., 659.

23. See Paul Willemen, "Remarks on *Screen*: Introductory Notes for a History of Contexts," *Southern Review* 16:2 (July 1983): 296.

24. See Douglas Gomery, *The Hollywood Studio System* (London: BFI/Macmillan, 1986).

25. Op. cit.

Martha Wolfenstein

Movie Analyses in the Study of Culture

This paper will be concerned with the analysis of the content of fiction (or entertainment) films in relation to the study of culture. Other kinds of films and other modes of approach will not be discussed. So, for instance, I shall not attempt to deal with propaganda, documentary, or experimental films. I shall leave aside the investigation of such topics as film history, film production, film technique, the relation of visual to sound effects, comparison of the film with other media such as the novel, questions of aesthetic evaluation.

First, I shall consider briefly the theoretical background of film analysis in relation to cultural studies. Second, I shall elaborate and illustrate procedures for the analysis of movie content. (I shall confine myself to questions of interpretation and shall not discuss observational procedure, for instance, with respect to frequency of viewing the same film, methods of note taking, etc.) I shall attempt to indicate how recurrent movie themes are related to variables of dynamic psychology, and how one can on this basis characterize groups of films within a given culture and compare films of different cultures. Third, I shall indicate some relations of movie themes to their cultural context, pointing out certain of the problems involved in connecting movie plots with real-life behavior and character.

From *The Study of Culture at a Distance*, edited by Margaret Mead and Rhoda Métraux. Republished by Berghahn Press, 2000, as part of a series from the Research in Contemporary Cultures Project, edited by William Beeman. Courtesy of the Institute for Intercultural Studies, Inc., New York.

1. Background of the Cultural Study of Movies

It is useful to bear in mind the relation of movie plots to stories and dramas in other and older media, and to recognize some of the theoretical antecedents of the recently developed skill of movie interpretation. The analysis of literary and other art forms in relation to their cultural contexts has developed from the convergence of a number of trends in modern thought. Of these the following may be noted here:

a. Philosophical theories of the differences of art styles of different epochs. The German and French romantics attempted to express what they felt to be major and discontinuous differences in the outlook on life of the ancient world and that of the modern world, and connected with them differences in what they called classic and romantic art styles. A late and elaborate expression of this view appeared in the work of Spengler (1918), in which for each of a number of cultures the styles of art, religion, philosophy, science, technology, and social organization were seen as interrelated.

b. The interpretation of folklore as a culture trait. Traditional tales, having been variously interpreted as concealing remote historical happenings, containing allegories or figurative explanations of events in nature, and so on, came increasingly to be regarded as expressions of the attitudes, daydreams, ethics, and mode of life of the people among whom they were told. This approach, as formulated by Boas and by Benedict (1931), parallels on a more empirical level the approach of the romantic philosophers to the productions of historical cultures.

c. Universal psychological motifs as sources of recurrent mythological themes. After Freud had recognized the relation of the Oedipus myth to a universal human conflict, Otto Rank wrote *Der Mythus von der Geburt des Helden* (1909), in which he showed a common pattern in myths of various sources (of the birth of Buddha, of Jesus, et al.), Rank carried this approach further in *Das Inzest-Motiv in Dichtung und Sage* (1912), in which he also applied the idea that the manner of expressing certain common themes varies through time. The relation of mythology to universal human fantasies has been most elaborated by the school of Jung (cf., for instance, the recent *Hero with a Thousand Faces* by Joseph Campbell, 1949).

d. Studies of the work of individual artists in relation to their life histories. This was also initiated by Freud (1943), in his study of Leonardo, and has remained the preferred approach to art of the Freudian school (cf., for instance, Marie Bonaparte's book on Poe, 1933; Ella Sharpe's essays on Shakespeare, 1950).

Contemporary cultural anthropology combines something from each of these approaches in interpreting art productions. It looks for regularities running through all the productions of a culture: its religious rituals, secular dances, myths, ornaments, and the like. At the same time it relates these to genetic psychological material drawn from the typical life cycle of individuals of the given culture. The universal psychological motifs serve to guide the observation both of the life course of members of the culture and of their artistic and other productions. The analysis of Balinese dances in their relation to other aspects of Balinese life, and especially to the characteristic parent-child relations, in the work of Margaret Mead, Gregory Bateson (Bateson and Mead, 1942), and Jane Belo (1949) is illustrative.

While a variety of considerations are combined in the analysis of a work of art from the point of view of its cultural relevance, such an analysis is also selective. This selectivity may be expressed in terms of grouping: With what other works are we going to group this one for the purpose of our study? For the purpose of cultural studies, we group the work with others that have been produced by members of the same culture. That we choose to work with this grouping of material does not exclude the usefulness for other purposes of other groupings. A particular work of art may be grouped with other works of the same artist and we may try to see what are his characteristic themes and ways of treating them. It may be grouped with other works of a particular school of art, with other works of its period, with other works in the same medium, with all other productions growing out of human fantasy. According to the grouping we choose we will get formulations of different levels of generality and pay attention to different orders of likeness and variation. The generalizations obtained from one kind of grouping do not preclude those from another. Thus, for instance, we may want to consider *Oedipus, Hamlet,* and *The Brothers Karamazov* from the point of view of their common aspect as Oedipal tragedies. If we want to take into consideration the culture and epoch in which these various works were produced, while not denying their common features, we should proceed to analyze the different ways in which they deal with their common problem. For this purpose we should look for relations between each of these works and others of its culture and epoch, and so on.

In the analysis of works of art for the purpose of cultural studies, cross-cultural comparisons, whether explicit or implicit, are indispensable. Without such comparisons we may attribute to a particular culture tendencies that are more widely shared (cf. Spengler, 1918). Thus, for instance, an attempt to reconcile goodness and badness in a woman is common to the literature and the drama of a number of Western cultures (and also, among other things, distinguishes them from cultures in which this emotional problem does not occur). If we want to distinguish between, let us say, French and American cultures, we must analyze the different ways in which they proceed to reconcile goodness and badness in their dramatic heroines. (A useful exercise for the beginner in cultural analysis of films is to compare films of two or more cultures that deal with a common topic such as the one mentioned.)

2. Procedures in Analyzing Movie Content

A general approach to the interpretation of movie content is as follows: (1) We have a set of concepts and propositions from dynamic psychology (e.g., those having to do with Oedipal conflicts). (2) These suggest a number of *variables* that can be illustrated in film content (e.g., father-son relations). (3) A particular way of handling such a variable in a film constitutes a *theme* (e.g., the father figure attacking the son figure). (4) Such a theme may be interpreted by applying propositions of dynamic psychology. We formulate a hypothesis about the derivation of the theme from underlying psychological motives (e.g., the son's hostility is projected onto the father).

In practice our observations and interpretations do not necessarily follow this logical sequence. We may observe a theme and subsequently attempt to relate it to variables derived from our psychological presuppositions. We may also be led by our observations to enlarge or modify our general psychological formulations. In other words, there is an interplay between observations and general ideas; the movement between them is in both directions.

To elaborate further on variables and themes, a variable indicates a general area to be observed, such as father-son relations, mother-son relations, father-daughter relations. A theme is the way in which a particular variable is repeatedly concretized in the productions of a particular culture. Thus, for instance, the moral superiority of a son (or son figure) to a father (or father figure) is a theme of American films; the moral superiority of a father (or father figure) to a son (or son figure) is a theme of British films. These two themes represent different positions in relation to the variable of father-son relations. Their relation to a common variable provides a basis for comparison.

A theme is a unit that recurs. That we look for recurrences is not a peculiar point of film analysis, but is rather a requirement of scientific method, which is concerned not with the unique instance but with regularities. In the preliminary phase of our analysis, what we take as a theme is a matter of convenience. It can be anything from a single image to a total plot configuration. Eventually one attempts to work out interconnections among the themes one has observed in the films of a particular culture. The procedure might be described in somewhat this way. To begin with, if we have seen one film of a particular culture, or several, or a considerable number, but have not yet begun any analysis of them, we are apt to have some vague overall impressions of their atmosphere. If we think of going to see a French film, an Italian, a Russian, a German, or an American film, we will anticipate a certain quality or flavor of each of these experiences, a certain recognizable world, characteristic of each. The aim of our analysis is to substitute for such inarticulate impressions a structured account of what has happened to produce them. In the transition from impressions to analysis, we work with themes of various degrees of particularity and inclusiveness.

We may cite as illustration a variety of themes, and also suggest in part the way they work into larger constructs. A recurrent theme of British films is the image of a bowed blond head. We get some idea of the significance of this image in relation to the recurrent temptation and danger in British films of men destroying women they love. Kracauer (1947) has observed in pre-Nazi German films the often repeated image of a man leaning his head on a woman's bosom (and we may note that this persists in post–World War II German films). This is associated with a total plot theme in which the hero attempts to rebel against a petty and stuffy family existence but fails, and returns to it beaten and chastened. A certain character type may be taken as a theme, as for instance the good-bad girl of American films, or the prostitute redeemed by love in French films. The good-bad girl fits in with the larger thematic constellation of eating-your-cake-and-having-it in American films and the pervasive trend of denying painful experiences. One can have both the attractiveness of the bad girl and the loyalty of the good; and it is not necessary to acknowledge any disappointments in love. In the French alternative, even though the prostitute becomes exclusively devoted to the hero, her previous involvement with other men is recognized.

The ways of characterizing certain groups may be taken as themes, as for instance the way in which the police are depicted. In American films the police are often mistaken, and the private investigator must solve the mystery. In British films, the police are almost always right. In both cases, the image of the police corresponds to the image of the father.

The quality of relationships may be taken as a theme. Thus in American films the hero remains tentative in his feelings for an attractive unknown woman; if she turns out to be bad, he can always detach himself. In French films, the hero is more apt to become hopelessly bound to the beautiful unknown and is unable to free himself even when he learns of her wickedness. These alternatives are related to the general tendencies already mentioned to deny love disappointments in American films and to evoke them in French films.

One may also take a total plot configuration as a theme, for instance the recurrent plot of American film comedies in which the hero, alternating between delusions of strength and craven apprehensions of weakness, meets with a series of accidental circumstances, or events contrived by others without his knowledge, of such a sort that they confirm his fantasies of omnipotence. As a result of the benevolence of the environment he ends up ecstatically triumphant despite his almost complete incompetence.

The level of concreteness or abstractness on which one works is largely a matter of convenience and individual preference. However, it is probably useful on the whole to work initially with themes of considerable specificity, to stay close to the concreteness of the material. Eventually a number of related themes will group themselves together. This may be illustrated from a study of American movies (cf. Wolfenstein and Leites, 1950). One of the most inclusive themes turned out to be that of false appearances. We found that forbidden wishes tended to be expressed as false appearances, and the eventual clearing-up of the false appearance had the significance of demonstrating that no one should be blamed or feel guilty for mere wishes. This generalization only emerged after we had observed a number of themes on a lower level of generality the interrelations of which were not at first evident. Thus we had observed the theme of the good-bad girl, the heroine who looks promiscuous but turns out to be quite innocent. We had similarly noted the recurrent predicament of the melodrama hero who is falsely accused, who looks guilty, but in the end succeeds in clearing himself. Comedies repeatedly presented situations where to an inquisitive but mistaken bystander a young couple seemed to be having an illicit affair, a husband seemed to be sharing his wife with his best friend, and so on. Presumably we might by an intellectual leap have arrived at the general concept of false appearances at an early stage of our analysis, in which case we would have had to proceed to observe in detail the various subthemes in which this major theme was illustrated. Proceeding in either direction is feasible, but it seems likely that if high-level generalizations are attempted at too early a stage, insufficient attention may be paid to the wealth of illustrative variations.

Within any one film a number of themes are apt to be repeated. For instance, Gregory Bateson (1945) analyzes the two occasions on which the hero confronts death in *Hitlerjunge Quex,* the first in which his mother commits suicide by turning on the gas and the hero barely escapes, the second in which he is murdered by the Communists. The attendant circumstances of each of these deaths are remarkably similar. Each follows an achievement on the hero's part, and is associated with a beloved woman. Each is represented by a billowing movement on the screen (of gas, of a fluttering flag), and by a change from darkness to light. Each marks a change in the hero's status and is preceded by words of his anticipating a wonderful future. This repeated sequence within the film was underscored by analogous sequences in other Nazi films, and was interpreted by Bateson as expressing a mystical expectation of passing "through death to a millennium."

Similarly, Erik H. Erikson in his study of the film *The Childhood of Maxim Gorky* (1950) observes how repeatedly the young hero, confronted with family scenes of intense emotional excitement, watches but does not participate. Thus nonparticipation is interpreted as expressing resistance to emotional temptations that would bind the young hero to the old way of life. By nonparticipation he reserves himself for another world of the future.

We may proceed to make more explicit the characteristics of variables and themes used in the kind of film analysis described here (cf. Wolfenstein and Leites, 1950). Any number of other variables besides those so far illustrated might be chosen. For instance, we might observe the number of characters who appear on the screen at any moment. How many and how long are the sequences in which no characters appear, in which one character appears alone, in which only two characters appear, or three characters, or more, and what is the pattern of alternation of such sequences? We should be inclined to say that variables of this sort would be likely to be meaningful for us only in relation to other variables, of more direct psychological import, as, for instance, the emotional significance of being alone, the meaning of the larger group in relation to the individual's wishes, and so on. The main variables with which we work are chosen because they are related to what we presume to be major emotional concerns of the producers and the audiences. On the whole our assumptions about what is emotionally important derive from contemporary dynamic psychology. Having observed certain recurrent themes that illustrate a certain variable, we proceed to interpret them in terms of the underlying psychological presuppositions which guided us in our selection of the variable. In this we are advancing hypotheses about the emotional processes in the producers and the audiences. These hypotheses would require verification by more direct study of members of these two groups.

To indicate schematically these interrelations, suppose our variable is father-son relations. Behind our choice of this variable is our knowledge of Oedipal conflicts and their role in emotional development. We find in a certain group of American films that father figures appear as criminal and dangerously attacking; the hero would be justified in killing them in self-defense, but usually someone else does this for him. In interpreting such a fantasy, we regard it as a variety of solution of Oedipal conflicts, one in which a particular combination of defenses has been employed. So, for instance, the Oedipal hostility of the son appears to be projected into the father; it is denied in the son, thus relieving him of guilt. The son is given a moral justification for attacking the father, since the father attacks him first. However, the son does not destroy the father; someone does it for him. His hostility, even though justified, is again projected. Here the mechanism of projection seems to operate to reduce guilt for Oedipal hostility both by denying it and by justifying it. In making such an interpretation we are assuming that this sort of transformation of Oedipal conflicts has gone on in the producers in their invention of such plots and that the film may offer similar emotional solutions to the audiences. (We do not infer that in actual life producers and audiences resolve their Oedipal conflicts in this way. We consider only the derivation and the impact of the fantasy conveyed in the film. We shall have something to say later about the relations between such fantasies and actual character.)

We may now illustrate more fully the relation of a variable to a group of themes. Let us take as our variable a situation in which one character is the onlooker in the relation of a man and woman to each other. If we consider some of the emotional undertones we would expect such a situation to evoke, we note that it is obviously related to Oedipal conflicts. However, it is more specific; it focuses on the situation where the child discovers, or further observes, the relationship between the parents and reacts to the fact of his exclusion from it. We would consider this to be a major background experience contributing to the emotional significance of scenes where an onlooker observes a couple. It is often useful for purposes of observation to choose as our variable a situation of this sort which is close to the level of concrete content. In practice we do not choose such a variable in advance, but decide to work with it when we find that themes illustrating it occur in our material. We have found the variable of the onlooker and the couple frequently illustrated in both American and French films. (British films seem to be less often concerned with it.)

Some of the most recurrent themes dealing with the onlooker and the couple in American films are the following:

1. The hero sees the heroine with another man and suspects that there is some intense relation between them. He later learns that the relation he imagined between them never existed (*Gilda; The Big Sleep*).
2. The hero observes a couple together but what happens between them is repulsive or pitiable rather than enviable. For instance, the hero sees through the window that the husband shoots his wife and then commits suicide (*The Strange Love of Martha Ivers*).
3. A comic character sees the hero and heroine together and mistakenly imagines they are having an illicit affair, or sees the hero or heroine with another partner and again imagines an illicit relation. Nothing is really happening between the observed couple (*She Wouldn't Say Yes; Guest Wife*).
4. A friend of the hero observes the hero and heroine and assumes a bored, little-boyish attitude toward their being so romantic: "Do I have to listen to all this mush?" (*Pardon My Past*) This is closely related to the instance where a kid brother, not yet eligible for romance, finds the amorous entanglements of an older brother and sister "all very dumb" (*Kiss and Tell*).

5. A friendly onlooker promotes the relation of the couple. This may be an elderly parental character, but it may even be the heroine's rival for the hero's love who, having lost out, quickly shifts to becoming a friend of the family (*Love Letters; The Bells of St. Mary's; Adventure*).

To summarize the main trends in this material: The observed couple do not do anything, or if they do it is not anything that could arouse jealousy or envy, but just the opposite. If the onlooker is jealous, he learns that this feeling was ungrounded (the couple did not do anything). More often the onlooker is not affected by what he observes, or thinks he observes. He may be just a comical passerby, unrelated to the couple. Or he may be a friend, but then he is humorously indifferent to their involvement with each other, or else he may help to promote it.

French films frequently present the following themes in the treatment of the the onlooker and the couple:

1. The hero first sees a beautiful woman alone, thinks of her as pure, and falls in love with her. Later he sees her together with another man with whom she is seriously involved. This disastrous discovery does not undo the hero's attachment to the woman, which proves fatal for him (*Panique; La Passionelle; Martin Roumagnac*).

2. An onlooker who is debarred from love sees an amorous couple and reacts with despair or rage. A precocious bespectacled twelve-year-old girl, for instance, sees her aunt's lover enter the aunt's bedroom. As the door closes, she bursts into a storm of tears (*Le Corbeau*). A hideous dwarf or an embittered spinster may react to their experiences as onlookers of others' happiness with vindictive fury (*L'Eternel Retour; L'Amour autour de la Maison*).

3. A man who has suffered disappointment in love directs a play in which the woman he loves and his successful rival appear as happy lovers while he looks on (*Les Enfants du Paradis; Le Silence Est d'Or*).

The main tendencies expressed in these scenes are the following: The relation between the observed couple is an intense and enviable one. The onlooker experiences great suffering in observing them. He may already be in love with one of them so that the discovery of their relation is a painful surprise and disappointment to him. But even if he is not closely involved with them, the realization of his loveless and excluded position is extremely bitter. The onlooker's involvement with the couple may be fatal for him, or may move him to destructive rage toward them. The onlooker may re-evoke his suffering by repeating the occasion of it in a dramatic performance.

The French treatment of the onlooker and the couple is in marked contrast to the American treatment. We may now proceed to an interpretation of these alternate themes. If we assume that a major source for fantasies about the couple and the observer is the childhood situation in which the child observes the parental couple and discovers a relation between them from which he is excluded, it would seem that French and American makers of films have handled very differently the emotions evoked by this experience. French films seem to repeat with relatively little distortion the painful feelings involved in the original situation. The observed couple are indeed intensely bound to each other. The onlooker suffers from the awareness of his exclusion. The experience of the little boy who has loved the mother before he became aware of her relation to the father is repeated in the plots where the hero makes a corresponding discovery about the woman he loves, whom he has first seen alone and then later sees with the other man. The difficulty of giving up this loved woman (the mother), the possible disastrous consequence (for the man who cannot free himself from his involvement with the parental couple), the chagrin, the despair, and the murderous rage, are recognizably reproduced. A probable motive for this re-evocation is suggested by the plots in which the hero as dramatist transforms his love disappointment into a play. Through such a transformation one can experience actively what one previously has undergone passively, and one may by going over it inure oneself to the painful experience. Further observations have suggested that this may be a fairly pervasive motive in the formation of plots of French films—we can reduce suffering from the numerous inevitable frustrations of life by again and again facing the painful situations. In this way our unrealistic wishes may become chastened and our tolerance for frustration be increased. The principle is similar to that of Mithridates, who by taking a little poison every day succeeded in becoming immune to it.

In American film plots the experience of the child with the parents seems to have undergone much more distortion. The device of denial seems to have been extensively applied. Nothing happens between the observed couple, or at least nothing enviable. The onlooker, whether involved with the couple or just a passerby, is unaffected by envy or jealousy. Though he may himself be loveless, the sight of the couple's happiness does not rouse any longing in him. The sequence of childhood events in which the little boy first loves his mother and then discovers her relation to the father is reversed in the plot where the hero first sees the heroine with another man, then later learns that there is no relation between them. The choice of this sort of solution to an emotional problem is illustrated in other aspects of American films. As we have already remarked, there is a tendency to deny painful feelings or feelings that involve conflict (as, for instance, hostility toward the father). There is a tendency to deny disappointing experiences. Also emotional involvement with the past, with the family one comes from, is apt to be represented as tenuous or easily dissolved. But even more recent attachments, if they threaten to lead to danger or distress, are relatively easily abandoned. The hero does not remain hopelessly bound to a woman who turns out to be bad. He is apt to keep his feeling for her rather tentative until he has investigated her sufficiently. Liability to serious disappointment or frustration appears as much less an inevitable part of life than it does in French films.

To sum up, in the treatment of the onlooker and the couple, French films seem to re-evoke the feelings of disappointment of the child in order to inure us to them. American film plots tend to solve the problem by denying that anything painful has happened. The differences in themes are derived from the choice of different devices for resolving a common emotional problem.

Our actual procedure in the study of films is somewhat less neat and simple than this account may suggest. Scenes involving an onlooker and a couple occur here and there in the scores of films we see. They are recorded along with a large number of other themes and

tentatively interpreted in a variety of ways, depending on their varying contexts. As we begin to organize our data, we may decide to
group some of it around the variable of the onlooker and the couple.
The material we group around this variable will be at least in part relevant to a number of other variables, for instance, goodness and badness in women, the significance of looking. That is, some of the
onlooker and couple material will also be classified with other material relating to goodness and badness in women, and so on. Moreover,
we will be working throughout on continually modified formulations of a fairly inclusive sort in which we attempt to connect up a
large number of themes in French films or in American films. The
analysis of the onlooker and couple themes given here is not arrived
at until a rather late stage in our overall analysis of French and
American films.

3. Movie Themes and Their Cultural Context

Let us now turn to consider the relation between the psychological
processes we take to be characteristic of a particular culture in the
development of movie plots and the prevailing real life character
structure of the producers and the audiences. On this extremely difficult question we can at least say that the relation is complicated and
probably not uniform for different cultures. For instance, we have
noted that French film plots seem frequently to derive from the
motive of inuring oneself to the painful aspects of reality, while
American film plots seem to be more often derived from the operation of projection and denial. Can we infer from this that French
character is more dominated by the reality principle, while American character gives freer sway to unrealistic infantile mechanisms?
Such an inference would not be warranted. Americans may be read-
ier to regress for purposes of fantasy enjoyment. The French, on the
other hand, may strive to achieve in art an attitude of wise resigna-
tion that they do not necessarily maintain in real-life situations. In
other words, the possible relations between character and preferred
fantasies are numerous. We cannot simply infer one from the other.
It is necessary to have independent evidence on both topics.

We may, however, attempt to indicate, on the basis of admittedly fragmentary evidence, some possible connections between movie fantasies and character structure. These connections are suggested less for their substantive value than as illustrative of the kinds of relations that may be found. In films, as in drama generally, we experience vicariously the carrying-through of violent impulses to a degree that few of us can manage in actuality. This unleashed dramatic violence assumes a variety of forms. For instance, frequently in British films (as, for instance, also in many British novels, from *Clarissa* on) the victim is a woman. We see numerous heroes who are driven by an impulse to destroy the women they love, or for whom this is a terrible temptation, or who, despite their struggles, are carried away by this impulse, or who, though blameless, suspect themselves of such tendencies. A good father figure warns and guards the hero against his destructive tendencies towards the woman (cf. Ghost of Hamlet's Father: " 'Taint not thy mind, nor let thy soul contrive/ Against they mother aught"). One of the indictments against an inadequate father figure is that he fails to prevent the hero from destroying the beloved woman.

We may assume that the kind of defenses that are erected against destructive tendencies are related to the aim of these tendencies, which is variable, and to which fantasies give us a clue. If a major British fantasy of what would happen if destructive tendencies were set loose involves the destruction of a beloved woman, an appropriate defense against such tendencies would be their transformation via a reaction formation into tenderness and protective concern for the weak. Some observations of British character tend to suggest that this is a chosen defense against destructiveness. The protection of the weak, as exemplified in the well-known British preoccupation with prevention of cruelty to animals, seems to be a prominent British tendency. In other words, if fantasies as embodied in films show what unopposed impulses would look like, they can give us clues as to why certain defenses have been chosen in the struggle against impulses.

In American films, by contrast, violence appears much more often as an attack against the hero by dangerous and powerful agencies. For protection against violence envisaged in this form, toughness rather than tenderness would seem to be an appropriate character trait. And it would seem that American men do value toughness to a higher degree than is the case with Britons.

These instances suggest one possible kind of relation between chosen fantasies and character, but they also raise many more questions. We should like to know what sort of life experiences, starting with the family situation, have favored such different fantasies of what unleashed violence would look like. In the case of the British, why is male violence aimed to such a degree against women? In the American instance, what has encouraged the projection of destructiveness and consequent justification of toughness? We do not propose to answer these questions here, but raise them to indicate the extent of the problem.

We have suggested one possible kind of relation between chosen fantasies and character structure—that the fantasies represent impulse completion while the related real-life character is constituted of defenses against these impulses. However, there are other possibilities. In some cases impulses may be carried through to a greater extent in actuality; fiction and life might parallel each other. There is some evidence to suggest that in Russian life there is a distinctive tendency to act out extreme fantasies. Literature and drama would thus tend to repeat or to anticipate actual events. For example, certain novels written in the period immediately following the Russian Revolution anticipated in remarkable detail the later extreme regimentation of life and also the trials of the Old Bolsheviks (cf. Zamiatin's *We*; Rodonov's *Chocolate*).

Within a particular culture there may be certain areas where chosen fantasies and actual behavior are complementary, others where they are similar. In American films we find some themes that seem to correspond to real life. There is, for instance, the good-bad girl. This type of heroine, who looks so promiscuous, whose attractiveness is enhanced by her apparent involvement with other men, but who in the end turns out to love only the hero, seems to be a dramatic version of the American popular girl, who is attractive because she dates so many men, but who manages not to get too deeply involved with any of them until she finds the right one.

There is the further possibility that in life certain impulses are carried through while in art defenses against these impulses are expressed. Erikson, in analyzing the film of Maxim Gorky's childhood, is reminded of certain events of Russian history. There is a scene in the film in which the grandfather, after having beaten the boy, sits beside the boy's bed and tries to conciliate him. Erikson (1950) recalls in this connection the famous painting of Ivan the Terrible holding in his arms the corpse of his son whom he has murdered. And he recalls that not only Ivan, but also Peter the Great, murdered his son. We do not know whether in fact Ivan held his son in his arms after having murdered him. Possibly this posthumous love, guilt, and longing to undo appears in art more than in life in Russian culture. The serfs who killed the father of Dostoevsky probably did not feel the complicated repercussions of conscience of the sons of the murdered Karamazov. If this would be the case, we would have an instance where the crude unleashing of impulse is more extreme in life than in art. This would be the reverse of the relation we thought might obtain in British culture, where destruction raged in literature and gentleness was more the rule in life.

We have considered the following possible relations between fiction and character: that a similar form of impulse gratification occurs in both; that fiction shows freedom of impulse and character defenses against it, and that conversely impulses are released in actuality while fiction expresses defenses against these impulses. There is a fourth possibility, that defenses against impulse are expressed both in fiction and in real-life character. This could probably be illustrated in some Victorian literature (e.g., Coventry Patmore's *The Angel in the House*). Clearly it would be an oversimplification to suppose that a particular culture might be characterized by a single type of relationship between fiction and life. One would have to work out, given adequate data, in which areas which kinds of relationships obtained.

Let us consider briefly the relation between the circumstances of real life—for instance, in the kind of family relations that prevail—and the preferred fantasies of a given culture. In American life it would seem that children are encouraged to outgrow and surpass their parents. We do not need to go into the various factors that contribute to this. We will only remark that it is not considered ideal or adequate simply to reproduce the life of one's parents, to live in the same house, to pursue the same occupations. The expectation that the children will surpass the parents would seem to contribute to several of the fantasies we have found to be recurrent in American films. The projection of the son's bad impulses onto the father may be facilitated by the circumstance that from an early age the son is encouraged to regard himself as potentially superior to the father. Similarly, the fact that children are encouraged to strike out on their own rather than to wait for a paternal inheritance may facilitate the fantasy that old emotional bonds are easily dissolved. The converse would seem to have been the case in France, where family property was transmitted and preserved from generation to generation, and children often had to wait well into middle age to achieve independence, which only came with the parent's death. The theme of French films having to do with the difficulty of detaching oneself from from old involvements may be related to this. What accounts for the preference for one or another arrangement of family life is a further question, and one we cannot answer.

In view of what has just been said, we should perhaps qualify our earlier remarks about French and American handling of the onlooker and couple situation. In interpreting these contrasting treatments we implied that different defenses were being employed to cope with the same emotional experience. We should now add that not only in fantasy productions but also in life the original family situation has been treated in different ways. The disappointment that an American little boy feels in discovering the love relation between his parents is qualified from the start by his being treated by both parents as one who is bound to surpass his father. In French families, the childhood experience may well have been more poignant insofar as the little boy felt that it would be long before he succeeded the father, whom he would never surpass. It seems that the fantasies about father figures in American films may be on a more infantile level because in life the son's conscious concern with the father is apt to come to an end as soon as the son is grown up. In France, where the grown-up son was still much involved with his family of origin, the image of the father was apt to be worked over in the light of adult experience, and the more complicated and sympathizable father figures of French films (so often portrayed by the late Raimu) would seem to have developed from this.

To sum up these latter points, which are intended to be merely suggestive, the way in which family and other relationships are styled in a particular culture probably contributes to the preference for certain fantasies. The form the real life relationships assume may be reflected in the favored fantasies. Depending on the defensive structure embodied in prevailing character types, preferred fantasies may coincide with or represent the opposite of actual behavior. Since the possible relations between the preferred fantasies of a culture embodied in films, and other art forms, and actual character are so various one cannot infer one from the other; it is necessary to have independent information on both in order to see how they are related.

WORKS CITED

Bateson, Gregory. *An Analysis of the Nazi Film* Hitlerjunge Quex. (New York, N.Y.: Institute for Intercultural Studies, 1945); mimeographed.

Bateson, Gregory and Margaret Mead. *Balinese Character: A Photographic Analysis* (New York, N.Y.: Special Publications of the New York Academy of Sciences, II, 1942).

Belo, Jane. "Bali: Rangda and Barong," *American Ethnological Society Monographs* 16 (1949).

Benedict, Ruth. "Folklore." In *Encyclopedia of the Social Sciences* (New York, N.Y.: Macmillan, 1931).

Boas, Franz. "The Social Organization and the Secret Societies of the Kwakiutl Indians." In *Report of the U.S. National Museum for 1895* (Washington, D.C., 1897), 311–737.

Bonaparte, Marie. *Edgar Poe, étude psychanalytique* (Paris: Denoel et Steele, 1933).

Campbell, Joseph. *The Hero with a Thousand Faces* (New York, N.Y.: Pantheon Books, 1949).

Erikson, Erik H. *Childhood and Society* (New York, N.Y.: Norton, 1950).

Freud, Sigmund. "Eine Kindheitserinnerung des Leonardo da Vinci." In *Gesammelte Werke* vol. VIII (London: Imago, 1943), 128–211.

Kracauer, Siegfried. *From Caligari to Hitler* (Princeton, N.J.: Princeton University Press, 1947).

Rank, Otto. *Der Mythus von der Geburt des Helden* (Leipzig: Deuticke, 1912).

———. *Das Inzest-Motiv in Dichtung und Sage* (Leipzig: Deuticke, 1914).

Sharpe, Ella Freeman. *Collected Papers on Psycho-Analysis*, ed. Marjorie Brierley (London: Hogarth Press and the Institute of Psycho-Analysis, 1950).

Spengler, Oswald. *Der Untergang des Abendlandes* (Munich: Beck, 1918).

Wolfenstein, Martha and Nathan Leites. *The Movies: A Psychological Study* (Glencoe, Ill.: Free Press, 1950).

National Cinemas

Tom O'Regan

Australian Cinema as a National Cinema

Introduction

"What does Australian cinema *have in common with other national cinemas*—no matter how diverse?" This chapter answers this question by establishing the characteristics of national cinemas generally through a survey of different aspects of Australian cinema. In inspecting Australian and other cinemas, I aim to generalize the shape and outlook of national cinema as a category. Like all national cinemas, the Australian cinema contends with Hollywood dominance, it is simultaneously a local and international form, it is a producer of festival cinema, it has a significant relation with the nation and the state, and it is constitutionally fuzzy. National cinemas are simultaneously an aesthetic and production movement, a critical technology, a civic project of state, an industrial strategy and an international project formed in response to the dominant international cinemas (particularly but not exclusively Hollywood cinema). Australian cinema is formed as a relation to Hollywood and other national cinemas.

National Cinemas and le Défi Américain

> *Alternative cinemas gain their significance and force partly because they seek to undermine the common equation of "the movies" with "Hollywood."*
> —Kristin Thompson,
> *Exporting Entertainment,* 170

From *Australian National Cinema* by Tom O'Regan (Routledge, 1996). Reprinted by permission of Taylor & Francis Books Ltd. and the author.

> *If you can't stand the heat, get out of the kitchen, living in the twentieth century means learning to be American.*
>
> —Dusan Makavejev quoted in Elsaesser, "Putting on a Show," 24

The American cinema looms large as a term of reference for every national cinema in the West and many beyond. Curiously, cinema in the United States is in many respects like other national cinemas. It relies in the first instance on the certainties of its domestic market, it is embedded in a particular industrial, policy and aesthetic milieu, it has dynamics that are simultaneously local and international, and it negotiates particular social, cultural and ethnic differences within the United States. But Hollywood is not usually thought to be a "national cinema."

The term is reserved by critics, filmmakers, policy makers, audiences and marketers for national cinemas other than that in the United States. For them, national cinemas provide a rubric within which cinema and television product can be differentiated from each other and from the dominant international Hollywood cinema. There is Hollywood, and there are national cinemas. Hollywood is an avowedly commercial enterprise. National cinemas are mixed-commercial and public enterprises. While the United States government assists Hollywood's commercial ends, in other national cinemas there is a higher degree of formative government assistance involved in creating and sustaining them. Australian cinema, for example, is what it is today because of the ongoing governmental assistance to it since 1969. From the end of World War II to 1969 Australian feature production was sporadic and marginal because it lacked such assistance.

The American national cinema is in its reach the most international of national cinemas. It is the preeminent supplier of international products in various national markets. It is the closest thing we have to an audiovisual lingua franca in the world. It also has had an historical stranglehold over many of the world's cinema and more lately video markets—and this market presence is most evident in Europe, the Americas and Australasia. These countries are culturally closer to the United States than those in Africa and large parts of Asia. This makes Hollywood a particularly important term of reference.

Along with India, Hollywood is one of the few cinemas that consistently dominate their domestic box offices. In the United States and India the national cinema *is* the cinema. Differences are disclosed mostly *within* the local cinema. There is, to be sure, a minor United States market for the product of other national cinemas in its ethnic cinemas and its "art cinema" circuits; indeed Elsaesser argues it was the "US distribution practice of the art-house circuit which gave the term 'art cinema' its currently accepted meaning" (Elsaesser, "Putting on a Show," 24). Within the United States, other national cinemas occupy minor niche markets and do not threaten Hollywood's American hegemony. It makes little sense to think of these cinemas in the same "national/international" terms that we do for national cinemas. Differentiations between the American cinema and imported product is not something producers in the United States need to negotiate, marketers to market as "their advantage," and American politicians to concern themselves with (unless it is to try and remove barriers to its international circulation in other national markets). Yet these are the things of central concern to film workers in other national cinemas. Rather, in the United States producers, politicians, etc., are primarily concerned with differences within the American cinema.

In most countries which have their own national cinema, cinema-going, cinema distribution, cinema viewing and cinema criticism are not primarily oriented to the local national cinema, but to the cinema more generally, and more particularly the dominant international cinema. Most national cinemas do not dominate their domestic market. American and to a lesser extent British and European cinema is central to the Australian audience's experience of the cinema, television and video. So too the local production component of the cinema, television and video industries in Australia makes up only a fraction of their total turnover. So, for example, Australian features made up between 5 percent and 21 percent of the local cinema box-office in the 1980s (AFC, 71), which means that Australian cinema-goers saw an Australian film "between 5 and 20% of the time depending on the films available in any particular year" (AFC, 71). This situation is repeated in television drama, where in 1990 local television drama comprised 16 percent of total drama programming on the commercial television networks, 7 percent on the foremost public service broadcaster, the ABC and a negligible proportion on the SBS (ABT, 32).

The international cinemas are more naturalized parts of the cinema landscape than are the various local cinemas. Within most countries people experience the cinema more as another cinema than as their own national cinema. Andrew Higson notes that this international cinema, particularly Hollywood cinema and television, has become "an integral and naturalized part of the national culture . . . of most countries in which cinema is an established entertainment form" (Higson, 39). One of the consequences here is that, as Geoffrey Nowell-Smith writes of Britain, the American cinema is "by now far more deeply rooted in British cultural life than is the native product" (Nowell-Smith, 152). Diane Collins puts this case in its strongest form for Australia:

> For most of this century Australians have watched little else but American movies and America's domination of Australia's film culture extended far beyond the screen. Australians saw (and see) these films in American-style picture shows; news of the latest releases came (and comes) via the American industry's publicity methods. It was not long before locally made films were modelled on Hollywood production styles and America's movie world meant more to many Australians than homegrown celebrities. (Collins, 2)

At best, Australian films supplement the audience's and the exhibition and distribution industry's mostly Hollywood diet.

National cinemas are structurally marginal, fragile and dependent on outside help. In their own domestic market and internationally, they are often structurally dispensable in that exhibitors, distributors and audiences can make do without their product, though they cannot do without international product. The 1991 figures for Australian theatrical releases well illustrate this point: of the 238 theatrical releases, 60 percent were sourced from the United States, 10 percent from the United Kingdom, 14 percent from

Europe (7 percent France), 9 percent from Australia; of the remainder 3 percent were from the Far East, 2 percent other, 1 percent Canada and less than 1 percent from New Zealand (calculated from Curtis and Spriggs, 75). The lack of distributor and exhibitor interest in Australian cinema is a continuing leitmotif of Australian film history. The exhibition and distribution combined entity, Union Pictures, chose to consolidate itself and expand during World War I and immediately after at the expense of local production. Film activists of the 1960s regarded with justification the Australian film trade as simply an extension of the American film industry. They saw themselves as representing Australian interests, while the dominant exhibitors—Hoyts and Greater Union—represented American interests.

While most national cinema producers face difficulties in their home market, this same domestic box-office is generally crucial to all national cinemas (even Hollywood has historically relied on 45 percent to 75 percent of its revenues from its domestic market). National cinemas generally need as good an access to their domestic box-office and to the international market as they can get to be viable. But only part of their local box-office is available—in the Australian case between 3 and 21 percent of the box-office from 1977 to 1993 (Reid, 82). Clearly they need help—and this is where government is important, as is other non-cinema backing and international involvement, whether by way of direct investment, co-productions, or simply revenues from having had a major international success.

Every national cinema activist negotiates to win ground for its national cinema in this market context. "The aim of a national cinema is one of producing a local presence alongside the dominant imported presence in both the local and international markets." The task of a national cinema is to graft itself as a minor component on to the existing communication circuits and networks of cinema and television. The aim of a national cinema in this market and cultural environment is not to replace Hollywood films with say Australian films so much as to provide a viable and healthy local supplement to Hollywood cinema. National cinema producers hope, at best, for some limited import substitution and some limited overseas presence. And this is the case for all bar the largest of national cinemas—in the 1992/93 financial year, the value of Australia's audiovisual exports were $65 million, while its import bill was a massive $437 million (Given, 19). Policymakers recognize the limits of import substitution given the cultural and economic characteristics of the Australian market; and generally the limits in export.[1] Naturalizing a local contribution to the cinema and local and international audiences to a national cinema is an unending and fraught process. A sense of the minor and subordinate role of domestic production is never far away from debates or writings on any national cinema. The local cinema needs to be worked for anew and presented to every new generation of critics, viewers, exhibitors, distributors and politicians. National cinema activists and filmmakers have to think out, work at, legitimate, lobby for, self-consciously articulate and market their difference from the dominant international cinema and each other.

"[T]he cinema," Geoffrey Nowell-Smith writes, "has always been international, both culturally and economically" (Nowell-Smith, 154). In this context, national cinemas routinely negotiate the extraordinary internationalism of the cinema. They do so from an unequal basis. National cinemas can expect to be no more than a junior partner to the dominant international cinemas. As Elsaesser observes, "'national cinema' makes sense only as a relation, not as an essence, being dependent on other kinds of filmmaking, to which it supplies the other side of the coin" (Elsaesser, "Putting on a Show," 25–26). A national cinema necessarily "functions as a subordinate term" (26).

A national cinema, as it is understood on everything from festival schedules to publishers lists, is a production industry operating in the context of a more significant international, usually Hollywood, market presence. For Australian and European cinema alike the "shape" of the national cinema was partly defined by the impact of and competition provided by the North American film production and distribution industry (Thompson, *Exporting Entertainment*, 168) and a subsidiary component of "runaway" and "offshore" productions of that industry—like Stanley Kramer's *On the Beach* in 1959 or Steve Gordon's 1993 *Fortress*.

National cinemas like Australia's evolve strategies to respond to Hollywood's pre-eminent place on the cinema horizons of the Western world and beyond (I make the "Western" qualification here to allow for the significant circulation of Indian and Hong Kong cinema in African and Asian contexts). They are thus, local film production, film policy and critical strategies designed to effectively *compete with, imitate, oppose, complement* and *supplement* the (dominant) international cinema. The relation between the local and the international cinema provides many "national cinemas" with their identity and force.

Because Hollywood looms large for those cinemas culturally closest to Hollywood cinema such as the English-speaking cinemas of Canada, Australia, the United Kingdom, and New Zealand, the need to imitate and oppose Hollywood is felt especially keenly. British, Australian and Canadian film producers often tackle the competition head-on at home and abroad: with titles like *Crocodile Dundee, Four Weddings and a Funeral* (Newell 1994), and *The Fly* (Cronenberg 1986). These sorts of films circulated as Hollywood major product: Warner Brothers, for example, handled the international distribution of the *Mad Max* films. At times various British studios, distributors and exhibitors have sought to try to become a British Hollywood major. Being directly competitive, internationally, is an option mostly available to the English language cinemas.

This means producing films that are, if not imitative, then consonant or interchangeable with the international product. Australian filmmakers are often held to "imitate" American films, whether it be Carl Schultz's Sirkian melodrama, *Careful He Might Hear You* (1983) or Dr. Miller's "revenge/road movie" *Mad Max* (1979, 1981, 1985) cycle. As local cinema and television drama markets are dominated by imports, the local product is shaped by these imports. The prevailing international styles, techniques, technologies, programme concepts and sensibilities are used, adjusted, and transformed in their local enactment in national productions and criticism. In such circumstances of "internationalization" and "hybridization," it is often difficult to ascertain where the local ends and the other national or international begins (Dermody and Jacka, *The Screening of Australia*, 20).

Another strategy to "counter" Hollywood competition is to compete indirectly by seeking complementarities. This market niche option can take a number of directions. It can seek local specificities in domestic social events, issues, stories and myths foregrounding the coherence of the national cultural system such as the shearers in *Sunday Too Far Away* and the famous racehorse *Phar Lap* (Wincer 1983). Elsaesser notes the "importance of the texture of speech and voice for our idea of a national cinema" (Elsaesser, "Putting on a Show," 26); there are the Australian accents in the work of scriptwriter and playwright David Williamson in the 1970s with *Don's Party, Stork* (Burstall 1971), *The Removalists* (Jeffrey 1975) and *The Club* (Beresford 1976) which foregrounded the Australian vernacular. These may draw on what Alison Butler has called "more localized approaches to cultural codification" (Butler, 419). Alternatively it can seek an aesthetic distinction by promoting cinema product as "Art." Sometimes a national cinema takes on an avant-gardist opposition to Hollywood style" (Butler, 419). Or it can do both. Doing both is central to the "art cinema" as a strategy for a national cinema. As Elsaesser notes, "one function of auteur cinema, before the advent of television, was to transcribe features of a nation's cultural tradition as figured in other art forms (the novel, theatre, opera) and to represent them in the cinema" (Elsaesser, "Putting on a Show," 26). This can be seen in the coincidence of Australian auteurs and the literary *oeuvre*: Armstrong and Miles Franklin's *My Brilliant Career*; Weir and Joan Lindsay's *Picnic at Hanging Rock* and Weir and Christopher Koch's *The Year of Living Dangerously* (1982); Schepisi and Thomas Keneally's *The Chant of Jimmie Blacksmith*; Beresford and Henry Handel Richardson's *The Getting of Wisdom* (1977) and Beresford and David Williamson's *Don's Party*. It can also be witnessed in the focus on the Norman Lindsay legend in John Duigan's *Sirens* (1994). Lindsay was not only a painter, novelist, poet, children's story writer and publisher but a cultural phenomenon in his own right, who scandalized Sydney society for three decades. Steve Neale argues that Art and national identity are fused for the Germans in the 1920s, essentially for market niche reasons. Australia did not have this fusion until 1970 or thereabouts.[2] This doubling was first an explicit project of Australian film policy and later embodied in Peter Weir's *Picnic at Hanging Rock*. Here, for the first time, a nation's character seemed embodied in a personally idiosyncratic and poetic cinema as opposed to slick Hollywood commercial entertainment (and its Australian predecessors that sought to be only entertainment).

Critics and filmmakers oppose Hollywood screen dominance, seeing in the local product alternatives to Hollywood norms and values. They invoke Australian film's humanist values, its black humour, its quirkiness. For Australia's festival cinema—*Breaker Morant, Sweetie*—the aim is not to directly compete so much as to complement Hollywood product. It has what Butler would call its "nationally specific styles," its "misreadings" of Hollywood norms (Butler, 418).

National cinemas provide a means to identify, assist, legitimate, polemicize, project, and otherwise create a space nationally and internationally for non-Hollywood filmmaking activity. Just as "the international" makes no sense without nations, so, in cinema terms "national" makes no sense without "le défi américain."

National Cinema as a Local and International Forum

So, national cinemas can be seen as a response to the internationalization of the cinema. They are not alternatives to internationalization, they are one of its manifestations. National cinemas, whether in the guise of a local film industry producing a variety of films or of a purveyor of the national culture or whatever, are from inception vehicles for international integration.

In Australia's case, the project of a national cinema in the multifaceted sense advanced so far, did not emerge until 1969, well after Hollywood had consolidated its international reach and control over the Australian market. At that point, formative government assistance was put into place and an Australian national cinema became a project capable of enlisting a large array of local and international actors—politicians, arts bureaucrats, voters, critics, audiences, filmmakers. Before that, it was simply a struggling commercial industry, producing, or striving to produce, popular entertainment capable of intermittently enlisting government support, or it was a producer of unaffiliated product showing great promise but achieving no theatrical release like Cecil Holmes's films *Captain Thunderbolt* (1953) and *Three in One* (1957).

As one of the forms the internationalization of the cinema takes, national cinemas *localize* the cinema and explicitly *contribute* to the international cinema at one and the same time. As Kristin Thompson observes:

> few national cinema industries operate in isolation; through foreign investment, competition and other types of influence, outside factors will almost invariably affect any given national cinema. Such effects have implications for most types of historical study—whether of film style, industry working, government policy, technological change or social implications.
>
> (Thompson, *Exporting Entertainment*, 168)

National cinemas work to be local while streamlining themselves to be of interest to audiences outside Australia. Bruce Beresford's *The Adventures of Barry McKenzie*—a classic comedy of an "ocker" in England—came out of a period where film policy and criticism emphasized securing a local following and gave near exclusive priority to representing Australia to itself. But the film was also from its inception international: self-consciously made for the British and Australian market, it was successful in both (the Barry Humphries comic strip on which the film was based was more popular in the United Kingdom than in Australia). *Barry McKenzie* has as its erstwhile hero the monstrous Barry McKenzie who in order to acquire his inheritance must visit the "old country," England. Apart from the opening sequence in Sydney and a brief sequence in Hong Kong immediately following, the rest of the film is concerned with Bazza's assorted English adventures. If, with his double breasted suit, airways bag, and his braggadocio, McKenzie is a camp parody of a by then outdated Australian masculinity (his clothes belong in the 1940s and early 1950s not the the 1960s or 1970s) he is also the Australian abroad, the colonial Candide. Episodically structured, improbably connected, the film has a farcical structure in which narrative is clearly at the service of set piece performances by Barry Crocker (Bazza), Barry Humphreys (Edna Everage and other roles), Spike Milligan and Peter Cook. In many ways the film can be regarded as a "rewriting" of *They're a Weird Mob* (Powell 1966). It encourages not so much the "identification" with its Australian-ness, but a suspending of illusionist belief, thereby producing its fantasy of the "hyper-Australian" intersecting with an equally "hyper-Britishness." The film could be simultaneously, depending on where you stood: "us sticking it up the Poms" and "us dealing with those frightful Australians."

This process of streamlining has a bearing on what is selected from the cultural archive—British/Australian implications in the colonial or post-colonial eras are foregrounded in many Australian films, including notable successes like *Gallipoli* and *Breaker Morant*. Michael Blakemore set his film, *Country Life* (1994) in turn-of-the-century Australia. The metropole/province relation was configured as a British/Australian relation within an Australian family. Sometimes it can be updated, as in Mark Joffe's *Spotswood* (1992) where the English efficiency expert comes to an Australian moccasin factory. The workers here are more interested in racing slot cars than working and he is eventually "bent" towards his eccentric workers. Here again the British connection not only lies with Anthony Hopkins's presence in the lead role but in the many ways the film evokes the Ealing comedies of the 1940s and 1950s. In *Film Review 1993–4* James Cameron-Wilson described it as "an exquisitely judged social comedy, which is written, directed and played at just the right pitch, evoking fond memories of Ealing" (in Cameron-Wilson and Speed, 99).

Similarly the "American in Australia" and, to a lesser extent, the "Australian in America" are constant figures in the local cinema. Sometimes American "innocents" are done down but eventually triumph over the disturbed, psychotic, murderous or rampaging monsters who happen to be Australian. Stacy Keech and Jamie Lee Curtis are the only "normal characters" in *Roadgames* (Franklin 1981). They do battle across the Nullabor plains with an odd assortment of weird Australians including a sex murderer, unfriendly police officers, and cranky drivers. Jimmy Smits is the charismatic American

University Professor in Melbourne falsely accused and imprisoned for rape in *Gross Misconduct* (George Miller 1993). He is the victim of the overheated sexual gaze of a beautiful female student who turns out to be a victim too—of incest—which retrospectively explains and justifies her actions. In *Razorback* (Mulcahy 1984), Carl (Gregory Harrison) comes to Australia to avenge the death of his wife at the hands of the eponymous wild pig, and in the process he also sorts out the malevolent local kangaroo shooters who have a symbiotic relationship with the pig.

American men provide love interests for Australian women in Chris Thomson's 1989 film *The Delinquents*—Charlie Schlatter is Kylie Minogue's love interest in this film of love on the wrong side of the tracks, and in the World War II story *Rebel* (Jenkins 1985)— Matt Dillon plays a GI deserter in Sydney hidden by a night club singer, Debbie Byrne.

Americans are often "problematic" figures and presences which Australians need to negotiate and come to terms with—often making the Australians feel inferior. In Mora's *Death of a Soldier* (1986), James Coburg plays a senior American commander in Australia during World War II dealing with the lines of demarcation between the American military police and the Australian civil police force over an American soldier wanted by both for a series of murders of local women. Eric Roberts in Dusan Makavejev's *The Coca-Cola Kid* (1985) is a Coca-Cola executive sent to Australia to bring Coke into the back-blocks—like the Anthony Hopkins character in *Spotswood* he achieves his goal but in the process is changed. *Dallas Doll* (Turner 1993) has Sarah Bernhardt as a morally questionable character who is simultaneously desired by and repelled by nearly every character (all Australians) in this film. She seduces nearly everyone in the family—the father, the son and the mother. Eventually the Australians turn the tables on her, or, in the case of the mother, simply assert themselves.

Finally, American actors sometimes play Australian characters. Notably Meryl Streep in *Evil Angels*, Robert Mitchum and Deborah Kerr in *The Sundowners* (Zinnemann 1960), and Richard Chamberlain in *The Last Wave* (where the Chamberlain character is given as having a South American heritage).

Equally, there can at times seem to be an almost seamless web between working to be local and being internationally successful. Indeed just about every national cinema at some stage goes local in order to go international. It was an article of faith in the 1970s for the national cinema to be local in front of and behind the camera and even to be substantially locally financed. Film critics like the influential critic of *The Age* (Melbourne), Colin Bennett, in the 1970s found evidence of the wisdom of this position in Schepisi's 1970s classics—*The Devil's Playground* and *The Chant of Jimmie Blacksmith*, Armstrong's *My Brilliant Career*, Miller's *Mad Max*, and Noyce's *Newsfront*. The presence of international actors in Australian films of the decade became another, and sometimes unwanted and distracting "noise."

If this local orientation is now explicitly repudiated as the only model for a national cinema, it persists because it is a structural necessity in the Australian cinema—which like the New Zealand and German cinemas—relies so critically on the work of first and second time directors for success. Their best directors, cinematographers and actors become expatriates after a decade or less in filmmaking. Some of the most successful and high profile Australian films of the 1990s were either their director's first feature: Jocelyn Moorhouse with *Proof*, Geoffrey Wright with *Romper Stomper*, Baz Luhrmann with *Strictly Ballroom*, Paul J. Hogan with *Muriel's Wedding*, Ray Argall with *Return Home* (1990), John Ruane with *Death in Brunswick* (1991), Geoff Burton and Kevin Dowling with *The Sum of Us*, or their second feature: Stephan Elliott with *The Adventures of Priscilla, Queen of the Desert*. Additionally, many highly regarded—although not always commercially successful 1990s releases—were also the work of first-time or second-time feature directors: Jackie McKimmie (*Waiting* 1991), Tracey Moffatt (*beDevil*) and Pauline Chan (*Traps* 1994) and Alexis Vellis (*Nirvana Street Murder* 1991). By definition, first time directors are not that internationally integrated, as they are yet to prove themselves. Their locally set, locally produced and locally acted productions are their international calling cards. Australian cinema of the 1990s was— with the exception of international blockbusters set outside Australia—increasingly dependent on "sleepers": low budget films that exceeded all expectation for success. But these were not "sleepers" of the *Mad Max* variety. They were films from directors whose national and international careers were often established in advance through international film festival screenings of their shorts and features.

The 1990s cinema looked a lot like that of the mid- to late 1970s when there was a similar turn towards Europe and attention was being paid to gaining recognition in the international European and North American festivals. As in the earlier period, there was a shortage of Australian investors, the industry needed to rely on "first time" directors to give the Australian industry a palpable form, and the state funding institutions played a much larger role than they did in the 1980s. It is worth noting that these "local productions" were sometimes underwritten by state investment and subsidy in partnership with international financing, for example *Muriel's Wedding* was underwritten by French finance through CIBY Sales, with a principle involvement of Film Victoria and subsidiary involvement of the Queensland Pacific Film and Television, the NSW Film and Television Office, the AFC and the FFC.

"Going local" does not only hold out the prospect of a culturally authentic, low budget cinema just possibly able to recoup its money from the domestic market and attractive to international audiences in its Australianness (using the local to go to the universal). It also opens on to two other possibilities:

1. the prospect of a commercially oriented exploitative cinema—a crassly commercial cinema, recycling possibly regressive notions and ideas (the 1970s "sex comedy" classically embodied by *Alvin Purple* is often taken to be an instance here, as was the first *Mad Max* at its time of release); and
2. the prospect of a quirky, eccentric cinema to one side of the international norm as a means of establishing international attractiveness. In *Sweetie* and *Strictly Ballroom*, *Muriel's Wedding*, and *The Adventures of Priscilla, Queen of the Desert* a space is created for what has become an international expectation of Australian "quirkiness," "eccentricity," and "individuality."

In these features, the banality and richness of contemporary, usually urban settings and culture, are foregrounded and turned away from their usual moorings in realist social problem filmmaking. So Peter Castaldi praises *Strictly Ballroom* for its combination of the conventional romance fairy tale and Australian suburbia, its back streets and its dreams. This combination "liberates the suburban from the grip of the realists and lets fantasy run free" as the filmmakers "took the back streets of any town and dressed them up in the most colourful, outrageous and wickedly witty way." In making *Sweetie,* Campion took the "short films" for which she had become internationally famous and made them longer without sacrificing their signature "look." As Campion reported,

> When I made them [my short films], I never thought in the future I'd have the opportunity to make such personal, off-the-wall films. But then I saw how people enjoyed them, and I thought I'd like to make a feature which went even further than they did. I decided I didn't want to ape the kind of films made by other people: I wanted to invent my own.
>
> (Quoted in Stratton, 373)

In so doing, she legitimated the AFC's policy of developing talent and stylistic and plot innovation through the short film. Campion provided an example for subsequent filmmakers: filmmakers would be encouraged as much as possible to keep and extend the concerns and signatures of their short films into their features. In critical and marketing terms, her short films' prestigious international circulation created expectations for the director's long awaited first feature. *Sweetie*'s enumeration of what Anne-Marie Crawford and Adrian Martin called "a world defined, at a fundamentally banal and everyday level, by alienation, irresolution and incohesion" (Crawford and Martin, 56–7) provided a larger statement of the work in her short films. These same characteristics are also the domain of the many everyday stories of *No Worries* (Elfick 1993), *Return Home,* and *A Woman's Tale* (Cox 1991).

So to be "wholly local" in a pure form in front of and behind the camera is not the natural condition of a national cinema—even when it looks to be doing precisely that. Most national cinemas seek to involve international players (actors, directors, distributors, festival organizers, composers, television buyers) in the creation, financing and circulation of national cinema and television texts. A feature filmmaker's domestic career often hinges on getting their film into and comporting themselves appropriately at the Cannes, New York, Venice, Montreal, Toronto and London film festivals. In their choice of actors, locations, production personnel, story and dialogue, local producers routinely take into account the requirements of international circulation. Such considerations are crucial to getting films to circulate internationally, to bringing in international distributors, to securing pre-sales and co-production partners. National cinema filmmakers keep abreast of contemporaneous international technical, stylistic, storytelling, and organizational instruments for filmmakers indigenizing them to local circumstance.

Particularly when we move to its higher budgeted form, every Western national cinema strives to be explicitly international in its textual form. No national cinema can survive on "sleepers." Those who make sleepers want to operate with higher budgets and a bigger scale. At some stage each national cinema has to produce expensive films and this means becoming more explicitly international. This is riskier though because more money is at stake. It also entails enlisting a lot of international allies in advance. But it is the only way of escaping the low yields and lower production values typical of the purely local product. Compared to *Crocodile Dundee* and *The Piano, Strictly Ballroom* and *Romper Stomper* were minor successes internationally. Half of *Strictly*'s global revenues were generated in Australia; compared to 10 percent of *The Piano*'s $112 million (US) (Given, 13). The sleeper *Mad Max* could never hope to compete with its high budget successor *Mad Max II* (aka *The Road Warrior*)—it was the latter, not the former, that changed international filmmaking, sparking many imitations, the latest of which is Kevin Costner's *Waterworld* (Reynolds 1995). Higher budget productions also benefit the local and international image of the Australian cinema. They raise the industry's infrastructure, update its domestic technological base, employ and train a large number of professionals to industry standard and drag the smaller Australian films in their wake both locally and internationally. They help create the international currency of the local cinema. (Securing an attachment on Jane Campion's *The Piano* was important to Margot Nash making the transition from documentaries to low-budget features with *Vacant Possession*.) As one Australian-based director, Werner Meyer, put it to me in 1992: what the Australian industry needed was another *Crocodile Dundee*—not because this was the sort of film he made or liked but because "it made everything easier for everyone else in the industry." But, of course, this is harder to achieve successfully. Sometimes the international requirements in the makeup of international films change: liberal tax concessions made it possible in the 1980s to make a "quality" blockbuster with a predominantly Australian cast, finance and explicitly foregrounded Australian connections with titles like *The Man from Snowy River*, *Mad Max II*, *Gallipoli*, and *Dead Calm* being the result. But, in the 1990s, it required a project with an international setting and connection—often co-productions with Australian involvement more behind than in front of the camera, in titles like *The Piano*, *Black Robe* (Beresford 1992), and *Green Card* (Weir 1991), which I will discuss later.

If all national cinemas are implicated internationally, Australian cinema has been remarkably implicated. This can be measured in a variety of ways, like the international financing of Australian features and televison dramas (between 1988/89 and 1992/93 financial years foreign investors accounted for 39 percent of production funding, government agencies 33 percent and Australian private and commercial investment 28 percent [Bean and Court, 37]), or the international actors appearing in Australian cinema (some American actors not already mentioned include Tina Turner, Lee Remick, Kirk Douglas, Linda Hunt, Tom Selleck!), or, indeed, the international directors working behind the camera in Australian productions. British, American, Canadian, German, Polish and Yugoslav directors have made films in Australia from Australian stories and sometimes with Australian financing. Sometimes the films of major international directors have had a lasting impact on the subsequent shape of the national cinemas they worked in, however briefly.

There can, at times, be a happy mutuality between Australia as the location for other imaginings and these imaginings as "ours." Some of these films became owned by Australians as theirs. The most obvious examples here are: Harry Watt's *The Overlanders* (1946), Jack Lee's *A Town Like Alice* (1956), Fred Zinnemann's *The Sundowners*, Robert Powell's *They're a Weird Mob*, Nicolas Roeg's *Walkabout*, and Ted Kotcheff's *Wake in Fright*. These directors took Australian cultural artifacts—literature for Powell, Zinnemann, Kotcheff and previous "images" of Australia for Roeg—and transformed them into films.

Some "location" filmmaking projects have been crucial to Australian cinema providing models and opening out new territory for local filmmakers to follow. *The Overlanders* may have been an Australian/British western but it was also a "docu-drama" and possibly the first Australian art film. It opened the "outback" to a different fictional emplotment and eschewed the melodramatic norms which had been essential to the 1920s and 1930s Australian cinema. Romance was downplayed. There was an absence of closeups. The "vast open spaces" were shot as spectacle (a repertoire still in evidence). More important was the space it created for a mutually advantageous British-Australian partnership. Through it Australia became an on-screen presence in Britain—something that was, at best, unevenly achieved in the preceding decades.

The post-1970 Australian cinema revival is particularly indebted to the Australian work of the British directors Powell (for *Weird Mob*) and Roeg (*Walkabout*); and to the Canadian Ted Kotcheff. They prepared local and international audiences and critics for the Australian films that followed in the 1970s and beyond. Powell's *They're a Weird Mob* was a forerunner to the "ocker" films of the 1970s and the multicultural cinema of the 1990s with its repertoires of ethnicity, ethnic mixing and cultural non-comprehension—still in evidence in *The Heartbreak Kid* and *Romper Stomper*.

Wake in Fright's prototypical middle-class male school teacher experiencing a vernacular working-class male regional culture fashioned the male ensemble film. With its dystopian view of mateship and misogyny, *Wake* introduced the idea of endemic and structural evil to Australian cinema. These rhetorical figures have persisted through to the present and have helped organize the terrain of much subsequent Australian storytelling from *Don's Party* to *Romper Stomper*. The preparedness to accept, exploit, entertain and at times exaggerate this possibility provided an important maturity to Australian filmmaking and undoubtedly aided its circulation in the international festival market. It helped create—after the figure of New German Cinema's "unmastered past"—an unsavoury Australian past and present centred largely on the deeds, misogyny, limited horizons, and xenophobia of white (Anglo) males. Kotcheff's film prepared the way for that mix of hyperrealism, excessive masculinity, ambiguous sexuality, and misogyny so insistently present in subsequent Australian cinema.

In Roeg's *Walkabout* landscape was worked into the film as a "character." As the British critic Dilys Powell wrote on its release: "it is to the eyes that *Walkabout* speaks. Mr Roeg has painted an Australian landscape, blazing, enormous; and his desert really is a red desert; the sand burns brick red" (Powell, 261). Such an emphasis on landscape as character is evident in many later films but notably Peter Weir's *Picnic at Hanging Rock*, Paul Cox's *Exile* (1993), and Robert Scholes's *The Tale of Ruby Rose* (1988). Roeg's emphasis on the uncanny and the otherworldly, the mundane and the spiritual, and the tragic clash of Aboriginal and non-Aboriginal peoples in the Australian continent opened directly on to Weir's *The Last Wave*, Schepisi's *The Chant of Jimmie Blacksmith*, Moffatt's *Night Cries— A Rural Tragedy* (1989), the children's films *Storm Boy* (Safran 1976) and *Manganinnie* (Honey 1980), and even Barron film's remake of *Bush Christmas* (Safran 1983).[3] Roeg's observations about the film are pertinent to this discussion: "It couldn't have been made anywhere else and it was an utterly Australian film. . . . But it did something, I think, and I like to hope that it touched emotional chords that were international. I think that helped in some way to open doors for Australian movies" (quoted in White, 25).

Walkabout and *Wake in Fright* were seminal films for the Australian film revival to critics, audiences and filmmakers alike. Actor Jack Thompson claims both films to be "searching looks at the Australian ethos" and credits them with demonstrating "not only to the rest of the world of filmmakers but to ourselves that we were capable of making feature films" (quoted in White, 27). While neither was particularly successful in Australia, Thompson notes that they were "transitional films" signalling the transition between a feature industry marked by the "almost totally foreign-made films being made in Australia" and an "Australian cinema." These two films became particularly important to the 1970s film revival, in that they created Australian cinema as an international territory in the cinema and provided directly for an Australian place. They were noticed by critics and industry figures.

National cinemas are one of the means by which the local and the international reconfigure each other. Our above example foregrounds British, American and Canadian filmmakers refashioning the audiovisual representation of Australia and Australians and more than this, reconceptualizing the form, approach and stylistic means of the Australian cinema that followed—which was largely Australian produced, directed and scripted. But such refashioning is only part of the general circulation of any national cinema as it "travels" outside its domestic context and enters new contexts. Thomas Elsaesser writes of how "European films intended for one kind of (national) audience or made within a particular kind of aesthetic framework or ideology, for instance, undergo a sea change as they cross the Atlantic and on coming back find themselves bearing the stamp of yet another cultural currency (Elsaesser, "Putting on a Show," 25). The international appreciation of national cinemas in, for example, festivals "assign different kinds of value" to the product and in the process the films acquire a "new cultural capital beyond the prospect of economic circulation (art cinema distribution, a television sale)." Quite provocatively Elsaesser claims that "the New German Cinema was discovered and even invented abroad, and had to be reimported to be recognized as such" (Elsaesser, *New German Cinema*, 300). Australian cinema from the 1970s fashioned this international process as an intrinsic part of marketing Australian cinema to local audiences. Selection at Cannes provided an imprimateur for local audiences. It also rehabilitated local directors.

When Fred Schepisi's *The Chant of Jimmie Blacksmith* came out it died at the box-office after eleven weeks. Schepisi lost a lot of his personal savings accumulated over a decade of working as a television commercials director. He was attacked from all sides: filmmaker Terry Bourke claimed this film and Weir's *Last Wave* had led Australian filmmaking away from commercial values and genre filmmaking. Veteran director and former Channel 9 boss Ken G. Hall weighed in by claiming that Schepisi should have known that films about Aborigines are box-office poison. From the other direction, James Ricketson weighed in claiming *Jimmie Blacksmith* was a "dinosaur," an "ersatz Hollywood monster" and that the industry would be better funding "four potential [low budget] *Mouth to Mouth* [Duigan 1978] than in funding one *Jimmie Blacksmith*" (Ricketson, 226–67). The film's humanist values were attacked by an academic screen criticism inimical to humanism. Mudrooroo (then known as Johnson, 50) questioned the novel and the film's politics. He later wrote that the film's lingering image was that of "a beserk boong hacking to death white ladies." He noted the consternation among the Aboriginal family of Jimmy Governor and how they, on seeing the film, sought legal advice to try and stop its screening. It was left to Pauline Kael to salvage the film's Australian reputation somewhat. Albert Moran and I incorporated Kael's 1980 *New Yorker* review of the film into our 1985 collection *An Australian Film Reader,* partly because it provided a different view on the film as well as providing an instance of the importance to Australian cinema's international circulation of the New York critical establishment. Susan Dermody and Elizabeth Jacka noted how the republication of this review suggested that *Jimmie Blacksmith* "may be one of the underestimated and overlooked films of the 1970s" (Dermody and Jacka, "*An Australian Film Reader* in Question," 148). Through this and similar critical rethinkings, Schepisi was brought home, even though his subsequent career was now mostly in the United States.

The local as much as international terrain informs perceptions and the success of the dominant, imported cinema and national cinema product in international circulation. Historically, cinema and television is international in its outlook and sensibility, while local in its national configurations. Borders—especially national borders—are significant to explaining the circulation of Hollywood and national cinemas alike. These influence the viewing of international cinema as surely as they do the local product. In answer to the question of "what happens when a text crosses national or other borders" Alison Butler writes:

There is mounting evidence that the refunctionalization of texts is not just a manifestation of occasional resistances, but the very condition of possibility of such border crossings. Pro-ductive—and indeed unproductive—misreading is perhaps the paradigmatic operation which governs the reception of films outside—and sometimes inside—their original national contexts. (Butler, 419)

If this is the terrain of an imagined "America" bearing sometimes a limited relationto the actual United States, it is also the terrain of the "imagined" Australia or "Britain." Both *Crocodile Dundee* and *Four Weddings and a Funeral* were criticized at home for providing a "tourist's–eye view" of Australia and Britain. They both exported a view of Australian and British life "which is more like the rest of the world wants it to be than it actually is" (Roddick, 15). Here, the worry is that the "imagined Australia" (an outback "ocker" doing battle with crocodiles and New York escalators) or "imagined Britain" (upper middle class twits "off to a smart wedding in a battered Land Rover" [15]) directly impinges and shapes domestic film production. But if Butler is right, such repositionings are an unexceptionable part of the cinema landscape—and a part that filmmakers are acutely aware of. Take Stephan Elliott's account of the different audience responses in France, Australia and the United States to his film, *The Adventures of Priscilla, Queen of the Desert:*

At a screening we had for an Australian audience, they laughed at all the Australianisms. The Americans laughed too, but at different jokes. There is a line where Tick says, "Bernadette has left her cake out in the rain. . . ." Last night, they [the French audience] didn't get it, whereas the Americans laughed for ten minutes. (Quoted in Epstein, 6)

Elliott went on to observe that his film—like *Strictly Ballroom* (Luhrmann 1992) before it—was changing from "territory to terri-tory" to become "a different film in different territories" (Elliott, quoted in Epstein, 6). This difference Elliott observed extended to its public meaning: it could be seen in the gay response in the United States which saw it "as the big one that will bring gay lifestyles into a mainstream" while Australian audiences "embrace it as just another successful Australian film"—"a musical with actors who are really recognizable" (7). And so it was for *Crocodile Dundee* too (see Crofts).

Such a situation leads Elsaesser to declare that "national cinemas and Hollywood are not only communicating vessels, but (to change the metaphor) exist in a space set up like a hall of mirrors, in which recognition, imaginary identity and miscognition enjoy equal status (Elsaesser, "Putting on a Show," 26). The local dimension of a national cinema does not only reside in the specifically local cultural codifications or domestic production traditions, but also lies in the movement of localization, the movement of indigenizing other nations' cinema product and their production models. National cinemas are one of the means by which cultural transfers are routinely accomplished in the international cinema. More than this, these cultural transfers embodied in the locally produced cinema are themselves a form of localizing and indigenizing processes. Localizing becomes the means of internationalizing; internationalizing the means of localizing. The local and the international are ineradicably mixed in the constitution of the national cinema project.

National Cinemas as Festival Cinemas

> We [Americans] want Australian films to seem real and convincing (as if there are real films of real Australia), certainly more real and convincing that most people imagine Hollywood films to be. I suppose this is the defining characteristic—a prejudice to your advantage, really—we have towards Australian cinema, perhaps Australia as a whole. . . . Your cinema is to us a "specialized cinema," an art house cinema supported by festivals, critics and filmgoers who want something different . . . but not too different, who want a more real and convincing cinematic experience, who want to experience this sense of "Australianicity," an Otherness that is, in fact, not all that Other.
> —Tony Safford (29)

Tony Safford was here speaking to the Screen Producers Association of Australia conference in 1994. He was not only defining the particularity of Australian cinema to Americans but defining as well the space of a festival cinema more generally. Like part of the output of any national cinema, Australian cinema circulates in that principally non-Hollywood ("festival") space of the "foreign film" in world cinema markets. Since the 1970s film revival, there have been a handful of internationally recognized Australian cinema auteurs (notably Peter Weir, Bruce Beresford, Fred Schepisi from the 1970s generation; Gillian Armstrong, Phil Noyce, George Miller of the 1980s generation; more lately, the Australian-trained Jane Campion) and avant-garde cinema stylists (Albie Thorns in the 1960s, Tracey Moffatt in the 1990s), internationally renowned documentarists and ethnographic filmmakers (David Bradbury, Denis O'Rourke, David and Judith MacDougall, Bob Connolly and Robin Anderson), feminist experimental filmmakers (Helen Grace, Laleen Jayamenne), indigenous filmmakers (Moffatt and Prattan) and a band of recognizable, adaptable actors used by accomplished mainstream and art cinema directors (Judy Davis, Jack Thompson, Sam Neill, Russell Crowe). Their works mark out the routine Australian membership and presence at the Cannes, Berlin, Toronto and even Singapore film festivals as something from Australia now becomes an unexceptional though minor norm at international festivals and subsequently in repertory film and "quality" television markets.

Bill Nichols has made a number of points about the function of this film festival cinema:

> The festival circuit allows the local to circulate globally, within a specific system of institutional assumptions, priorities and constraints. Never only or purely local, festival films nonetheless circulate, in large part, with a cachet of locally inscribed difference and globally ascribed commonality. They both attest to the uniqueness of different cultures and specific filmmakers and affirm the underlying qualities of an "international cinema."
>
> (Nichols, 68)

This festival context adds "a global overlay to more local meaning" (Nichols, 68) providing "a continuous, international pattern of circulation and exchange of image-culture." Here Australian cinema can be seen to observe John Orr's dictum that "cinema is often at its more powerful in filmmakers who emerge from distinctive *national* traditions" and that what he calls "the neo-modern moment has its origin in the national cinemas of Western Europe and the United States where it engages with Western capitalist modernity" (Orr, 6).

The different European national cinemas of the 1950s to the present and the Asian, African and Latin American cinemas of the present provide the Australian cinema audience and local filmmakers with an important social and cultural experience of modernity, and not just in the cinema. That Australian filmmakers should want to contribute to it should come as no surprise. Furthermore Nichols suggests that within this festival optic Hollywood occupies an "oppositional rather than an inspirational position" (Nichols, 74). The film festival circuit displaces this centre rather than "bolstering" it (74). It provides a way of valuing its own product at the expense of Hollywood. And therein lies its attraction for Australian filmmakers and audiences alike. It naturalizes the local as internationally acceptable, just as it provides a space to one side of the mainstream Hollywood competition. In doing so, it does not so much compete, as circulate and organize an alternative space to the common vernacular of Hollywood. As noted, an important component of this festival circuit is the art cinema, whether in its major and still dominant form of the European art cinema, or in its emergent form as films from outside the "Western, Eurocentric centre" (Nichols, 74).

Director Paul Schrader once described the difference between the European and the Hollywood film as one of attitude: "American movies are based on the assumption that life presents you with problems, while European films are based on the conviction that life confronts you with dilemmas—and while problems are something you solve, dilemmas cannot be solved, they're merely probed or investigated" (quoted in Elsaesser, "Putting on a Show," 24). Elsaesser contends that this "might explain why a happy ending in a European art film is felt to be a cop-out, a fundamentally unserious mode of closure" (Elsaesser, "Putting on a Show," 24). He asks: "isn't one of the characteristics of 'modern' cinema (until recently synonymous with the art film) its metaphysical doubt about master narratives of progress, preferring to be sceptical of linear time and the efficacy of action?"

Consequently the largely European-derived "art film" model and its televisual equivalent in "quality television" has had an impact on Australian production schedules and television priorities. This poses its own obligations upon Australian cinema: a cinema created for the representation of modernist cultural themes (existentialism, the absurd, alienation, "boundary situations") and modern political issues (class, gender, race) providing the doubling of aesthetics and politics. The best representatives of this tendency in Australian cinema usually combine fragments of all of these: from Peter Weir's *Picnic at Hanging Rock*, to Paul Cox's *Man of Flowers* (1983), to Gillian Armstrong's *The Last Days of Chez Nous* (1992), to *Sunday Too Far Away*, to *Don's Party*; from *The Piano* to *The Chant of Jimmie Blacksmith*.

Not surprisingly many of Australian cinema's narrative resolutions and thematic preoccupations (though not necessarily their means of realization) are classically those of the international art cinema. As Debi Enker observes about Australian cinema's thematic preoccupations:

> Characters are repeatedly alienated and driven apart, condemned to loneliness, or at the very least to being alone. In this context, the dearth of happily resolved love stories is entirely appropriate. . . . Australia's filmmakers have concentrated more on the spaces that separate people, on communities that stifle the spirit and circumstances that drive lovers apart. It is a much darker and despairing vision than that of a frontier paradise promising freedom and unlimited scope for fulfilment.   (Enker, 224–25)

Enker goes on to note that this includes films as diverse as *Mad Max* and *Picnic at Hanging Rock*, *Caddie*, and *Nirvana Street Murder*, *Breaker Morant*, and *Monkey Grip* (K. Cameron 1982).

More than any other filmmaking project before Campion's *Sweetie*, Cox's *My First Wife* (1984) fits in with European art cinema protocols. Perhaps this is why his films easily fit within local and international art film circuits. The chief interest in the film is in the break up of a relationship seen from the man's (played by John Hargreaves) perspective. The viewer is invited continually to identify with his sense of grief, remorse, betrayal. In consequence, the wife remains both a cipher and an enigma for him and for us as viewers. To realize this narrative structure, *My First Wife* entails the strategies (the feelings, intensities, excesses, and neuroses) of art cinema. There is a trading in of narrative development for a vivid tableaux. It relies on an interiorizing of conflict, upon states of mind, feelings, sentiments which find their expression in repeated scenes. One such scene is the flashback to the wedding scene which provides the film's narrative image. The image here is of the Wendy Hughes character, the first wife, in her wedding dress (it's also the image used on the video dustjacket). It promises literally what is not in the present time of the film. The image of the wife at her wedding is recalled as his memory. It is insistently returned to: a counterpoint to the present of a conjugal relationship in crisis.

My First Wife invites interpretation. It is, as Bill Routt and Rick Thompson (Routt and Thompson, 32) would put it, a text which despite its attractive surface is not "for everyone," as it contains, and has wrapped itself around enigmas and secrets. The enigma to be explored by viewer and filmmaker alike is the meaning for the John Hargreaves character (and we viewers) of his previously unquestioned relationship with his wife. This enigma distilled in the film's narrative image—the Wendy Hughes character at her wedding happy in love with the John Hargreaves character—is the pretext and subtext of the film.

The film is built around what Horst Ruthrof calls a "boundary situation" in which "a presented persona, a narrator, or the implied reader in a flash of insight becomes aware of meaningful as against meaningless existence" (Ruthrof, 102). David Bordwell sees this situation as a defining characteristic of much art cinema (Bordwell, 208). Certainly *My First Wife*'s impetus wholly derives from the main character's recognition that he faces a crisis of existential significance. Cox's film insists upon a degree of psychologizing as the protagonist's state of mind is visualized. This messes up the dividing line between reality and fantasy, past and present, suggesting an uneasiness with the literal present. In this Cox's bears comparison to some of Peter Weir's films—*The Last Wave* particularly—where liminal states of mind are externalized into a heightening of reality, into a literal present gone awry.

In nearly all of Cox's films there are clear moments of excess which suggest the relation of the filmmaker to the apparatus. In *My First Wife* there are the sequences which are distorted, which refuse to show clearly, which de-representationalize, and thus diminish the scope for us to see anything clearly. Because they go on just a shade too long, they carry more than the existential weight of the husband's state of mind. They draw attention to themselves as play with film stock, with the form of film. They pose another disrupting enigma, that of film play. The viewer is encouraged to read different meanings into the film—not only in the end there is only the family, but also in the end there is only film and its experience.

With its invitations to psychological depth, its dislocations, its willingness to fragment, its use of the "boundary situation"—Paul Cox's cinema is one for which readings of personal vision are appropriate, fit easily and are encouraged by the films themselves. The figure of John Hargreaves in *My First Wife* is irresistibly a stand-in for the author. If like so many 1980s films the central journey is "His" journey, it's a journey which we are advised to speak of in personal terms.

But it's not only the kernel of interpretation at the heart of Cox's films that is refracted in their critical circulation. There is also the drive to make cinema meaningful, to reinvent it, to place oneself, one's whole being at its service. If this involves the cinematizing of the personal it also carries the megalomaniac's dream of total control and total risk. This licences his films to come stuffed with chaotic excess, prejudices, intellectual and physical obsessions, unreasonableness—thereby encouraging the reader in his or her turn to engage with them. There are few directors in Australian cinema who so insistently invite the labour of the auteurist as Paul Cox.

The festival circulation of director as auteur and the close proximity of self-expression and personal vision to national and intersubjective vision, ensures that the kind of attention the festival and related circuits confer upon a film generates a certain kind of public reputation. It gives Australian cinema generally more value, just as it permits the construction (as with all auteur-based projects) of a singular career and a star persona. As Nichols goes on to note, a transformation is involved in this passage from the local to the international: "The entry of national cinemas and the work of individual filmmakers into the international film festival circuit itself constructs new meanings, and it is these new meanings that we, as festival-goers, are most likely to discover" (Nichols, 71).

While this international standing and circulation may have little to tell us about what, if anything, connects any of these Australian directors, filmmakers and actors it does signpost cultural estime (however liminally as birthplace or site of training) and public relations value. Both are critical to sustaining the domestic reputation of the industry on governmental and other horizons within Australia.

National Cinemas and the National

Only by being aware of its national identity can a film industry be international.
—Volker Schlondorff 1977, quoted in Elsaesser,
New German Cinema, 306

If national cinemas are an intrinsically international form, they are also national forms. As Schlondorff's comment suggests, national cinemas do not only persist as a means to counter or accommodate Hollywood, they are sustained and shaped by local purposes of a social, economic, cultural and national nature. Moreover they need to be conscious of these. Recently Phillip Adams reflected on his and Barry Jones's insider involvement in bringing about federal government support for a film industry in 1968–1969. Here Adams explicitly brings together "national identity" and film export—associating the former with a "boutique industry":

> We [Phillip Adams and Barry Jones] weren't arguing for a major film industry. Just a modest effort that would allow us to explore our national identity (whatever that was) and to export it to the world's film festivals. At no stage did Jones or I believe it was either possible or useful to make more than ten or fifteen features a year, but our travels had convinced us that there was an opportunity for a boutique industry, that would make culturally specific films for up-market audiences everywhere.
>
> (Adams, ix)

Every national cinema attempts at some point to turn its national distinction into an asset, not a liability. It strives at some point to be locally attached. National cinemas have to do so because the national cinema's place on the horizons of local (and international) cinema and television drama viewers is more marginal than is its international counterpart. Consequently the local connection to government, to non-cinema kinds of backing, and to international involvement whether by way of direct investment or co-productions are going to be all the more important. For this reason there is no clearer instance of this localizing moment than in the ways national cinema producers, promoters and activists call on and mobilize local resources to naturalize their films on the local industry, on local governmental, private enterprise and community horizons. These agents routinely move outside the "film world" and call on whatever vehicles are at their disposal to bind audiences to the local product and naturalize the local cinema. They characterize the national cinema product as a story of the local people-among-themselves framing their histories, their stories, their lifeways, their locations. Going local at some point is a way of securing the resources with which to compete at home and abroad.

The vehicles drawn on are often "outside" the typical film communicative circuits. The educational apparatus was enlisted for Peter Weir's *Gallipoli* (1981), as schools around the country organized matinée visits to the cinema during school time for its screening. This had been done before with John Heyer's *Back of Beyond* (1954)—a documentary film commissioned by the Shell Film Unit to capture the "essence of Australia." Schepisi drew on a dramatic local incident: the Lindy/Michael/Azaria Chamberlain story of a dingo, Uluru (Ayers Rock) and the ensuing court case which made world news in *Evil Angels/Cry in the Dark* (with Meryl Streep and Sam Neill in the lead roles). David Elfick drew on the late 1980s and early 1990s story of rural crisis, with a generation of workers on the land walking off, for his film *No Worries*. National cinemas often work to produce social purposes as a means of enlisting local audiences. Again *Gallipoli* is an instance where the film's launch and the public discussion surrounding it provided a national lesson in civics. It also provided a marketable Australian image abroad in the historical film. Elsaesser argues that countries like Australia and the United Kingdom "without a strong and continuous tradition of film-making may have to depend on an ability to 'market' the national history as spectacle for international success." National history like the dramatic contemporary public event provides filmmakers with a "common currency" which they might otherwise lack. It "establishes a signifying system of motifs, oppositions, antinomies and structural binarisms: the very stuff of narratives" (Elsaesser, *New German Cinema*, 293). Elsaesser was thinking here of historical titles like the British *Chariots of Fire* (Hudson 1981) and the Australian *We of the Never Never* (Auzins 1982). This history need not be glorious either. It can be ignominious as in *The Chant of Jimmie Blacksmith*'s insistence on white Australia's racist history (the Aboriginal survival becomes Australia's "unmastered past" like the Holocaust for Germans); it can be about national defeat in World War I at *Gallipoli;* and it can be about the sacrifice of principles of justice for the sake of a postwar order, as Japanese war criminals are set free and an innocent Japanese man is convicted as a scapegoat in *Blood Oath* (Wallace 1990).

These different survival options are connected to the strategies and agencies of "nation-building" of the state and private sector. The two dominant filmmakers of 1930s and 1940s Australian cinema—Charles Chauvel and Ken G. Hall—operated in a period where there was just not the same degree of formative state support as there was after 1969. Yet these commercially minded directors were explicitly nationalist. Chauvel proclaimed his mission to be one of "featuring Australia" as a character in his films. Later national cinema producers had outside help to survive in what Elsaesser calls "the politics of culture [support]" of the state (Elsaesser, *New German Cinema*, 3). As Tim Rowse observed, "[n]ation states promote a sense of nation-hood. That is one of the functions of cultural policy" (Rowse, 67). Curiously this enabled them to be less explicitly nationalist.

A. D. Smith distinguishes two features of the common national culture that are important to any discussion of a national cinema (Smith, 129–39). There is the *national political*—the common political and civic culture involving citizenship and equality before the law; and there is the *national cultural*—the cultural core of memories. values, customs, myths, symbols, solidarities and significant landscapes shaping "Australian" identity. For Smith no state can be workable without both a national political and national cultural sense of itself. The cinema and television matter to public policy makers, interest groups, lobbyists, filmmakers and audiences as targets for their national cultural and national political projects and ambitions.

Filmmaking and film industry policy sustains both kinds of national definitions. The agitators for Australian cinema in the 1960s and early 1970s sought national political support for Australian cinema as a national cultural institution concerned with identity and self-expression—"dreaming our own dreams, telling our own stories." A measure of a self-respecting mature nation was the possession of a national cinema. Their emphasis on an open-ended national cultural ambition for the cinema helped legitimate the creation of filmmaking infrastructures which sustained mainstream, oppositional and peripheral cinemas. It also created a space for alternative Australian identities. If this last had been dressed up as an explicit national political project, rather than as part of a national cultural project, it might well have not got off the ground.

Filmmaking and film and television policy can sometimes emphasize each at the same time. In 1980 the beginnings of a fifth television network—the SBS-TV—started in Sydney and Melbourne. It was legitimated by a policy of multiculturalism that was initially conceived as a national political project, highlighting those ethnically and culturally diverse NES background peoples in Australia. At the same time, the establishment of a generous tax concession régime encouraging private investment in film and television production (called 10BA) largely underwrote a film and miniseries boom in which the "national cultural" was consistently foregrounded and with it the established settler culture and its Australian history. It should be noted that the 1980s was that decade in which the Australian state played the least important role in the selection of film properties and funding (reduced to 16 percent compared to the 1990s' 39 percent)—but it still had an indirect role through its certifying of film and miniseries as Australian to qualify for tax concession purposes. This role limited the degree of internationalization of production through the decade and inhibited the development of story properties set outside Australia. Some of the most popular Australian cinema and miniseries television of the 1980s revisited formative national moments in the national symbols-myths complex, such as the Boer War in Bruce Beresford's international "breakthrough" film, *Breaker Morant,* World War I in *Gallipoli;* the legend of the eponymous racehorse of the 1930s in *Phar Lap;* the bodyline cricket controversy of the 1930s between Australia and Britain in *Bodyline* (Schultz, Ogilvie, Marinos, and Lawrence 1984). These productions restated and updated old myths "dedominionizing" Australia by accentuating its "non-English" characteristics (see Kapferer, 167 and Davidson, *passim).* The most popular features of the decade—*Crocodile Dundee* and *The Man from Snowy River*—revisited Australian "bushman" archetypes and in the *Snowy River's* case the famous poem once taught universally in Australian schools.

While this was happening some policymakers, critics and filmmakers subscribed to a different national political object. This was a reconstructed objective of a "multicultural" Australia which was to become an increasingly important definition of Australian nationhood from the mid-1980s, culminating in the 1989 National Agenda for a Multicultural Australia. As Rowse observed in 1985, it "yields an Australianism defined by inner diversity, rather than by a homogeneous sense of being different from Britain" (Rowse, 75). It envisages an "Australia linked in a relaxed diversity of inheritances to all the nations of Europe and Asia by the encouragement given to ethnic plurality among migrants" (75). Cathy Robinson, current Chief Executive of the AFC, observed in November 1991 that multiculturalism ensured that "cultural policy and cultural nationalism could no longer be so easily equated" (Robinson and Given, 20).

The two movements for locating a national cultural identity and a multicultural reality found some congruence in a handful of the miniseries of the late 1980s foregrounding the NES experience of the Australian mainstream, in programmes like *The Dunera Boys* (1985, Jewish refugee experience of Australian internment), *Cowra Breakout* (1985, Japanese prisoner-of-war internment in World War II), *Fields of Fire* (1987, 1988, 1989, Italian-Australian experience

in the cane fields of north Queensland) and *Always Afternoon*
(1988, a German national's experience of discrimination during
World War I).

Sometimes the two can be in conflict. With the increasing importance of multiculturalism as an official policy of state over the 1980s
and a sense of the inevitability of industry internationalization by the
late 1980s, film policy makers and bureaucrats certifying films as
Australian for investment purposes gave policy a more national
political hue. They became concerned with industrial markers—
how many were involved in the making of it and in which positions.
At the same time, broadcasting regulators at the then Australian
Broadcasting Tribunal were concerned to evolve national cultural
terminology and notions, seeking textual markers for something to
be Australian (see Cunningham, 56–60). For the first the issue was
an employment and deployment one involving principles of equity
and access. For the second it was a national cultural issue. The conflict between these two arms of government confronted a national
political assessment with a national cultural one.

Both critical commentary and film industry thinking had, by
the late 1980s, moved towards the notion that, in Rowse's words,
"Australianness should mean nothing more than that a number of
residents of Australia were employed in the making of it" (Rowse,
75). This had the advantage of "not beg[ging] the question of what
people who live in Australia are concerned with" (79) and therefore
living up to the promise of multicultural ism. It also had the advantage of opening the industry to what Ross Gibson has called "international contamination" in which Australian cinema could be
envisaged as a large family of projects made with some Australian
involvement (Gibson, 81). This entailed a significantly more com-
modious notion of what could be "Australian" in order to permit
some exploitation of the opportunities afforded Australia as a cultural producer in the English language, like the French-Australian co-
production *Green Card*—the vehicle for Gerard Depardieu to reach
a wide English-speaking audience—or Vincent Ward's remarkable
Map of the Human Heart (1993), with its tale of an Inuit's unre-
quited love, and Pauline Chan's *Traps*—a story of a marriage falling
apart set in Vietnam of the 1950s. The preferred Australian was now

what Ghassan Hage has usefully called a "cosmopolite"—a "'mega-urban' figure, detached from strong affiliations with roots and consequently open to all forms of otherness" (Hage, 76). As Deborah Jones writes in the context of *Strictly Ballroom*, "to be Australian now is to be much more like other people, anywhere, than we may have admitted in the past" (Jones, xiv). And it produces a filmmaking whose "identity" is uncertain, like *The Piano* and *Sirens*.

When Elsaesser writes that "no other European country, it seems, is as unsure of the meaning of its culture as Germany, or as obsessed with its national identity" (Elsaesser, *New German Cinema*, 49)—he could just as well be writing of Australia. As with the New German Cinema, the Australian cinema since the 1970s has resolutely set about problematizing its national identity, taking on, or perhaps "trying on" successive identities, holding together apparently incompatible national cultural and political objectives and using the nation as a means of questioning and interrogating its very national possibility and merit as such. Because of the importance of "nations" to a national cinema, national cinemas inevitably involve questions of relative national merit.

In their own ways, Germany and Australia have problematic international identities and these influence what their cinemas can be and how they can be taken up. Both have as part of their very cinematic identity this movement of problematizing the nation, the culture, and even the society itself. Germany's Nazi history is sometimes compared to Australia's Aboriginal and Islander genocide. But mostly Australia's problem is not Germany's one of the specific kind of cultural value it musters, but rather the absence of (any) value and therefore any distinguishing culture in international circulation.

Like the German cinema, the Australian cinema has also been "innovative and coherent" (Elsaesser, *New German Cinema*, 61) in its margins: its women's cinema, its films about marginal groups (the skin-heads of *Romper Stomper*, the bikers of *Stone*—Harbutt 1974), the sub-cultural lifestyles (*Monkey Grip*'s Carlton milieu, the transvestites of *The Adventures of Priscilla, Queen of the Desert*), and minority interests (the displaced persons of *Silver City*, the Greeks of *The Heartbreak Kid*, the Japanese war brides in *Aya* (Hoaas

1991), the disabled in *Struck by Lightning* (Domaradzki 1990), the Murri Aborigines of *Fringe Dwellers* (Beresford 1986)—and perhaps, most significantly, in its documentary tradition. Films produced under this logic are often seen as the true heart of Australian cinema: not only where it is at its most experimental, innovative and coherent but where it deals with the toughest issues and where it is "most Australian."

Yet, as with the New German cinema, films produced under this logic also suffer a legitimation gap in that they are marginal to a significant part of the audience. At times their audiences are more virtual than actual—films to mark time, to develop talent, to get noticed to make a high budget film. But equally, as with the New German Cinema, Australian cinema in its minor streams has highly specific audiences in mind making films appealing to a small part of the audience "from a sense of shared values and assumptions" (Elsaesser, *New German Cinema*, 154) but running "the risk of being either parochial (the in-group film) or esoteric." The cinema here "served an audience for confirming or validating individual experience and feelings" opening on to a "desire . . . directed at the filmmaker, to represent only a 'correct' political or ideologically unambiguous standpoint." There was a constant "need for self-confirmation and self-validation in the guise of criticism and ad hoc political theory on the part of the spectators" (159). If this is particularly true for the independent cinema in Australia with *Filmnews* until 1995, Cantrill's *Filmnotes* and *Metro* serving as vehicles to make it so; it is also true of a critical milieu seeking as a matter of some urgency to work out whether the mainstream *The Sum of Us* or *Bad Boy Bubby* or *The Piano* have got their respective sexual politics right—establishing in short whether these films can legitimately speak to "us" in the way Campion's short films, and Ana Kokkinos' *Only the Brave* apparently do/did.

Like the New German Cinema, the search for an audience is continually foregrounded as a problem in Australian cinema. Even the villains were the same: the exhibition and distribution sector concerned with exhibiting American pictures, the local audience trained to accommodate the wrong product, the Americans who have colonized our subconscious in a thoroughly mediatized landscape—

Kings of the Road (Wenders 1975) meets *Newsfront*! To some degree the responses are also similar: Kluge's experimentation with form in his 1970s films echoes the experimentation in distantiation found in Australian feature "documentaries" like Cavadini and Strachen's ethnographic experimentation in the service of a political cinema in *Two Laws* (1981) or in John Hughes's Walter Benjamin–inspired film *One Way Street* (1993). As in New German Cinema, there is considerable attention to getting the film processes right—ethically and politically—to obtaining the right forms of consultation particularly with respect to marginal groups. Herzog's propensity to "test borderlines, limits and extremes" finds its Australian equivalent in Denis O'Rourke's dramatic gestures on the Pacific rim—in his documentary features *Cannibal Tours* (1988) and most extraordinarily in *The Good Woman of Bangkok* (1992). Schepisi's treatment of the media and the courts in *Evil Angels* (aka *Cry in the Dark*) as instruments of systemic harassment replicates Margarethe von Trotta's *The Lost Honour of Katharina Blum* (1975).

Elsaesser notes that "Australia . . . has seen a revival as a national cinema similar to that in West Germany" (Elsaesser, *New German Cinema*, 309). He also notes the parallel with the new Australian cinema. Elsaesser and Dermody and Jacka make the state central to their account. For their part, Dermody and Jacka see Australian filmmakers as having three different responses as handmaidens to the state, its reputation and its ethos. One has been to subscribe to state purposes, to the dominant national cultural purposes in a bland mainstream feature filmmaking, which they call the AFC-Genre; another has been to subscribe to and stress the industry and therefore commercial purposes espousing genre filmmaking; and yet another—and this is by far the most dependent one on the state—is to resist both. This estimation very much consigns the mainstream product to the sidelines as either nakedly commercial or as a bland product. It certainly has been incoherent and less evidently "innovative" in a formal and minoritarian sense. Yet this "absent centre" at the heart of mainstream Australian features—this seeming dependence on "other cinemas" and their norms, genres and so on—is actually one of the most fascinating aspects of Australian cinema, enabling it to speak so powerfully to local and international audiences alike in *Strictly Ballroom, Mad Max II (The Road Warrior), My Brilliant Career,* and *Crocodile Dundee.*

The Messiness of National Cinemas

If there is a considerable "local" aspect to national cinemas, there is considerable fuzziness surrounding them. At some time or other most national cinemas are not coterminous with their nation-states. As we have seen, production funding is international. Formal co-production treaties between countries provide frameworks to produce films which may have little to do with either country. Peter Weir's romantic comedy, *Green Card*, is typical of the high budget strand of Australian filmmaking in the 1990s: it has an Australian director, it is funded by French and Australian investors and its post-production was carried out in Australia. This is a French/Australian co-production set and filmed in New York and is the story of a "marriage of convenience" between a French man played by Gerard Depardieu and an American played by Andie MacDowell. He marries in order to gain permanent residency in the United States and she to secure an apartment only available to a married woman. The comedy and the developing romance between the two evolves once they are subject to an official investigation over the status of their "marriage." Yet unlike the rapid-fire comedy dialogue of similar Hollywood romantic comedies casting opposites—physically, emotionally, intellectually—*Green Card* has a slower delivery of dialogue, and is consequently more muted, slow and observed. It remains true to the green card experience of the Depardieu character speaking and mastering English as a second language. This and the film's ending, where the Depardieu character is deported at the precise moment the couple realize they love each other, signifies the intrusion of the European-Australian "reality principle" which refuses to solve the problem in a happy ending but instead substitutes a new dilemma for the old. There are no Australians in front of the camera, yet. It is, with its FFC backing, Peter Weir's "Australian film" of the 1990s.

Many smaller national cinemas are also in product, orientation, industry and language at some stage a part of each other. Deciding where the national leaves off and another national begins is difficult in these cases because the "national" involves both. This is particularly so for Australia and New Zealand. Close cultural, language and historical links forge an Australasian filmmaking and identity. Vincent Ward, Jane Campion and Cecil Holmes (regarded by some as filmmakers, whose promise made evident in *Three in One* and *Captain Thunderbolt*—was tragically not able to be fulfilled) are all New Zealanders. Franklyn Barrett—with Longford and McDonagh—the finest of Australian silent filmmakers, came to Australia after a filmmaking career in New Zealand. There is a long history of Australian directors making New Zealand films which includes Longford's *A Maori Maid's Love* (1916). Some silent films—like Beaumont Smith's *The Betrayer* (1921)—managed Australian and New Zealand locations. And New Zealand actors have always had a strong presence in Australian films from "the clever New Zealander" Vera James (whose father secured the New Zealand distribution rights for her film *A Girl of the Bush* (Barrett 1921),[4] to Sam Neill in *My Brilliant Career, Dead Calm*, and *Death in Brunswick*.

Campion's explicitly Australian-based work is sometimes claimed for New Zealand cinema. *Sweetie* was screened in Sydney as part of a festival of New Zealand cinema. Is Campion a New Zealander or an Australian? Sometimes she describes herself as an Australian; just as often she associates her work—particularly her New Zealand based stories—with her Kiwi identity. This gives rise to debates over whether *The Piano* is an Australian or a New Zealand film. Does her work spanning the Tasman Sea and that of Vincent Ward (*The Navigator: A Medieval Odyssey* 1988—the AFC and the New Zealand Film Commission's first co-production) presage the development of a more integrated "Australasian" film market to undergird an Australasian identity?

The Piano was set in New Zealand and made by a New Zealand director and of its three principals two were American and one a New Zealander. The Australian connection is solely that the AFC provided Campion with script development money and that Campion is Sydney-based, has lived in Australia for seventeen years, was trained at the AFTRS, and has used Australian film subsidy and production regimes to develop her talent and film properties. Yet *The Piano* is not simply another international production with some Australian involvement, it also represents Australasian filmmaking and a growing convergence and integration of the Australian and New Zealand filmmaking, exhibition and distribution sectors in the 1990s. This emerging situation is reminiscent of the integrated market that existed before television fractured what was a highly integrated Australasian audiovisual market.

Sweetie, The Piano, Map of the Human Heart, and *An Angel at My Table* are just some of the high profile "mixed productions" involving Australian and New Zealand collaborations of creative personnel which became an unexceptionable part of the cinema landscape in the 1990s. The 1990s also saw the return of New Zealand to the Australian imagination after so long being the "poor relation." Films set and shot in New Zealand gained significant audiences and acclaim from the Australian market, as *An Angel at My Table* and *The Piano* were followed up with Lee Tamahori's *Once were Warriors* (1994) and Peter Jackson's *Heavenly Creatures* (1995). Campion's films project in these terms an Australasian identity reflecting the close economic, cultural political, social and historical links between Australia and New Zealand and the significant New Zealand migrant presence in Australia. It is worth remembering in this regard that every Western national cinema is, at some stage, as a matter of national cultural policy interested in fostering international values, cooperation, mutual understanding and economic integration. The rethinking of the Australian–New Zealand relation on both sides of the Tasman at virtually every level in the late 1980s and through into the 1990s is a case in point. *The Piano* is one consequence of this rethinking. For David Robinson the film becomes "in its combination of Australasian and Hollywood practices . . . a paradigm of new international art cinema" (Robinson, 125).

Many smaller national cinemas are also at some stage part of larger national cinemas. Think of Austrian cinema with respect to German cinema; or Australian and New Zealand cinema with respect to English and American cinema. The Australian cinema of the 1930s consciously foregrounded its diasporic links to Britain—

both as a means to create product suitable for sale in the United Kingdom and as a way of giving expression to a dominant (but by no means uncontested) cultural ideal of the day projecting Australia as a British-defined society. In 1930, W. K. Hancock wrote in his authoritative work on Australians: "If such a creature as the average Briton exists anywhere upon this earth, he will be found in Australia" (Hancock, 28). Ken G. Hall's *The Squatter's Daughter* (1933) set up a seamless movement from Australia to Britain and then back again. The talented musician denied opportunity within Australia in *Broken Melody* (Hall 1938) goes to England to claim his destiny as a composer of merit, to return later to Australia and reclaim his romantic love and retrieve his place in his father's affections and bail out the family farm.

The postwar Australian feature cinema up until the decisive explosion of the 1970s was significantly—and mostly—a consequence of the outreaching of other national cinemas—British, American and even French and Japanese cinemas. The 1966 film *They're a Weird Mob* is a pivotal transition film between the "outreaching of others" and the "on local terms" of the 1970s. It looks back to the British and American location films of the 1950s and 1960s; and it looks forward to an "Anglo- Australian film industry" characterized by creative partnerships like that between J. C. Williamson and Powell and Pressburger. Post-1970 Australian cinema used subsidy and television industry consolidation to forge on its own terms international partnerships in place of the off-shore productions of the 1950s and 1960s.

So too, nation-states are only one among a number of organizers of films, their circulation, production and meaning. Large regional international organizations such as the European Community are taking over some of the functions of nation-states and evolving film policies fostering international cooperation. So too it is a policy priority of the Australian, Canadian, English and New Zealand film organizations to pursue greater production, policy and industry links between themselves to better coordinate and integrate their markets to mutual benefit. This parallels and updates the relatively integrated "Commonwealth" film market of the 1950s involving these same countries. *Black Robe* is an example of this

increasingly formalized association between the government funding agencies of these Commonwealth countries. This film is veteran director Bruce Beresford's "Australian film" of the 1990s.
There are a host of Australians in the crew and one in the cast, in
Aden Young (who grew up in Canada). It is a Canadian/Australian
co-production. It is also a Canadian film set in Canada telling the
story of colonization and most particularly the religious colonization of the Indian peoples of Quebec. At my local video library *Black
Robe* is located on the "festival" shelves and marketed on the dustjacket as being in continuity with the director's 1980 classic,
Breaker Morant.

Other organizers of film production and circulation are multinational distributors, satellite television networks, international
festivals, television networks and co-production arrangements. Most
of this is not new. The transnational European film ideal of today had
its predecessor in the Film Europe movement of the 1920s and early
1930s (cf. Thompson). Co-productions emerged in the 1960s to
facilitate continental European filmmaking.

Sometimes this fuzziness in the national cinema is structural
to the nation. Take for instance the language and regionally based
"national" cinemas within India and Canada. The Canadian state,
for example, supports two national cinemas: an English-speaking
one based in Toronto and Vancouver and a French-speaking one
based in Montreal. And there are the various diasporic cinemas
which in some guises have the stature of a cohesive "national" cinema—like the "overseas Chinese," "Indian" and Jewish cinema
which gains Australian audiences. Jewish film festivals have
become a phenomenon in Australia and the United States, whose
product is drawn from across the world including Australia. Australian cinema's contributions to a Jewish cinema have been limited: they include Henri Safran's comedy *Norman Loves Rose*
(1982) and Jackie Farkas's searing short film *The Illustrated
Auschwitz* (1992) which recounts a survivor's experience of the
Holocaust and how her memory of that is connected to her first
post-Holocaust cultural experience of watching *The Wizard of Oz*
(1939). Are the growing body of short films shot in Italian, Spanish and Greek a contribution to the Italian, Spanish and Greek

"national cinemas" or are they "Australian cinema"? Although not part of any larger diaspora, diaspora-like structures have emerged surrounding "first peoples" or "Aboriginal" filmmaking and screening events, which bring together culturally diverse first peoples who have been marginalized in different parts of the world by processes of colonization. Is there an Aboriginal and Torres Strait Islander cinema we can call an indigenous national cinema emerging from the spaces of non-Aboriginal and Aboriginal partnerships? The AFC sponsored a touring season of films in 1995 called *Hidden Pictures*, promoting an indigenous cinema whose beginnings are located in collaborations between non-Aboriginal filmmakers and Aboriginal actors and individuals—in Ned Lander's tale of an Aboriginal band on the road in *Wrong Side of the Road* (1981) and Phil Noyce's low-budget road movie *Backroads*. The openness of these filmmakers to Aboriginal input and their preparedness to allow that input shape the final product prepared the way for Aboriginal filmmakers like Tracey Moffatt and Anne Pratten and a greater role for Aboriginal voices.

Like many national cinemas, Australian cinema operates within the multiethnic context. Fourteen percent of Australian households spoke a language other than English at home and these homes sustained "ethnic video" and cinema outlets for screening imported, culturally appropriate product and for the screening of locally produced materials. With 22 percent of its population born outside the country courtesy of a large post–World War II migration programme and a generous refugee programme (on a per capita basis Australia accepted more IndoChinese refugees than did any other country; see Lombard, 18), Australian cinema may not be the natural non-Hollywood cinema of a minor but not insignificant proportion of the population. With such a multiethnic society the "typical Australian" is now a product of several ancestries to the extent that Australia's cinema audience is shaped by a variety of cultural influences—which are increasingly seen in its cinema—as in the Spanish family in *Strictly Ballroom* and the Greek family in *Death in Brunswick* and *The Heartbreak Kid*.

National cinemas function within internally divided provincial contexts sustained by provincial governance and regional identities.

Because many nations are, like Australia, Canada, the United States, and Germany, federations, state or provincial authorities are also organizers of film production and circulation through, for example, various state film authorities and the local basis for censorship provisions. Elsaesser notes Germany's "long established reflex of regionalism, and centuries of decentralization" commenting on its impact on German cinema and the politics of culture support (Elsaesser, *New German Cinema*, 49). Australia is like Germany in this respect: regionalism is a standard reflex—the Australian states existed before "Australia" did as a governing entity and decentralization is not only intrinsic to the European settlement of Australia but to Aboriginal and Islander society before it. Some Australian states, notably the populous New South Wales (Sydney, its capital, was the major centre for film production and still is) imposed film quotas in the 1930s. One of the important features of the Australian film revival was that production funding has been provided by the different states since 1972. Some Australian exhibition chains have been locality- and state-specific. And various kinds of sub-national identities provide alternative cultural materials and spaces to exploit.

A good example of this regionalism is Argall's *Return Home.* Its Adelaide setting stresses the cultural particularity of regional Australia. It foregrounds the significant migration to the metropolitan city from provincial Adelaide. It is also about diminishing living standards and downward mobility that is a marked feature of the lower middle class and working class experience over the 1980s and 1990s. One of the characters, Noel, is rehabilitated by his journey home from Melbourne. The film is structured as a dialogue between two brothers, Steve (Adelaide) and Noel (metropolitan Melbourne). Each has what the other lacks. Steve owns a failing small garage business but he has family. Noel has no family but is successful and has big city Melbourne values. We are invited to read their different values in relation to the changing geographic "landscape" of Australia. The narrative is resolved in favour of provincial Adelaide and family, as Noel returns to lend his skills to rejuvenate his brother's business. His affirmation of home has a utopian dimension, as Adelaide and South Australia have bleaker prospects compared to the booming economies of Queensland and Western Australia and the industrial heartlands of Sydney and Melbourne. Here Adelaide can be remade by the return of sons and daughters it has lost to the metropolis. Watching *Return Home* I was struck by the many parallels between it and Edgar Reitz's miniseries *Heimat* (1984). Both Australian and German cities have a deeply provincial character, with competing regional centres having different outlooks. There is the same "rootlessness," as a postwar order was made and fashioned as a significant "break with the past." Both have seen significant internal migration—in Australia's case north to Queensland and west to Western Australia, and to Australia's two metropoles of Sydney and Melbourne. *Return Home*'s regionalism is achieved through its suburban characters, language, and the minute, often nostalgic descriptions of everyday life in the spacious single-storey suburbs of Adelaide. The film interweaves ideas of provincialism and homeland—giving voice to that other side of Australian life—its provincial character. Here the suburban heartland is centred on the nuclear family, its local horizons, the immediate and locality-bound networks which are gently opposed to the modern city, Melbourne and its alienated vision of glass. Like *Heimat, Return Home* consistently exploits the tension which Kaes identifies there between "staying and leaving, between longing for distant places and homesickness" (Kaes, 168). Argall's film is a troubling objection to the changes wrought on traditional Australian communities struggling to keep their provincial lives, hopes and lifeways intact in the face of declining economic circumstance and profound structural change.

NOTES

1. The only exception I can think of is the 1979 Peat Marwick, Mitchell Services report on the Australian Film Commission, which imagined unlimited horizons for Australian cinema, enacting the dream so chimerically available to the non-Hollywood English-language producers, in gaining equivalent American success. See Peat, Marwick, Mitchell Services, 18–20.

2. Bill Routt, personal correspondence, August 1994.

3. The earlier film—a British location film—was directed by Ralph Smart and released in 1947.

4. The "clever new Zealander" quotation is taken from the trade press of the time (see Berryman, 26).

WORKS CITED

Adams, Phillip. "Introduction." In *A Century of Australian Cinema*, ed. James Sabine (Port Melbourne: Reed Books, 1995), vii–xi.

Australian Broadcasting Tribunal (ABT). *Broadcasting in Australia* (Sydney: Australian Broadcasting Tribunal, 1991).

Australian Film Commission (AFC). *Analysis of the Performance of Australian Films since 1980: A Paper for the House of Representatives Standing Committee on Environment, Recreation and the Arts Inquiry into the Performance of Australian Film—"The Moving Pictures Enquiry"* (Sydney: AFC, October 1991).

Bean, Jeremy and David Court. "Production." In *Get the Picture*, 3d ed., ed. Rosemary Curtis and Shelley Spriggs (Sydney: Australian Film Commission, 1994), 30–67.

Berryman, Ken. "*A Girl of the Bush.*" In *Focus on Reel Australia*, ed. K. Berryman (Hendon SA: Australian Council of Government Film Libraries in association with the National Film and Sound Archive, 1990).

Bordwell, David. *Narration and the Fiction Film* (London: Methuen, 1985).

Butler, Alison. "New Film Histories and the Politics of Location," *Screen* 33:4 (Winter, 1992): 413–26.

Cameron-Wilson, James and F. Maurice Speed. *Film Review 1993–4 Including Video Releases* (London: Virgin Books, 1993).

Castaldi, Peter. "Movie of the Week," *Sunday Herald Sun*, TV Extra (October 23, 1994). In *Cinedossier* Issue 656 (October 25, 1994): 52.

Collins, Diane. *Hollywood Down Under—Australians at the Movies: 1886 to the Present Day* (North Ryde, Sydney: Angus & Robertson, 1987).

Crawford, Anne-Marie and Adrian Martin. "Review of *Sweetie*," *Cinema Papers* 73 (May 1989): 56–57.

Crofts, Stephen. "Cross-Cultural Reception: Variant Readings of *Crocodile Dundee*," *Continuum* 5:2 (1992): 213–17.

Cunningham, Stuart. *Framing Culture: Criticism and Policy in Australia* (Sydney: Allen & Unwin, 1992).

Curtis, Rosemary and Shelley Spriggs, eds. *Get the Picture: Essential Data on Australian Film, Television and Video*, 2d ed. (Sydney: Australian Film Commission, 1992).

Davidson, Jim. "The De-dominionisation of Australia," *Meanjin* 38:2 (July 1979): 139–53.

Dermody, Susan and Elizabeth Jacka. "*An Australian Film Reader* in Question," *Continuum* 1:1 (1987): 140–55.

———. *The Screening of Australia. Vol. 2: Anatomy of a National Cinema* (Sydney: Currency Press, 1988).

Elsaesser, Thomas. *New German Cinema: A History* (London: BFI and Macmillan, 1989).

———. "Putting on a Show: The European Art Movie," *Sight and Sound* 4 (April 1994): 22–27.

Enker, Debi. "Australia and Australians." In *Australian Cinema*, ed. Scott Murray (St. Leonards, Sydney: Allen & Unwin in association with the Australian Film Commission, 1994), 211–25.

Epstein, Jan. "Stephan Elliott: The Adventures of Priscilla Queen of the Desert, Interview," *Cinema Papers* 101 (1994): 4–10, 86.

Gibson, Ross. *South of the West* (Bloomington and Indianapolis: Indiana University Press, 1992).

Given, Jock. "Review: 1992–93." In *Get the Picture*, 3d ed., ed. Rosemary Curtis and Shelley Spriggs (Sydney: Australian Film Commission, 1994), 12–28.

Hage, Ghassan. "The Limits of Anti-Racist Sociology,'" *UTS Review* 1:1 (1995): 59–82.

Hancock, W. K. *Australia* (1930; reprint, Brisbane: Jacaranda Press, 1961).

Higson, Andrew. "The Concept of National Cinema," *Screen* 30:4 (1989): 36–46.

Johnson, Colin (Mudrooroo). "Chauvel and the Centering of the Aboriginal Male in Australian Film," *Continuum* 1:1 (1987): 47–56.

Jones, Deborah. "Waltzing out of the Outback into the Ballroom." In *Strictly Ballroom. From a Screenplay by Baz Luhrmann and Andrew Bovell*, ed. Baz Luhrmann and Craig Pearce (Sydney: Currency Press, 1992), xiii–xiv.

Kael, Pauline. "A Dreamlike Requiem for a Nation's Lost Honour." First published in *New Yorker* (September 15, 1980); republished in *An Australian Film Reader*, ed. Albert Moran and Tom O'Regan (Sydney: Currency Press, 1985), 204–10.

Kaes, Anton. *From Hitler to Heimat: The Return of History as Film* (Cambridge, Mass.: Harvard University Press, 1989).

Kapferer, Bruce. *Legends of People, Myths of State* (Washington, D.C.: Smithsonian Institution Press, 1988).

Lombard, George. "The Australian Example," *Refugees* 93 (1993): 18–19.

Moran, Albert and Tom O'Regan, eds. *An Australian Film Reader* (Sydney: Currency Press, 1985).

Neale, Steve. "Art Cinema as Institution," *Screen* 22:1 (1981): 11–40.

Nichols, Bill. "Global Image Consumption in the Age of Late Capitalism," *East-West Film Journal* 8:1 (1994), 68–85.

Nowell-Smith, Geoffrey. "But Do We Need It?" In *British Cinema Now*, ed. Martin Auty and Nick Roddick (London: British Film Institute, 1985).

Orr, John. *Cinema and Modernity* (Cambridge and Oxford: Polity Press, 1993).

Peat, Marwick, Mitchell Services. *Towards a More Effective Commission: The AFC in the 1980s* (Sydney: Peat, Marwick, Mitchell Services, 1979).

Powell, Dilys. *The Golden Screen: Fifty Years of Films*, ed. George Perry (London: Pavilion Books [in association with Michael Joseph], 1989).

Reid, Mary Anne. "Distribution." In *Get the Picture*, 3d ed., ed. Rosemary Curtis and Shelley Spriggs (Sydney: Australian Film Commission, 1994), 67–129.

Ricketson, James. "Poor Movies, Rich Movies." First published in *Filmnews* 9:1 (May 1979); republished in *An Australian Film Reader*, ed. Albert Moran and Tom O'Regan (Sydney: Currency Press, 1985), 223–27.

Robinson, Cathy and Jock Given. "Films, Policies, Audiences and Australia." In *Film Policy: An Australian Reader*, ed. Albert Moran (Nathan: Institute for Cultural Policy Studies, Griffith University, 1994), 17–26.

Robinson, David. *Chronicle of the Cinema 1895–1995. No. 5: 1980–1994* (London: British Film Institute, 1994).

Roddick, Nick. "*Four Weddings* and a Final Reckoning," *Sight and Sound* (January 1995): 12–15.

Routt, William and Richard Thompson. "'Keep Young and Beautiful': Surplus and Subversion in *Roman Scandals*." In *History on/and/in Film*, ed. T. O'Regan and B. Shoesmith (Perth: History and Film Association of Australia [WA], 1987), 31–44.

Rowse, Tim. *Arguing the Arts* (Ringwood: Penguin, 1985).

Ruthrof, Horst. *The Reader's Construction of Narrative* (London: Routledge Kegan Paul).

Safford, Tony. "Two or Three Things I Know about Australian Cinema," *Media International Australia* 76 (May 1995): 27–29.

Smith, Anthony D. *The Ethnic Origins of Nations* (Oxford: Basil Blackwell, 1986).

Stratton, David. *The Avocado Plantation: Boom and Bust in the Australian Film Industry* (Sydney: Pan Macmillan, 1990).

Thompson, Kristin. *Exporting Entertainment: America in the World Film Market 1907–1934* (London: British Film Institute, 1985).

———. "The End of the 'Film Europe' Movement." In *History on/and/in Film*, ed. T. O'Regan and B. Shoesmith (Perth: History and Film Association of Australia [WA], 1987), 45–56.

White, David. *Australian Movies to the World* (Sydney: Fontana and Cinema Papers, 1984).

Eric Rentschler

The Testament
of Dr. Goebbels

Big Brother or Brave New World?

Siegfried Kracauer's *From Caligari to Hitler* presented the films of
the Weimar Republic as previews of coming Nazi attractions. About
National Socialist features themselves, however, Kracauer had very
little to say.[1] If German films prefigured Hitler, how they actually figured once Hitler rose to power is a contested matter. The Third
Reich's productions, administered by Joseph Goebbels's Ministry of
Public Enlightenment and Propaganda, remain today at once widely
reviled and yet undeniably resonant.[2] "Never before and in no other
country," Wim Wenders wrote in 1977, "have images and language
been abused so unscrupulously as here, never before and nowhere
else have they been debased so deeply as vehicles to transmit lies."[3]
In many minds, Nazi cinema is an infamous and abject entity: its
most memorable achievement is the systematic abuse of film's formative powers in the name of mass manipulation, state terror and
worldwide destruction.

Despite its adversaries, Nazi cinema has had and continues to
have many apologists and admirers. Outraged voices may have
demonised this corpus of film in the hopes of exorcising Goebbels's
legacy, but their interventions have in decisive ways gone unheeded.[4]
Nazi features are anything but universally proscribed or detested;
they are still shown today in many places. Most of the era's films
exist and remain in circulation. Films of the Third Reich have played

From *Film History* 8:2 (1996), pp. 317–326. Copyright © John Libbey & Company
Limited. Reprinted with permission from John Libbey & Company Limited and the
author.

an integral role on German television, for example, on the Second Channel (ZDF) and particularly on the Bavarian regional station (BR). In 1980, Nazi films comprised 8.7 percent of all features aired on West German stations, a total of 113 titles. By 1989 the number had risen to 169.[5] Invariably, these selections are cheerfully introduced as fond memories or old standards; announcers rarely say anything about these films' historical provenance.

Film sociologist Gerd Albrecht's positivistic compendium, *Nationalsozialistische Politik*, documents just how prominently generic productions figured in the Third Reich; they constituted 941 of its 1,094 feature films, including 295 melodramas and biopics, 123 detective films and adventure epics.[6] Almost half of all features—to be precise: 523—were comedies and musicals (what the Nazis termed "heitere," i.e., "cheerful" films), light fare directed by ever-active industry pros like Erich Waschneck, E. W. Emo, Carl Boese, Hans Deppe, Georg Jacoby and Hans H. Zerlett, peopled with widely revered stars like Hans Albers, Marika Rökk, Heinz Röhmann and Ilse Werner, as well as character actors such as Paul Kemp, Fita Benkhoff, Theo Lingen, Grete Weiser, Paul Hörbiger and Hans Moser. Such works seem to demonstrate that the Nazi regime created space for innocent divesions; they reflect, claim revisionist historians, a public sphere not completely subjugated by state institutions. Many of these films receive recognition as noteworthy achievements, as grand hallmarks of German cinema, in some cases even as bearers of oppositional energies. Were these illusions indeed harmless or were they malevolent or were they perhaps both at the same time? Were they sometimes subversive or, as ideological critics insist, always affirmative?

Seeking answers to these questions, one turns to sweeping panoramas and comprehensive surveys, all of which leave much territory uncharted. The standard accounts of the subject range in tone from dismissive to indulgent and in any case, they seem more concerned with thematic structures than with formal shapes.[7] Previous books on cinema in the Third Reich have little to say about Nazi film aesthetics, about the look and texture of these features, about the properties which made some of them so resonant and well-regarded.[8] Oddly, historians typically concentrate on the making and partaking of films during the Third Reich, acting as if its productions no longer existed. Crucial questions receive only partial answers or go unasked altogether. In what ways did the German dream factory of the 1930s and 1940s appropriate and consciously recycle Hollywood fantasies? What is the place of Nazi cinema in German film history as well as film history at large? What lessons does film under Goebbels import regarding the use and abuse of the mass media, and are those lessons perhaps timely?

Until recently, it has been customary to describe cinema in the Third Reich as a function of a "1984" rather than a "Brave New World." This was particularly easy to do as long as commentators could equate the Ministry of Propaganda with a Ministry of Fear. Goebbels, it was claimed, relied on "doublethink" and institutionalised cynical reason, manipulating the flow of information, lording over all sectors of the public sphere and infiltrating the private realm. Nazi Germany, in this understanding, resembled Orwell's dystopia: a regime in which there was no free space, a society where ultimately even one's dreams were monitored, an order that allowed no alterity. Big Brother represented a collective projection, the political construction of a party that demanded total and unquestioned allegiance.

Examining the era's mass culture more carefully, however, one does not encounter only the duty-bound, no-nonsense and angstridden society of lore. Photographs from the period (both official images and private snapshots) often displayed the cheerful faces and animated physiques of an invigorated German populace. This buoyant condition was, to be sure, not enjoyed by everyone. Contingencies of birth, political convictions or sexual preferences resulted in many people being denied membership in the Aryan nation, For those marginalised by National Socialism, life and being were an altogether different experience. These individuals were ostracised and persecuted; they were forced to leave Germany or to lead a shadow existence; many of them were incarcerated, tortured and executed. This racial state disciplined bodies in a variety of ways; under its auspices, euthanasia, sterilisation and genocide coexisted with a vast array of creature comforts and material compensations. Fear and loathing were crucial parts of the system, but National Socialism could not—and did not—rule by terror alone.

Hitler's Germany, similar to Huxley's *Brave New World*, was also an exercise in emotional engineering, a political order that openly proffered tourism, consumerism and recreation as dialectical complements to law order and restriction. Fascism had a sinister visage, but it also had a pleasing countenance—and cinema embodied the agreeable facade in its most scintillating incarnation. Very few Nazi features simply rant and rave; most of them appear to have nothing to do with politics. The distinction between political and unpolitical films is in fact one that the Nazi administrators implemented and which postwar commentators have continued to employ. The Nazi film industry wanted its cinema to appear both national and international, open and regulated, modern and eternal. Film under Goebbels was to become a *Volkskunst* that would foster an imagined community, a *Volksgemeinschaft*. A popular medium and a vehicle of mass culture, film preserved old forms of identity while offering a new (and powerful) vehicle of consensus-building.

As we scrutinise Nazi films more than fifty years since the end of World War II, we need to take pause and re-evaluate conventional wisdom. We cannot reduce all Nazi films to hate pamphlets, party hagiography or mindless escapism. This cinema, in fact, is neither singular nor aberrant; its conscious reliance on classical Hollywood conventions has virtually gone unnoticed as has the recourse of so many productions and so much of Nazi mass culture to American techniques and popular genres.[9] Much of its fatal appeal derived from a modern populace's desires for a better life. The utopian energies topped by the feature films of the Third Reich in a crucial manner resembled, indeed consciously emulated, American dreams. In this endeavour, I would like to offer some propositions about Nazi Germany's society of spectacle and ponder its relationship to the mediadriven culture which surrounds us and the world of mass-produced images in which we live.[10]

The Dream of a Dominant Cinema

Feature films in the Third Reich were principally the function of a genre cinema, which in turn was part of an elaborate mass culture.

This cinema sported titles, figures and materials well-known to Weimar film which would persist in the postwar era.[11] Indeed, until the early 1960s and the revolt of the Oberhausen activists, most West German films did not take leave of yesterday; they continued as the endeavours of directors, scriptwriters and casts who had worked under Goebbels.[12] Films in the Nazi epoch employed well-known stars, ready-made formats, standardised productions and studio economies. Goebbels sought to create a popular domestic cinema which would be not only profitable and entertaining, but also ideologically effective and politically useful, both a stabilising force and an animating energy. The Minister of Propaganda announced his grand designs forthrightly: he wanted German cinema to be *the* dominant cinema. Speaking in 1940, he declared: "We must give film a task and a mission in order that we may use it to conquer the world. Only then will we also overcome American film, it will not be easily overcome. But it can be overcome."[13]

After the beginning of World War II, Nazi film became an extremely popular and lucrative entity, enjoying large audiences and enthusiastic followings. "The financial success of our films is altogether amazing," Goebbels noted soon after German troops invaded Poland. "We are becoming real war profiteers."[14] In October 1940, he wrote, "I shall not relax until the entire European film industry belongs to us."[15] Goebbels and the Ministry of Propaganda waged an all-out war against Hollywood, seeking to win over domestic viewers, overwhelm foreign competitors and conquer international markets. In his diary entry of 19 May 1942, Goebbels reiterated his resolve: "We must take a similar course in our film policy as pursued by the Americans on the North American and South American continents. We must become the dominant film power in Europe. Films produced by other states should be allowed to have only local and limited character."[16]

Under Goebbels's administration, cinema become centralised and consolidated; by 1942, four state-owned studios (Bavaria, UFA, Terra, Tobis) dominated the scene. In an attempt to control the articulation of fictional worlds, only a small proportion of films was shot outdoors or on location. Directors functioned above all as facilitators, not as distinctive auteurs. Film was to be artful and accessible, not intellectual or esoteric. Features of the Third Reich favoured carefully crafted artificial realms and showed a predilection for studio spaces, costume design and script logic. Films made under the Nazi regime amounted to an other-directed cinema, administered by a state apparatus which determined every aspect of production from a script treatment to a film's final shape, from its release and exhibition to its circulation in the public sphere.

In contrast to its Weimar counterpart, Nazi cinema denigrated the film of the fantastic as well as filmic realism. The one remained too open to irrational forces; the rightful place of the fantastic was to be an everyday of bright uniforms, hypnotic rituals and dazzling spectacles. The Weimar legacy of workers' films was likewise forsaken and left behind. Nazi cinema shunned the extremes of Weimar's "haunted screen" (*Das Cabinet des Dr. Caligari/The Cabinet of Dr. Caligari* [1920], *Nosferatu* [1922], *Metropolis* [1927]) and its socialist realism (*Mutter Krausens Fahrt ins Glück/Mother Krause's Trip to Happiness* [1929] and *Kuhle Wampe* [1932]), assuming a middle ground of historical period pieces, costume dramas, musical revues, light comedies, melodramas and petty bourgeois fantasies. The film culture of the Third Reich allowed at best a limited space for experiments. Trade papers and film journals spoke only rarely about avant-garde initiatives. Modernism persisted in Nazi cinema, to be sure, not in features, but rather in short subjects and nonfiction films (for instance, in the documentaries of Leni Riefenstahl, Willy Zielke and Walter Ruttmann).

Film narratives of the Nazi era generally privileged space over time, composition over editing, design over movement, sets over human shapes. Compared to Hollywood movies, most features of the Third Reich appeared slow and static. They were more prone to panoramas and tableaus than to closeups, decidedly sparing in their physical displays (very little nudity, few stunts and action scenes). Nazi film theorists stressed the importance of kinetic images as well as galvanising soundtracks.[17] Music worked together with visuals to make the spectator lose touch with conceptual logic and discursive frameworks, pulling "listener and viewer from act to act, from impression to impression ever more overwhelmingly."[18] The ideal film would spirit people away from the real world and grant viewers access to a pleasant, compelling and convincing alternative space.

Only a minority of Nazi features displayed what one might speak of as overt propaganda. There were two waves of films with manifestly strident overtones: the "movement films" of 1933 and the anti-Semitic, anti-British and anti-Soviet productions of 1939–1942. But to grasp how Nazi films captivated spectators and promulgated political meanings, one must comprehend the way in which films interacted with and resonated within larger social constellations. Ideology more often than not came sugar-coated, in gripping, engaging and pleasant packages of entertainment which coexisted with other emanations of everyday culture. Films were not isolated experiences in the dark; they circulated within a vast complex of orchestrated and high-tech efforts to control thought and meaning. The Third Reich constituted the first full-blown media dictatorship, a political order that sought to occupy and administer all sectors of perceptual possibility, to dominate the human subject's every waking and sleeping moment.

From its quality features to its run-of-the-mill products, Nazi film reflected the workings of the classical cinema with its deference to character motivation, the codes of realism, the strictures of dramatic development and closure. It was a cinema dedicated to illusionism. "The task that I have posed for myself as a director," claimed Veit Harlan, "consists to a great part in making spectators forget that they are sitting in cinemas."[19] Goebbels saw himself as a German David O. Selznick and sought to create a film world every bit as alluring as Hollywood. Nazi films to a great degree seemed unexceptional and resembled Anglo-European features of the era. They were steeped in Old World values and fond of traditional formulas; their favourite sites were urban localities, bourgeois interiors and lower middleclass settings. Government film administrators as well as studio executives eschewed films that put National Socialism directly on display. In so doing, they carefully fostered the impression that cinema was a world apart from party agendas and state priorities.

Films of the Third Reich often allowed viewers vocations from the present in fanciful spheres so that they could forget politics and civic responsibilities. With its utopian spaces sponsored by Goebbels's Ministry of Propaganda, Nazi cinema not only created illusions but often showed illusionists at work and, on occasion, self-reflected about the power of illusions (*Capriccio* [1938], *Der Florentiner Hut/The Florentine Hat* [1939], *Münchhausen* [1943]). Many films thematised the fascination of aesthetic illusion (Viktor Touriansky's 1941 film, *Illusion*, offers a programmmatic title), concentrating on mesmerisers and performers as well as offering glimpses behind the scenes at film studios (*Es leuchten die Sterne/The Stars Are Shining* [1938], *Die gute Sieben/The Good Seventh Wife* [1940]) or revealing tricks of magic (*Truxa*, 1937). Nazi film illusions coexisted with government oppression, political terror and after 1939, a world war and the Holocaust. Screen illusions cushioned people against grim realities, offering the solace of worlds which were in order and seemed to allow unencumbered movement, safe havens and playgrounds where one could dream freely. Nazi escapism, however, offered only the illusion of escape from the Nazi status quo.

Despite the postwar claims of filmmakers and revisionist critics, one finds very few examples of open resistance to the party and state in this era's productions. Such films either did not find their way into production or were banned after initial showings. Nonetheless, not all meaning could be controlled and various films lent themselves to alternative appropriations.[20] To a large degree, such responses did not really run counter to official designs. Goebbels and his coworkers allowed films on occasion to transgress borders, exploring seemingly resistant potential and apparent exceptions to the rule, even subversive contents and oppositional positions, all the better to discipline distraction.

Postmodernity's Secret Sharers

Nazi illusions continue to exercise a decided hold on postwar imaginations, both in how people view Nazi images and in what they make of National Socialism. The fantasy productions of the epoch are still very much with us today—in matinee screenings, television showings, festival programs, video catalogues and university curricula. They offer testimony from the Third Reich which would seem to suggest a less oppressive everyday. Many of them abide as classics and evergreens, objects of revery and nostalgia; they circulate widely and remain problematic. Goebbels's tools of political affirmation have undergone transformation to become national monuments and vehicles of subversion. Nazi films such as *Glückskinder* (*Lucky Kids*, 1936), *La Habanera* (1937) and *Münchhausen* as well as memories of UFA's grandeur fuel fond German dreams; they energise reassuring fantasies of how, even in a cinema watched over by Hitler and his minions, the better part of the nation resisted the Third Reich. Many critics and observers persist today in holding on to National Socialism's prime illusions, namely that the imaginary worlds and fantasy scenarios created under a state-administered film industry had little to do with that state's operations.

Young German Film and its extension, New German Cinema, once turned against the Nazi legacy and "its demagogic treatment of images."[21] The New German directors declared war on their elders, seeking to liberate German film history from a fatal heritage of abuse. Over the years, though, as the history of the Third Reich was integrated into a larger German history, a rapprochement between New German Cinema and Nazi cinema become increasingly apparent. Hans Jürgen Syberberg recycled UFA stars, Werner Herzog sought to revive Arnold Fanck's mountain films, Helma Sanders-Brahms celebrated Leni Riefenstahl's *Tiefland* (*Lowlands*, 1954), Edgar Reitz affectionately cited Carl Froelich's *Heimat* of 1938 in his own *Heimat* of 1984 and a recent Wim Wenders feature (*In weiter Ferne, so nah!/Far Away and Yet So Close*, 1993) poignontly exonerated the Nazi collaborator Heinz Rühmann. Niklaus Schilling insisted on maintaining a sense of German tradition which incorporated films made during the Third Reich. "Without them," Schilling asserted, "we ignore an important part of our film tradition."[22] In Reitz's *Die Nacht der Regisseure* (*The Night of the Directors*, 1995), Leni Riefenstahl takes her place amidst contemporary Germany's most prominent directors. Even filmmakers—and critics—whose look back in anger spawned a New German Cinema have increasingly come to gaze on the sights and sounds of the Third Reich with a kinder and gentler regard.

Watching *Jud Süss* (*Jew Süss*, 1940) today is unlikely to turn any-one into an anti-Semite, people often claim, so why should it be banned along with several dozen other feature films from the Third Reich? No official list of these proscribed titles (*Vorbehaltsfilme*) exists; such a list could only demonstrate that the German govern-ment considers the populace of its democracy in crucial ways politi-cally immature.[23] Right-wing radicals and neo-fascist groups still partake of Nazi films and there is a substantial German black mar-ket for banned war movies, newsreels and Hitler documentaries.[24] One wonders how these films now resonate in a climate of violence towards foreigners, in a nation casting about for a new collective self-understanding.

Surely the continuing and largely unquestioned presence of entertainment films from the Nazi era in the German public sphere shapes popular feelings about that past. Comedies with Heinz Rühmann and Hans Moser hardly threaten to undermine civic val-ues, but they do influence how people look back at the Third Reich. Films of the Nazi era are easy to enlist in campaigns to normalise and neutralise the Nazi legacy. "We are what we remember," says the narrator of Don DeLillo's *Americana*. "The past is here, inside this black clock, more devious than night or fog, determining how we see and what we touch at this irreplaceable instant in time."[25] Films can preserve memory and function as vehicles of history. They can also serve as a means of forgetting, a medium to stylise, distort or erase the past.

Cinema under the aegis of Goebbels blended sensory plenitude and sensual deprivation.[26] Film images defined the good and the beautiful while vitiating the capacity for spontaneity and the desire for experience. Perhaps the most striking thing about life in National Socialism was its vicarious quality. A vanguard site, Nazi mass cul-ture reformed the living in the shape of the mediated; the everyday was defined by mechanically reproduced sights and sounds, by sim-ulations and special effects meant to generate strong emotions while systematically militating against the capacity to think in terms of continuities. Nazi cinema exploited the limitations of human imagination, seeking to obliterate first-person consciousness and to replace it with a universal third person.[27] Even as a leisure being, this other-directed creature was to remain a loyal state servant, a modern golem cast in the shape of mass-produced images. The Nazis used the cinema as the fictional Cagliostro of *Münchhausen* employed magic; they granted Germans their dreams, but at a usurious interest.

The Nazis recognised well that political effects could never derive from political expressions alone. Entertainment, spectacle and diversion lent themselves remarkably to instrumental endeavours. Hitler and Goebbels were consummate narcissists enamoured of their media images, the Third Reich a grand production, the world war a continuing movie of the week. Standardised mass culture, Goebbels realised, was the secret formula for successful mass manipulation. Mass culture also became a crucial precondition for mass murder. The media enabled Germans to withstand awful truths and ignore hideous presentiments, serving as a shield and a blindfold, audio-visual instruments that ensured uplifting fictions no matter how bitter the realities. Nazi feature films—both as entities that circulated in German cinemas during the Third Reich and as entities that still enjoy much public attention today—teach us above all one thing: entertainment can be far more than innocent pleasure.

Nazi media culture demonstrated just how potent and destructive the powers of fascination and fantasy can be, especially when systematically appropriated by a modern state and strategically implemented by advanced technology. A nation faced with material hardship and a spiritual void hailed Hitler's promises of a better life while shunning enlightened rhetoric. The Führer's order propped up spirits with artificial means and strived to hyperstylise the subjects of a new Germany. Simulations supplanted direct experience and illusions superseded reality. In this endeavour, the Third Reich granted a preview of postmodern attractions. Abusing the utopian possibilities of mass-produced representations, the Ministry of Propaganda also exhibited their dystopic potential. The National Socialist state's production of death and devastation would not have been possible without Goebbels's dream machinery.

The unprecedented historical example of the Nazi media dictatorship lingers as a very disturbing prospect, especially now, as sophisticated and pervasive technologies for the transmission and manipulation of audiovisual materials increasingly define who we are and how we exist. We refer to Hitler and Goebbels as madmen and demons, consigning them to the shadows. No matter how studiously we cloak these figures in darkness, however, they are clearly more than just ghouls or phantoms. Indeed, one might speak of Nazi Germany's irrepressible image-makers as postmodernity's secret sharers, as grasping entrepreneurs who profited from the industrialised means of enchantment, as master showmen who staged extravagant spectacles as the ultimate political manifestations. These real-life Mabuses have enacted the worst nightmares of any community whose social viability and collective identity depend on the media and mass culture. More than fifty years since the demise of National Socialism, the testament of Dr. Goebbels continues to haunt us.

NOTES

1. Siegfried Kracauer, *From Caligari to Hitler: A Psychological History of the German Film* (Princeton: Princeton University Press, 1947). The volume does contain a supplement on "Propaganda and the Nazi War Film," a study of newsreels and documentaries (273–331).

2. Between January 30, 1933 and May 7, 1945, 1,086 German feature films passed the censors and premiered in the Reich's cinemas. (Three of these represented films made prior to 1933 which were re-released between 1933 and 1935.) A further eight films were submitted to the censors prior to 30 January 1933, but were not released until after that date. The total of 1,094 features encompasses a few films which would be banned after their first public screenings. This figure does not include 26 films which were banned and never premiered; nor does it take in 67 international co-productions, films made in Austria before the *Anschluss,* nor the Films which were banned in Germany but premiered abroad.

3. Wim Wenders, "That's Entertainment: Hitler (1977)," in *West German Filmmakers on Film: Visions and Voices,* ed. Eric Rentschler (New York/London: Holmes & Meier, 1988), 128.

4. An impassioned recent example is Rebecca Lieb's "Nazi Hate Movies Continue to Ignite Fierce Passions," *New York Times,* August 4, 1991. Do Nazi propaganda films, asks Lieb, still possess the power to stir up hate? "Are they dangerous or should they be shown? If they are to be shown, who will show them and under what circumstances? Is there anything to be learned from them or are they too horrifying even to contemplate?" More than two decades ago, Amos Vogel posed similarly impassioned questions regarding the reception and exhibition of Leni Riefenstahl's films in his essay, "Can We Now Forget the Evil That She Did?" *New York Times,* May 13,

1973. For a German contribution which articulates similar concerns, see Hilmar Hoffmann, *Es ist noch nicht zu Ende: Sollen Nazikunst und Nazifilme wieder öffentlich gezeigt werden?* (Badenweiler: Oase, 1988).

5. Alfons Arns, "Die halbe Wahrheit: Zum Umgang mit NS-Spielfilmen in Fernsehen und Kritik," *Medium* 21:4 (1991): 35. See also Friedrich Knilli, "'Perlen' der Leinwand. Zur Rezeption Yon NS-Filmen in der Bundesrepublik," *Film und Fernsehen* 8:8 (1980): 20–22.

6. Gerd Albrecht, *Nationalsozialistische Filmpolitik* (Stuttgart: Enke, 1969), 96–97. In generating these figures, Albrecht chiefly relies on the generic descriptions of the Nazi *Reichsfilmarchiv*. He distinguishes between films with manifest (intended and recognised) and latent (neither intended nor recognised) propaganda, that is, between political films and non-political films. In crucial and problematic ways, Albrecht's statistics reflect Nazi categories and conceptions.

7. The most-often used synoptic works, besides Albrecht's *Nationalsozialistische Filmpolitik* (see note 6), include David Stewart Hull, *Film in the Third Reich* (Berkeley: University of California Press, 1969); Francis Courtade and Pierre Cadars, *Histoire du Cinéma Nazi* (Paris: Losfeld, 1972); Erwin Leiser, *Nazi Cinema*, trans. Gertrud Mander and David Wilson (New York: Collier, 1975); David Welch, *Propaganda and the German Cinema 1933–45* (Oxford: Oxford University Press, 1983); and Boguslaw Drewniak, *Der deutsche Film 1938–45. Ein Gesamtüberblick* (Düsseldorf: Droste, 1987.)

8. See historian David Weinberg's comments regarding crucial gaps in Nazi film studies: "There have been few attempts at in-depth analysis of film content . . . There is a need to go beyond the manifest messages of films produced under nazism to explore their subtle impact upon the psychology of the individual viewer, Such an exploration necessitates not only interpretation of the film dialogue but also an awareness of the various visual techniques employed by filmmakers to create specific audience responses" ("Approaches to the Study of Film in the Third Reich: A Critical Appraisal," *Journal of Contemporary History* 19:1 [January 1984]: 117).

9. The German notion of the *Gesamtkunstwerk* was even extended to describe the totalising effect of Hollywood movies. See, for instance, H. Ch. M., "Amerikanische Filme," *Die Tat* 28:2 (May 1936): "Whereas German features only manage to present a few good dramatic performances with cinematic allure, good American films are total works of art. The spiritual quality, the richness of sensibility and emotion in a single role of a German film, is larger and deeper than an entire American film. But because American films are total works of art, even if very primitive ones, they have a significance that deserves future consideration" (151). The author concludes with a discussion of the overwhelming effect of Leni Riefenstahl's short, *Tag der Freiheit!—Unsere Wehrmacht* (*Day of Freedom*, 1935). Its high drama and artistic pyrotechnics achieve the same ends as its Hollywood counterparts, but remain decidedly less subtle. "As a means of expression, film surely comes much more easily to the American" (153).

10. These reflections derive from the conclusion of my study, *The Ministry of Illusion: Nazi Cinema and Its Afterlife* (Cambridge, Mass.: Harvard University Press, 1996).

11. Various Weimar films were remade during the Third Reich, including *Die Finanzen des Grossherzogs* (*The Grand Duke's Finances*, 1934), *Der Student von Prag* (*The Student of Prague*, 1935), *Schloss Vogelöd* (*The Haunted Castle*, 1936), *Das indische Grabmal* (*The Indian Tomb*, 1938), *Die Geierwally* (*Vulture Wally*, 1940) and *Kohlhiesels Töchter* (*Kohlhiesel's Daughters*, 1943). Willi Forst and Viktor Tourjansky provided ersatz Lubitsch fare and passages of Karl Ritter's *Verräter* (*Traitors*, 1936) resembled Lang's *Das Testament des Dr. Mabuse* (*The Testament of Dr. Mabuse,*

1933). Numerous Weimar generic legacies continued without a break in the Third Reich: Prussia films (especially military dramas featuring Frederick the Great and starring Otto Gebühr), Heimat—and mountain films, costume films with historical settings, musicals With matinee idols like Lilian Harvey and Willy Fritsch, action films with Harry Piel, *UFA-Kulturfilme* and big city symphonies by Walter Ruttmann.

12. See Hans-Peter Kochenrath, "Kontinuität im deutschen Film," in *Film und Gesellschaft in Deutschland: Dokumente und Materialien*, ed. Wilfried von Bredow and Rolf Zurek (Hamburg: Hoffmann und Campe, 1975), 286–92. Remakes of Nazi films during the 1950s, for instance, included Wolfgang Liebeneiner's . . . *und ewig bleibt die Liebe* (*Love is Forever*, 1954, based on *Johannisfeuer/Midsummer Night's Fire*), *Urlaub auf Ehrenwort* (*Leave on Word of Honour*, 1955, a recast of Karl Ritter's 1938 production), *Waldwinter* (*Forest Winter*, 1956), *Franziska* (1957, based on Helmut Käutner's film of 1941, *Auf Wiedersehen, Franziska!/Goodbye, Francisca!*). Hans Deppe redid *Heideschulmeister Uwe Karsten* (*Country Schoolmaster Uwe Karsten*, 1933) in 1954 with Claus Holm, Barbara Rütting and Katharina Mayberg. Carl Froelich's blockbuster of 1934 *Krach um Jolanthe* (*Trouble with Jolanthe*) became Rudolf Schündler's *Das fröhliche Dorf* (*The Happy Village*) of 1955. Some other retreads were *Bel ami* (1955, based on Willy Forst's hit of 1939), *Dunja* (1955, Josef von Baky's variation on Gustav Ucicky's *Der Postmeister/The Postmaster*, 1940), *Das Bad auf den Tenne* (*The Bath in the Barn*, Paul Martin, 1956, derived from Volker von Collande's colour film of 1943), *Kitty und die grosse Welt* (*Kitty and the Big World*, 1956, based on *Kitty und die Weltkonferenz/Kitty and the International Peace Conference*, 1939), *Wenn wir alle Engel wären* (*If We All Were Angels*, 1956, a spinoff of Helmut Weiss's *Die Feuerzangenbowle/The Punch Bowl*, 1944, which itself had been drawn on *So ein Flegel/Such a Lout* from 1934), *Der Maulkorb* (*The Muzzle*, 1958, after the political comedy of 1938) and *Robert und Bertram* (1961, a remake of the anti-Semitic farce of 1939).

13. Joseph Goebbels, "Rede vor den Flimschaffenden am 28.2.1942 in Berlin," quoted in Gerd Albrecht, *Nationalsozialistische Filmpolitik* (Stuttgart: Enke, 1969), 500.

14. *The Goebbels Diaries: 1939–41*, trans. and ed. Fred Taylor (Harmondsworth/ New York: Penguin, 1984), 26.

15. *The Goebbels Diaries: 1939–41*, 149.

16. *The Goebbels Diaries: 1942–43*, trans. and ed. Louis P. Lochner (Garden City, N.Y.: Doubleday, 1948), 221.

17. See Hermann Wanderscheck's lead article, "Die Macht der Musik im Film," *Film-Kurier*, January 19, 1942. Many scenes in popular films prove, claim the author, "that music often can be more essential than dialogues, actors or visuals. It can compete with the soul of the image—the image remains silent, but music resounds, roars, paints, rings out in major and minor keys, spreading itself out like a rug over the image or flickering upward like a flame to provide the most powerful expression of redemption and liberation."

18. Leni Riefenstahl, *Hinter den Kulissen des Reichsparteitag-Films* (Munich: Eher, 1935), 28.

19. Veit Harlan, "Der Farbfilm marschiert," *Der Deutsche Film 1943/44: Kleines Handbuch für die deutsche Presse*, ed. Karl Klär (Berlin: Deutsche Fllmvertriebs-Gesellschaft, 1943), 77.

20. Among the films made during the Third Reich, there were, however, a few notable exceptions: films from the transition era between the end of the Weimar and Hitler's rise to power, Austrian films before the *Anschluss* (especially the work of Werner Hochbaum), banned and proscribed films (from *The Last Testament of Dr. Mabuse* [1933] and *Liebelei* [1933] to *Titanic* [1943] and *Grosse Freiheit Nr. 7/Great*

Freedom No. 7 [1944]), isolated instances of aesthetic resistance after 1942 (Helmut Käutner's *Romanze in Moll/Romance in a Minor Key* [1943], Wolfgang Staudte's *Akrobat schö-ö-ö-n* [1943], Peter Pewas's *Der verzauberte Tag/The Enchanted Day* [1944]) and films produced during the confused last months of World War II (*Unter den Brücken/Under the Bridges* [1946] and *Via Mala* [1948]).

21. Wim Wenders, "That's Entertainment: Hitler (1977)," in *West German Filmmakers on Film*, 128.

22. "Tradition im Kino, 15.10.78," *Filmforum* (Düsseldorf) (December 1978): 61.

23. The Allies initially banned 700 German films in 1945. (This figure includes documentaries, short subjects and some productions made before 1933 as well as Nazi features.) During the postwar years, German self-censorship authorities (the *Freiwillige Selbstkontrolle*, founded in July 1949) assumed responsibility for the removal of individual films from the proscribed list and their commercial re-release, responding to the requests of petitioners. Some titles would be taken off without conditions, others only if offensive or questionable passages were deleted. In June 1953, 340 German films from 1930–1945 appeared on an updated inventory. By January 1954, 275 films remained on the list; by August 1977 there were 176. As of late 1995, between thirty and thirty-five feature films from the Third Reich are still barred to the German public, available only for special screenings and closed seminars. This figure is misleading insofar as some titles stay on the list only because rightholders, for whatever reasons, have not petitioned for the release of films.

24. See André Gerely's survey, "Rechter Geschmack am NS-Film," *Medium* 13:10 (October 1983): 35–37.

25. Don DeLillo, *Americana* (1971; reprint, New York: Penguin, 1989), 299.

26. See, for instance, Walter Berten, "Musik durch Film, Funk und Schallplatte," *Der Deutsche Film* 1:7 (January 1937): "Without question the majority of the populace finds its desire for entertainment and its hunger for music to a great degree satisfied by radio, films and records." The possibilities of mass reproduction, though, would not be fully realised until the popular media succeeded in "freeing people from time and space so as to free up more time for spiritual and intellectual life" (200).

27. See the discussion about modern media advertising in *Americana*, 270–71.

Noël Burch
Geneviève Sellier

The "Funny War" of the
Sexes in French Cinema

The decision to explore the French classical cinema from a gender-informed viewpoint is not, in our view, "one approach" to its history (others being "strictly" sociological or "purely" political, for example). We believe that a cinema (all cinema?) that takes for its permanent and central material, romance and male-female relations, can only be studied in its textual density from a gender-conscious viewpoint. It was Ginette Vincendeau who provided the point of departure for our work. Aside from her remarkable analyses of the "myth" of Jean Gabin (1985, 1993), her principal contribution to our understanding of French cinema of the 1930s is to have noted the recurrence of the image of an "incestuous couple" in the films of that period (1989). Our own examination shows that indeed, the most typical scenario of that time does, in fact, place an older man in a more or less explicitly romantic relationship with a very young woman.

As Vincendeau suggests, this structure was no doubt overdetermined by a web of historical elements, not the least of which was the relatively advanced age of the major male stars of the day—who stepped quite naturally into talkies from music-hall or the legitimate stage, where it was quite acceptable for older men to play "young" leads. This structure seems all the more "natural" as bourgeois norms favored marriages of this type, particularly after the carnage of 1914–1918 (MacMillan, 1981). But it also signifies, more powerfully than any other relationship, the prerogatives of the father,

Translated from the Introduction and Chapter One of *La Drôle de Guerre des sexes du cinéma français* by Noël Burch and Geneviève Sellier. Copyright © Editions Nathan, 1996.

his power over women being confused with his power over his children; he was assumed to keep them, as did French family and marriage laws, in the same state of submission.

But Vincendeau's suggestion that this narrative figure can best be defined as oedipal seems misleading; we will adopt the other formulation she proposes: incestuous. In point of fact, except for those few films associated with "realism" ("poetic" or not), where Jean Gabin would confront a "bad father," in the vast majority of prewar films, the fantasizing subject is never "Oedipus" (much less the early Freud's "Electra") but a Father-bearer-of-the-Law seeking to displace the "son" in order to take possession of the "daughter." The term "incest" also permits us to relate this screen thematics to a whole psychosocial paradigm in real life, which goes well beyond arranged marriages between an older man and a young woman—since the sexual abuse of girls by men having power over them is not merely a daydream, as Nancy Huston (1979) and Marie-Victoire Louis (1994) remind us.

[. . .]

In order to refine Vincendeau's observations, we have documented the existence of about three hundred films (out of the roughly one thousand films of French initiative produced in France between 1929 and 1939) where this "incestuous" father/daughter relationship may be found.[1] This is an astonishing number, which confers on French cinema of the 1930s a homogeneity comparable to that of the popular cinemas of Japan, Hong Kong, or of India, with their unceasingly recurrent narratives, and which distances it from the American cinema, where similarities are organized according to genre. But we have also observed that in the examples cited by Vincendeau (1989) she fails to distinguish between the three markedly different versions of this cinema's incestuous fantasy, which we have dubbed the "confident father," the "self-sacrificing father," and the "bad father."[2]

We encounter the "confident father" in roughly half of these films. Here, the power of the father is strengthened, sometimes in an explicitly sexual manner (*Vous n'Avez Rien à Déclarer?*), but most often implicitly (*Justin de Marseille, Abus de Confiance;* see below), where the denial of incest allows for no consummation, not even by displacement (as is the case in *Vous n'avez rien à déclarer?*). This type of father, literal or symbolic, is typically portrayed, in the period, by Raimu, but may also be played by Charles Vanel (*Carrefour*), Jules Berry (*Arlette et Ses Papas*), Pierre Blanchar (*La Nuit de Décembre*), etc. The rest of these incestous fathers are divided between the figure of a self-sacrificing father, primarily associated with Harry Baur but also often with Eric von Stroheim, and on the other hand a bad father, not so much "unfit to be a father" as viciously evil. Unlike the first two, this third father figure is not at the center of the film, but serves as antagonist to a younger male. Associated with the tiny handful of left-sympathizers in the French cinema of the period, the most memorable incarnations of this role are given by Jules Berry (*Le Crime de Monsieur Lange, Le Jour se Lève*) and Michel Simon (*Quai des Brumes*).

The Confident Father, easily dominant during the first half of the decade (period of the triumph of filmed vaudeville), begins a statistical decline in 1936; the motif of the Self-sacrificing Father grows more frequent after this date, though it was already in evidence at the beginning of the talkies. The Bad Father was essentially a post-Popular Front phenomenon, associated with the development (less significant than is often imagined) of "poetic realism." However, this periodization is only one indication among many that this thematics of incest is not the simple, overall reflection of an eternal patriarchy. Rather did it function as a ritual, at once reaction and exorcism, specifically originating in the film community. This was a small enough group of men, but one whose sensibility was over-determined by the social imaginary of their class and gender—and who may be said to have been working overtime to ward off the veiled dangers haunting patriarchal power, capitalist order, and national identity.[3]

For, notwithstanding its apparent solidity, patriarchal legitimacy receives, all through the 1930s in France, staggering blows that no man could fail to register: in 1935, the legislature revoked the paternal right to corporal punishment; 1938 would see the end of the husband's absolute marital rights. Three times the Chamber of Deputies would pass a law giving women the right to vote (the last time in 1936), always knowing that the traditionally conservative Senate would use its veto. For, in fact, the tyranny of the Napoleonic Code continued to weigh on women, and anxiety about the birth rate would lead, near the end of the decade, to the *Code de la famille*, which would imprison women even further in their maternal role. Meanwhile, however, strikes of an unprecedented magnitude followed the 1936 electoral victory of the Popular Front, traumatizing patriarchy's "societal shadow," the capitalist bosses. And these strikes follow upon the street-fighting of 1934, which appeared at the time as the definitive defeat of the Cagoule, the Mauraussians, and other right-wingers filled with "nostalgia for the Father."

We also know the anguish that was felt in certain strata of the middle and lower bourgeoisie, confronted with a "foreign invasion"—immigrant workers from Italy and Poland, refugees from Spain, Jews fleeing central Europe (Schor, 1985: 168–70)—thought to undermine that idea of national identity which the German language links, more clearly than the French, with the Law of the Father (*Vaterland*).[4]

The Father of the Nation and His "Ward"

The American scholar Lynn Kirby has made a pioneering study of the converging representations of xenophobia and of the "national identity crisis" in some important films of the period, notably Maurice Tourneur's *Justin de Marseille* (1934), Jacques Feyder's *La Kermesse Héroïque* (1935), and Marc Allegret's *Gribouille* (1937). Her analysis of Tourneur's film, in particular, gives a path-breaking view of the articulation between xenophobia and the reaffirmation of the power of the Father—in this case, a very confident father indeed.

Justin (Berval), a Marseilles gang chief who hates violence (this idealized figure was thought up by scenarist Carlo Rim with the explicit permission of the local underworld!), is the benevolant patriarch par excellence: he rules with cool humor and a kind hand over his sympathetic band of crooks, but also over a pseudo-family composed of two children and a grandmother, as well as a "street family" representing the People and composed of comely young women who open oysters on the Vieux Port. His struggle against the Other, which is the main substance of the film, begins, paradoxically, when he does a favor for a "good" stranger, a "decent" Chinese drug merchant. This is, of course, the old French stereotype of "peaceful Chinese who keep to themselves" (Schor, 1985); seen only in their place of business, via telephone, these Chinese are not part of Marseilles. Berval rights a wrong by pulling a fast one on a rival gang who has robbed the Chinese. This other gang is a much less honorable bunch, made up of Italians and led by "a man who dresses like an Englishman." Berval will finally kill their chief (very discreetly, off camera), thus ridding the city of a foreign element who doesn't "play the game" and who, besides, has killed his best friend, the sweet idiot of the band The Stutterer (Pierre Larquey).

And it is almost by chance, honorably and effortlessly, that Berval "inherits," at the end of the film, the innocent creature who was cynically seduced at the beginning by an aspiring pimp with the goal of having her "tour the world in a pink nightgown." This innocent young thing is fortunate indeed: in a key scene at the beginning of the film, the pimp, in a hurry to have his way with her, coaxes his victim into a seedy hotel, ignoring her sentimental effusions about the stars in the sky. By contrast, in the last scene Berval, having saved the young woman from suicide and taken her under his wing, turns his back on this same hotel and goes off with her, arm in arm, rhapsodizing about the stars and the beauties of Marseilles. Lynn Kirby demonstrates that Marseilles, here, stands in for France, and that this kind patriarch, who respects women's honor (but keeps them on tap), embodies the defender of the Nation who is faced with an alliance between an evocative suggestion of *"le perfide Albion"* (as the Anglophobia of the period would have it) and a brutal and vulgar Italian, suggestive of Mussolini's Fascism (Carlo Rim's anarchist populism is that of a left-wing intellectual).

In a totally different political register, Charles Vanel's composition in *Abus de Confiance* offers another face of the Confident Father. Actually, this father is not so confident as all that, for he hides a guilty secret. The film has a secret too, a covert nostalgia for the Old Regime, resurfacing in 1936. Henri Decoin's film is one of the rare works from this period to take as its main character a woman (the role goes to Danielle Darrieux, first young woman to reach star status in the French cinema), and to acknowledge the obstacles to women's emancipation, which was also very rare.

Throughout the first part of the film, where visual style is close to that of the new "poetic realism," Darrieux, a law student and an orphan, is exposed, with didactic rigor, to various forms of male agression: a pimp lurking around the cememtery where she has just buried her last relative; a hotel manager who wants to collect "in kind" payment for the rent he is owed; a prospective employer who prefers pretty Danielle for "evening work at his place" to the super-competent, multilingual but obese secretary who has applied for the same job; and a well-mannered student who tries to take advantage of her situation by getting her drunk and bustling her into a hotel. With the exception of the student, a socially unformed pre-adult, all these exploiters of poor women (including the restaurant owner who cuts off her credit) belong to what one could label, roughly, the petty bourgeoisie. The rare people who show her some disinterested solidarity during this first part of the film are, on the contrary, more working class: a waiter, a woman who prepares shellfish, and above all her best friend, who suggests the "abuse of confidence" that gives the film its title.

The plan is for her to call on a rich and famous historian bearing documents (found by chance by her friend) which would lead the man to believe that she is his illegitimate daughter, born of a youthful affair with a woman he abandoned and who now is dead. The historian (Charles Vanel) enjoys a tranquil happiness, surrounded by his books and the discrete attentions of his wife (Valentine Tessier) in their comfortable home in Verseilles (where the lighting and camera styles become those of boulevard melodrama). Not unexpectedly, his field of study is prerevolutionary France. And needless to say, this generous patriarch welcomes into his house the guilty "fruit of his loins" with a quiver of emotion whose equivocal nature is underlined by his wife's jealousy. She suspects a liaison, "wrongly" on the surface of the text, but for the spectator this sexual potential is emphasized by our knowlege that Darrieux is not, in fact, the historian's daughter. The couple will end up adopting the orphan, even after they learn the truth. They will witness her début as a trial lawyer and place her in the hands of a worthy husband, who is nothing less than the father-figure's double: his young assistant and professional disciple. Here, the choice of an actor of somewhat vapid charm (Pierre Mingand) renders the subtext singularly clear, already obvious in the film's posters and credit sequence: the true couple is the "incestuous" one, and this arranged marriage is a red herring designed to distract attention from the incest taboo.

In 1936, the social meaning of this fable is clear: a certain emancipation of young middle class women was seen as inevitable, but in order to maintain patriarchal control it was necessary not only to reassert the authority of fathers, but to return to the mythic era of a benevolent monarchy, to a society ruled by an elite of clear thinking intellectuals (the objective allies of "honest workers") who are both above sordid questions of money (associated with the petty bourgeoisie) and who know how to respect the honor of women. Without necessarily assuming that Decoin or his scriptwriter (Pierre Wolf) were readers of *Action Française,* all this certainly smacks of Maurras.

This character of the pure, enterprising young woman deserves further attention, if only because it was she who was most often the object of the attention of these pot-bellied fathers. This role of the energetic, modern young woman was portrayed by a large number of actresses with short-lived careers (from Madeleine Ozeray and Josette Day to Jacqueline Delubac and Jacqueline Laurent), but above all, after 1935 (*Quelle drôle de gosse,* Léo Joannon) by Danielle Darrieux.[5] With Viviane Romance, Edwige Feuillère, and Michèle Morgan, she is one of the four female stars to emerge in this prewar French cinema where leading roles for women are so rare (hardly more than 5 percent of productions were built on female stars). In the patriarchal imaginary, what was at stake through this figure of the "modern young woman," was what was sensed to be the increasingly necessary control over the "new woman" who, because she worked outside the home, might escape from her men.

Martyrs of the Sex-War

In 1931, Julien Duvivier directed an adaptation of the best-selling novel *David Golder* by Irène Némirovsky. This film, one of the first noteworthy representations in the sound cinema of the Self-sacrificing Father, has for us the heuristic advantage of linking a justification of laissez-faire capitalism with a certain "cultural" anti-Semitism, and of associating the fantasy (barely disavowed) of father-daughter incest with an all-pervasive misogyny. The core of the work accomplished by this film is in the chain of displacements which allows it to obscure these successive postulations by a kind of mutual naturalization.

David Golder (Harry Baur) is an important Jewish financier, one of those so frequently caricatured in the satirical newspapers, conveyers for more than half a century of an anti-Semitism that was both petty bourgeois and anti-capitalist. But in the film as in the novel, this particular Jew is a good Jew, an assimilated Jew—and in fact, the actor Harry Baur was not Jewish (Le Boterf 1995: 12–13). He is just an "ordinary financier" (first displacement), a self-made man who raised himself by his bootstraps out of the Odessa ghetto. But above all he is an "ordinary husband" (second displacement), ruining his health to make more and more money, in order to support his idle, spendthrift wife and daughter, who live in a luxurious villa on the Riviera surrounded by effeminate hangers-on.

In order that from the outset the Jew in Golder/Baur be hidden behind the implacable financier (in the first sequence, he drives a competitor to ruin and suicide), there must be at his side another "profiteer" whose Jewishness is highly visible, in terms of the conventions of the period. By splitting the object of traditional French anti-Semitism into a good object (assimilated Jew/cultivator of capital) and a bad one ("wop"/unproductive money hoarder), the film accomplishes in two sequences the ideological displacement that over the course of a century had gradually detached anti-Semitism from its anti-capitalist roots (Léon, 1946). In Némirovsky's novel, the character of Soifer (the "bad Jew") appears in only one brief paragraph near the end. In Duvivier's film, on the other hand, he is foregrounded in two long sequences. Sole friend and confidant of the great speculator, he is the caricature of the ghetto Jew, the target of scornful glances from his friend's manservant; he is worth millions (in diamonds, because he distrusts banks), but he walks on his toes, in order not to wear down the heels of his shoes. This is certainly one of the most anti-Semitic images of the cinema of this period—which was rife with them (Garçon, 1984).

The second operation of the film consists in covering over this anti-Semitism with banal masculine solidarity directed against the universally predatory tribe of Women. In this battle, modern and audacious finance can extend a hand to the most archaic Jewry: in his account of the funeral of his unfortunate competitor, Golder tells the bachelor Soifer of the disgust he felt at the cupidity of the ugly widow. This way of making of Baur first of all a victim of women has the effect of banalizing, of naturalizing the film's defense of speculation (presented as an exciting and productive game) and the anti-Semitic opposition between good and bad Jew. In the end, Golder/Baur is thus only an ordinary man, exploited "like all the others" by a shrewish spouse (who makes only bad, sumptuary uses of money). How could he not transfer his desire (sublimated, of course) to a young woman every bit as profligate as her mother but splendidly beautiful, and who responds just enough to his incestuous caresses? In effect, the more the daughter's affection is shown to be superficial, self-interested, the more the father's desire comes to seem natural and touching.

The climax of the film is the nerve-racking confrontation between Baur, struck down by a first heart attack, and his castrating wife Gloria (Paule Andral), who reveals to him at his bedside that he is not the father of his adored Joyce (Jacky Monnier)—which has the effect of spicing up the subtext, since the incest tabou is henceforth nullified. However, in order to save his "daughter" from the poverty to which she would be subjected by the inactivity necessary to prolong his life, Golder goes back to work. He returns to his roots, to the land of the Soviets (!), in order to browbeat his negotiating partners into a 99-year concession for the exploitation of rich oil fields. He then proceeds to die of exhaustion on the boat bringing him back to France, while on the crowded deck fresh immigrants sing sad folksongs. He has become just another immigrant, sacrificed on the altar of devouring female idleness.

The selective anti-Semitism of this film finds its origins in the internal contradictions of the Jewish community of the period, which comprised both Jews assimilated for generations and those recently arrived from central and eastern Europe; the defense of capitalist speculation comes from the private biography of the daughter of well-to-do bourgeois parents forced into exile by the October revolution (and who could identify with the cultivated Jews of France). But this anti-Semitism was also that of a goodly portion of the French press of the day, while from a ruling-class viewpoint, the defense of speculation could be aimed at counteracting doubts about the system that had emerged after the stock market crash of 1929. As for the film's extreme misogyny, while it certainly comes from the individuals Duvivier and Némirovsky (the latter seems to have had problems with her mother), is also that of a whole era; it is born of the threat represented for many men (and many women) by figures of modern womanhood such as the heroine of Victor Margarrit's bestselling novel *La Garçonne.*

The two faces of misogyny revealed by this film deserve closer attention, because this is a model that will hang on tenaciously in French cinema, informing many postwar works, from Yves Allégret and Jacques Sigurd's *Manèges,* to Chabrol's *A Double Tour:* that of a beautiful daughter flanked by a mother who has passed the age of being attractive (her lover is only after her money) and whose avarice and pettiness are so extreme as to appear as pure sadism—or as a retaliation for sexual neglect. This is the figure of the Bad "mother," in quotation marks because the same figure can be wife, mother-in-law, aunt, or whatever; it enough for her to be outside the circuit of desire, and to persecute the hero.

In Duvivier's film, on the other hand, Jacky Monnier's cruelty is unconscious: David Golder's "daughter" is as candid as her mother is devious. The innocence-of-a-spoiled-child is no doubt the underlying meaning of the bucolic vacation sequence in the Basque country, when the young woman lounges with her smug lover while back home her parents are at one another's throats. The English-sounding names of these two women (again, perfidious Albion!), and their parallel predations, demonstrate clearly that Gloria is merely Joyce's future, and that it is his physical intimacy with this young enemy-in-spite-of-herself which in the end is fatal to the Father, incapable of resisting her charms simply because he is a man. This is a logic of the same order as that which in France is often used to justify prostitution as a means of preventing rape—given that masculine sexuality is "irrepressible" (Corbin, 1978).

One of the clearest formulations of this double-edged misogyny—"ugly or beautiful, they're all bitches"—is a greatly admired film by Jean Renoir, *La Chienne* (1931). The prestige of its maker is such that no analyst of this film seems to attach much significance to the hatred that it pours out onto women—on Michel Simon's wife (Madeleine Bérubet), who sadistically prevents her timid husband from indulging in his inoffensive hobby of painting, and on the stupid and cruel prostitute (Janie Marèze) whom the unassuming bookkeeper has the misfortune to fall in love with. Critics who recognize this as a defect at all tend to regard it as a temporary feature of Renoir's work, to be explained away by his problems with his actress-wife Catherine Hessling, from whom he had just separated.[6] In fact, this misogyny will later return in nearly all the films Renoir made in France, from *French Cancan* (1954) to *Le Déjeuner Sur l'Herbe* (1958). And on the other hand, one need only compare *La Chienne* with films like *David Golder, La Belle Equipe, Mollenard, L'Homme de Nulle Part,* and many, many others, to understand that, at the time, these were stock figures of the French cinema.

The figure of Michel Simon does have one original characteristic: he is a "father" who is more persecuted than sacrificing, and he attains, through regressive male bonding, a sort of tragicomic tranquility as a Boudu-like vagrant fleeing all women, side by side with his wife's first husband. This ironic ending, along with the power of Renoir's direction, does somewhat offset the film's aggressive misogyny, expecially in its assumption that Women's relation to artistic creation can only be negative (the wife keeps the artist from painting; the prostitute who pretends to be an artist is punished by death).

Berry, or the Father Burned in Effigy

It would, without doubt, be overly auteurist to credit Jean Renoir and Jacques Prévert with the "invention" of the figure of the bad Father in that celebrated utopian film of 1936, *Le Crime de Mon-*

sieur Lange, meant to herald the end of capitalist exploitation and the dawn of a new era. Batala (Jules Berry), the debauched, petty bourgeois boss who exploits women who are in his power even more than he exploits his workers, is a figure with an extensive tradition in the imaginary of the French workers' movement—with which the film's authors and the October Group (who were among its actors) had become intimately associated. Analyzing the discourse on women in the working-class press at the end of the nineteenth century, and notably the oppression of the working woman by the "fat bourgeois," Christine Dufrancatel (1979) establishes that:

> Women's destiny is not thought of as a separate problem. Women would be, first of all, symbolic of moral and social questions. . . . The degradation of the woman of the people when she was obliged to work, the inhuman conditions for motherhood, the reduction to the status of a sexual object, these represented a degradation of the entire class, striking at men through the women. . . . The body of the man depended on the body of the woman. And the body is one of the stakes of class struggle (167).

Possessing very young women on the couch in his office with no concern for the consequences, using their charms to manipulate his adversaries, the contemptable Berry is an abusive father by virtue of his class position. The first decisive victory against him—after his flight from his creditors and from justice, and before his return dressed as a priest and his death at the hands of René Lefèvre—comes when one of his female victims has a stillborn child, and the event is received by the neighbors with a great burst of laughter.[7] An optimistic film par excellence, *Le Crime de Monsieur Lange* valorizes women's work, gives us a gentle man as its hero (Lefèvre, a sort of anti-Gabin), and exiles violent masculinity to a cartoonish America (this is the other meaning of Arizona Jim, the righter of wrongs in Lange's serial novels).

It is generally recognized that the three utopian films which were Jean Renoir's "gifts" to the Popular Front are unique for their day.[8] But in the films of poetic realism, conventionally considered the other, pessimistic side of 1930s left-wing cinema, the Bad Father is a stock character. We find him played by Michel Simon, for example, as the libidinous shopkeeper of *Quai des Brumes,* who threatens the virtue of the unhappy young woman who is his ward, and whom the deserter from the foreign legion must kill in order to liberate her. In fact, it is too often forgotten that this ending, very pessimistic from the masculine point of view, is much less so from a woman's point of view, since while Morgan loses the man she loves, she also loses her oppressor and stays alive. Here, perhaps, is a meaning which escaped the authors of this Manichaean and manipulative film, which parallels Morgan's final liberty with that of a stray dog, going back on the road after the death of his master-for-a-day (a curious echo of the cat in *La Femme du Boulanger,* released the same year). But in any case, this freedom is in the film—and in the libertarian hatred of patriarchy which permeates it throughout. It is accessible through a reading of the text "against the grain," always capable of bringing to light the contradictions of a film, of a social environment, of a period. And, indeed, with the coming of the Bad Father, previously stable categories of the feminine become blurred.

The most famous of the period's bad Fathers is the role played by Jules Berry in the masterpiece of poetic realism, *Le Jour se Lève,* a film which constantly flirts with the incest fantasy and with oedipal rivalry, the two wellsprings of this "genre." But the Bad Father is not confined to poetic realism. Thomas Elsaesser (1984: 278–83), in a suggestive study of the films of emigré German directors in France during the thirties, notes that these are characteristically hybrid; they mix genres, styles, and motifs from Berlin, Hollywood, or Paris. Directed in 1936 by the most prolific of these emigrés, Robert Siodmak, *Le Chemin de Rio* combines French paternal melodrama with German-American crime comedy, through two loosely linked plot lines: the efforts of a franco-german duo of stereotypically buoyant investigative reporters (Kate de Nagy and Jean-Pierre Aumont) to break up a white slavery ring; and on the other hand an astounding duel to the death between two fathers, one belonging to the confident category, however shady his dealings (Charles Grandval) and the other immediately perceived as bad (since the role is played by Jules Berry).[9] Here, significantly, it is the private sphere's impingement on the world of "work" that will cause the two men's downfall.[10]

Le Chemin de Rio begins with the suicide, in an elegant Latin American brothel, of an innocent young Frenchwoman (Sylvia Bataille). In Paris Jules Berry, who makes a business of the white slave trade, learns that a girl whom he had set his cap at was shipped to Rio, against her will and without his knowlege, by his partner (Grandval). Mad with rage and grief, he seeks vengeance; just when he is about to have his partner killed by a hired assassin (Dalio), he learns that Grandval is the father of a ravishing young woman whom he adores and who knows nothing of his ignoble activities. We now witness a family dinner on the terrace of a luxurious villa in an exclusive neighborhood, through the eyes of Berry and Dalio lurking in the shadows of the garden, like spectators at a play—a mise-en-scène which seems to underscore the hypocritical theatrics of the bourgeois family. The scene inspires Berry with a new vengeance, one which he imagines will be worse than death: he will seduce the young woman (a project the very implausibility of which attests to the cinematic power of the father) and have her sent to Rio with a shipment of gullible "dancers" in search of financial independence and freedom from parental authority. Berry waits until the ship has sailed before announcing the "good news" to the father in his office . . . who stabs him to death by treachery.

In the guise of a sardonic, many-layered caricature, this film seems systematically to review the major motif of the French cinema of the period and to announce, in its own way, the twilight of the fathers.

Gabin, Son of Nobody

In *Quai des Brumes* and *Le Jour se Lève,* these landmark works of poetic realism, an intercessor named Jean Gabin will step in between the bad Father and his putative "daughter." Ginette Vincendeau (1993) has brilliantly described the constitution of the Gabin myth beginning with Duvivier's *La Bandera,* the myth of a masculinity at once ideal and fated to die, an object of identification for men who doubt (and who project these doubts onto "the people"), an object of desire for women. She demonstrates, notably, by subtle analyses of

Pépé le Moko and *La Belle Equipe* how Gabin's masculinity is made an object of spectacle ("hommages" to music-hall), and is constituted as a sort of "zero degree" of acceptable masculinity in the midst of "excessive" masculinities (the womanizer, the violent one, the greedy one, etc.). However, Gabin's masculinity is also constructed with reference to by-and-large negative feminine figures: the Bitch—who may be poor (Line Noro in *Pépé le Moko*, Viviane Romance in *La Belle Equipe*) or rich (Mireille Balin in *Pépé le Moko* and *Gueule d'Amour*)—or more complex figures such as the Tragic Woman with a Mysterious Past (Michèle Morgan in *Quai des Brumes* and *Remorques*) or the Deceptively Innocent Girl (Jacqueline Laurent in *Le Jour se Lève*). [. . .]

The theme of the woman who with money and power, whose body can only be satisfied by a man of the people, will fuel the Gabin myth in two important films by Duvivier and Grémillon, filmmakers who are ideologically poles apart. Duvivier's *Pépé le Moko* develops the populist theme of the tragic hero whose situation as a Parisian gangster in the Casbah easily functions as the equivalent of the solitude of the newly arrived colonial worker; fleeing, not the police but the Depression, he is disturbed by an Arab society with strong sexual segregation, where male homosexuality is not hidden—suggested in the film by the strange figure of Inspector Slimane (Lucas Gridoux), fascinated by his handsome prey. The nostalgia for Paris embodied, for this plebian male, by a woman from the *beaux quartiers,* is a variant on the anxiety over national identity already noted. The film clearly associates all the themes of Difference which characterize the period. A right-wing anarchist like Duvivier, though his films were often steeped in misogyny, perceives the financial dependency of Mireille Balin (the object of Gabin's ill-fated love) more as a kind of societal fatality, rather than as proof of women's duplicity. It requires all the authority of the colonial police to bring the unhappy woman back under the control of her rich and portly protector (Charles Grandval).

At the hands of Grémillon, known today for his subsequent feminist films, Mireille Balin fares far less well. Initially, *Gueule d'Amour* is both a reflection on the Gabin myth and an excercise in sexual role reversal: the Don Juan of a regiment of colonial cavalry, the focus of every female gaze, finds that having left the service and without his spectacular uniform, that he is no longer the center of attention—and that Mireille Balin, kept mistress of a rich bourgeois, is not prepared to give up a life of luxury for the love of a typesetter. For a while, this character is treated like her equivalent in *Pépé le Moko,* as the prisoner of society's logic (even if her venal mother is the acme of boulevard theater cynicism). But when Gabin admits defeat and vanishes from the capital to open a shabby bistro in Orange, Balin becomes (a bit artificially) one of the most extreme Bitches of the period: she seeks out Gabin, taunts him with a sadistic scorn beyond belief—brutally breaking off, in front of him, with his best friend (René Lefèvre), who has fallen prey to her charms—until the hero finally kills her.

In André Beucler's novel, written ten years earlier, class differences are absent: Madeleine is an absolutely enigmatic creature who "devours" men out of "animal" needs. Grémillon and Spaak grafted onto this story a social criticism specific to their milieu and their decade. *Gueule d'Amour* embodies, in exemplary fashion, the contradiction within the left at this time between its discourse on class and its discourse on gender.[11] For Geneviève Sellier (1989: 26ff.), Grémillon and Spaak's conscious discourse here is one of class criticism: Gabin's fatal error is not being wary of the cynical and hypocritical mores of the upper classes and, "incidentally," the women—and especially the courtesans—associated with them. But in this film, as so often in the period, these "mores" are indistinguishable from the devouring power of feminine sexuality. In the same way that Jews, in these years before the Holocaust, are the banal emblem of the evil power of money (Grémillon and Spaak had no scruples in killing off an unpleasant caricature of a Jewish usurer in *La Petite Lise*)—similarly, these rich women, with their frustration, their nymphomania, their frigidity, are the symbol of the noxious decadence of their class. And this iconography is not the exclusive property of the Left. We could cite, again in Duvivier's work, the idle mistress basking in luxury provided by the vile schemer who has paid a sinister Oriental to murder his rich aunt (*La Tête d'un Homme,* 1932).

These are not "innocent" metaphors for political conflicts, as traditional male historiography would understand them. In *Gueule d'Amour*, Grémillon and Spaak, as left-leaning intellectuals, perceive clearly society's division into classes and the injustice which flows from it; but as men, they experience the inexpressible menace of "woman" as the "natural" vector of social contradiction. [. . .]

Edwige Feuillère, or the Taming of the Shrew

To complete this tableau of the family romance of French cinema of the 1930s (which has no pretentions to comprehensiveness) there is, finally, the Strong Woman, or rather, the "shrew-to-be-tamed," a figure principally embodied by Edwige Feuillère. A limit case but all the more revealing thereby, she demonstrates the lengths to which the patriarchal imagination could go in blocking a strong woman's access to power. Scarcely affected by the upheavals of defeat or liberation, from 1936 (*Lucrèce Borgia*) to 1948 (*L'Aigle à Deux Têtes*), whether as "gentlewoman" thief (*J'Etais une Aventurière, L'Honorable Catherine*), legendary spy (*Marthe Richard au Service de la France*), or temptress taking revenge on men "in the name of every woman" (*La Duchesse de Langeais*), Feuillere remains the same beautiful, haughty, inaccessible, and (above all) dangerously efficient woman. Which is why she must always be defeated in exemplary fashion.

Emblematic of this ever-repeated humiliation is the climactic sequence of *Marthe Richard* (Raymond Bernard, 1937), when Feuillère announces to her lover, a German intelligence officer (Eric von Stroheim), that she has succeeded in her mission by sinking the fleet of submarines under his protection. Without batting an eye, Stroheim stops playing the piano, takes a syringe, and injects himself with a mortal poison, while Feuillère, victorious in the male sphere of warfare, is vanquished in the woman's sphere of feelings—which we assume to be of more importance to her. Confounded by this supreme gesture of virility, she ends "her" story as a helpless onlooker, powerless to prevent her enemy-lover's tragic death. [. . .]

Under the Occupation, with the Catholic Right in power for the first time in over a century, this figure of the strong woman was to deviate unexpectedly, in a direction that one could qualify as more secular, more feminist: even when she "loses" (for she will to continue to be defeated at the end of all her films) she will score many points, so to speak, and there will no longer be the feeling that the "match" was fixed.

[. . .]

It is a commonplace in gender studies to note that men, on the whole, have shown fear and mistrust toward women at all times and in all places (Dinnerstein, 1978). From this perspective, under a French patriarchy which, during the 1930s, was particularly ponderous and behind the times, images of the sexual submission of a woman-child almost went without saying. Just as "naturally," from the Left, one finds a few images of revolt against the father. At our present stage of research, we must ask where, in social terms, the fear of women to which these films testify actually "comes from." From French men (as a facile generalization among feminist writers of previous decades would have it)? From the French petty bourgeoisie? From French intellectuals? From the community of male filmmakers and allied theatrical circles? For the moment, this last hypothesis seems the only one of which we are sure.

Alternatively, are we perhaps "simply" dealing with a displacement of more directly "political" fears into a gender register, merely in order to obscure them: fear of the war, fear of the loss of national identity, fear of the Other? This is the thesis privileged by French cinema historians whenever they observe a thematic consistency in the filmic representation of the relations between generations or between sexes during the period under study here (Bertin-Maghit, 1989; Garçon, 1984; de La Bretèque, 1977). Be that as it may, it is reasonable to assume that these representations also spring from a fear of women in flesh and blood, exacerbated by the modest social advances of women and the very reasonable demands of existing feminist organizations (Bard, 1995).

These questions become more pressing when one considers the surprising revelations which emerge from our examination of four-fifths of French film production between 1940 and 1944, the time of the German Occupation and the Vichy regime. In fact, from the very beginning of this period, and as long as it lasted, we see a veritable overthrow of the Law of the Father, in favor of a fantasmatic "law of the mother." This reversal, which virtually all of the films of the period testify to, can almost certainly be attributed to the trauma of defeat and to the discrediting of a Patriarchy associated with the Third Republic and the General Staff of a routed army. This hypothesis tends to confirm the concept of a male social imaginary (Laborie, 1992), even more than does the prewar figure of the incestuous father. The fear and hatred of women will disappear like magic (the change we observe takes place in a matter of months), to be replaced by either a frozen female effigy, placed on a pedestal (an attitude that typifies the traditional Right, in the manner of the edifying Catholic *Bonne Presse*), or else a dynamic, modern figure pointing to a future renaissance (this is a leftist figure, found, for example, in Aragon's *Aurélien*, 1944).

Indeed, this social male imaginary in crisis, which may be observed in the great majority of male filmmakers, still conforms to the traditional division Left/Right (unsurprisingly, for France).[12] But how to explain that so many films elicited (and still elicit today) different interpretations, and no longer offer such clear oppositions between the "bad fathers" of poetic realism and the "confident fathers" from boulevard theater or Pagnol's Provence? Pierre Laborie (1990) notes that the atmosphere of prewar France is one of political and ideological confusion; Yves Chalas (1985) proposes the hypothesis that the stunning defeat at the hands of the Germans, and the Occupation, aroused in all sectors of society the obscure yearning for "something else," which Chalas describes as "going beyond liberal capitalism"—from future resisters to up-front *collaborateurs*, from the Vichyists of the Right (Maurassians, traditionalist Catholics) to those of the Left (the *Paulfauriste* current of the Socialist party) and even among those "apoliticals" who wanted to "wait and see."

Let us dwell for a moment on this thesis—still scabrous, in France today—that progressive aspirations might have seen the light of day "under Vichy." The theme of regeneration through women that we find throughout the film production of the Occupation years parallels the famous Vichy theme of the "return to the land." Gérard Miller (1975) observes that this notion was first "launched" by the exodus of June 1940, when French people from the north, the east, and the Paris region fled the modern, urban, and industrial France—which had plagued them with its strikes since 1936, and which had proven incapable of shielding them from the invader—to an agricultural south which also provided an imaginary refuge in the past. Christian Faure (1989) has shown that, beyond Pétain's speeches, the Vichy desire to redeem rural life gave initial impetus to the ethnography of rural France (creation of the Musée des Arts et Traditions Populaires) as well as to a major school of documentary film production—whose crowning glory is Georges Rouquier's *Farrebique,* made after the war but in execution of an official Vichy program.

Today, when French farmers, the French countryside, the quality of French agricultural products are menaced by the more and more absurd logic of liberal capitalism, we can have a more dialectical view of this current: the aspirations embodied in Vichy France both by the official theme of the revalorization of rural life and by the concrete activities promoted under its sponsorship, may be seen as an anticipation of certain aspects of contemporary ecology. In this perspective, we can better understand that the ideological ambivalence that permeated civil society, at least during the first two years of the Vichy government, had its positive side.

And the same was true of other aspirations, materialized, for example, in the creation of schools for female managers, on the model of the famous Ecole d'Uriage, explicitly aimed at repairing the Third Republic's huge deficit with regard to the civil and social training of the female members of the national community.[13] These aspirations, for a more egalitarian sharing of social responsibilities between the sexes, but also for new relations within couples and for a new notion of fatherhood (Delumeau, 1990), massively inform the cinema of the Occupation.[14]

Almost alone among the writers of their day, Camus, Bové, Sartre, and Aragon will lay bare the crisis of male identity provoked by the

Defeat. However, in *L'Etranger,* as in *Le Piège* and *Les Chemins de la Liberté* (*Aurélien* constitutes an exception due to Elsa Triolet's influence, acknowleged by Aragon), masculine self-doubt is accompanied by an often violent misogyny—which is precisely what separates the intellectual elite's works from the positive vision of women in the great majority of films of the period.[15] This difference between literature and cinema is perhaps explained by the specificity of each of these artistic practices: the writer is alone, the inheritor of a French cultural tradition that valorizes a universal masculinity (Coquillat, 1982); a writer, though no doubt attentive to the murmurs of his period, disdains to write for it: he writes for eternity.

By contrast, the collective artist that makes a film (that is to say, the actual crew that makes that particular work and the larger community of cinema professionals) is more open to the world by the very fact of being a group, and the awareness of the ephemeral nature of a film (much stronger in the years before the advent of the New Wave than it is today) implied that its authors worked in the present, for the audiences of their day. Not to mention the explicitly commercial dimension of cinema, which has always made the collective author of popular films receptive (consciously or unconsciously) to the flavor of the times.

Such questions aside, this complementarity between the crisis of masculine identity and the regenerative vision of the feminine is nowhere manifested as massively as in the cinema. Certainly, a few plays (the theatre is another collective art) offered female effigies surrounded by men in crisis, following a model not unlike the most typical cinema of the period.[16] And Pierre Laborie (1993) has brought to light the use of Joan of Arc as a symbol of unity and national reconciliation in the Catholic press of the Southwest during the same period.

The massive nature of this phenomenon in the cinema, compared with its near-absence in popular literature, for example, leaves a number of questions unanswered, which touch on an area barely investigated up to the present, at least in France: the specificity of different (individual and collective) cultural practices, in a given society at a given time.[17] And as concerns the cinema alone, how do creators and technicians become the mediators of the social imaginary—to the extent that such a crisis of gender identity may be assimilable to this notion?

The crisis of masculine identity which regularly follows that supreme test of male values which is war (particularly when war leads to defeat) is beginning to be explored for other periods and other nations (Theweleit, 1977; Maugue, 1987; Silverman, 1993). For France in the 1940s, we can formulate the hypothesis that, because of the two national humiliations provoked by this war— defeat followed by occupation, then liberation by foreign armies— the crisis of masculine identity is divided into two stages: a breakdown, followed by a return of authority. Along two complementary trajectories, the active and autonomous woman of the Occupation is changed after the Liberation into a diabolical creature (*Panique*, 1946), while the gentle male of the war years evolves into a victim-figure (*Manèges*, 1949), like an echo of the self-image of the many prisoners of war, returning from captivity obsessed by the thought that women will no longer be willing to assume their submissive roles of the prewar period. However, the filmic representations of the postwar period are also strongly contradictory: alongside this mainstream misogyny, and at the very time of publication of *Le Deuxième Sexe* (1949, a best-seller during the 1950s), there emerge a considerable number of feminist films in the modern sense. Often remarkable works (*Casque d'Or*, 1952), these attempt to bring to light the mechanisms of patriarchal oppression, showing that it weighs also on men.

Thus the cinema bears witness—more than any other means of expression, it seems to us—to the destabilization of the relations between the sexes in French society of the 1940s, brought about by political and military events. We study here the repercussions of these in the private sphere, which has traditionally been considered as following another time scale: the *longue durée* of Fernand Braudel and the history of mentalities. (The sensitiveness of the cinema to the upheavals in gender relations due to the war and the Occupation prove, if this were necessary, to what extent the private sphere is political.)

Noël Burch and Geneviève Sellier

In another context, the bringing to light of a layer of meanings which seems thus far only observable in the fiction cinema, which is only a small subsection of cultural production, can also show the potential interest in approaching the history of cinema as an autonomous area, capable of teaching us much about the state of our societies—as soon as we cease to consider films as merely reflections of ideas elaborated elsewhere.

NOTES

Translated by Alan Williams and Noël Burch (with thanks to Dudley Andrew).

1. The pattern is confirmed by the analyses in *Générique des années trente* (Lagny et al., 177ff.), which are based on a systematic study of leading roles in the decade's films. We have excluded some three hundred films that are French versions of foreign productions (UFA, Paramount, etc.).

2. In spite of her taking into account the historical dimension of representations, Vincendeau (1989) concludes thus: "The question whether the figure of the father is in the end 'victorious' as in *La Femme du Boulanger*, or not, as in *Dernière Jeunesse*, matters little (this is . . . above all a matter of generic conventions). In structural terms, it is always he who is the subject of the quest." This conclusion, which contradicts certain developments in her article, shows clearly the point of convergence between structuralist reduction and a fatalistic vision of the social relations between the sexes, as is so often the case in the work of anglo-saxon feminists.

3. Henry Bataille's play *La Vierge Folle*, filmed in 1938 by Henri Diamant-Berger is, in the repertoire of boulevard theatre, one of the most explicit demonstrations of the fears, the misunderstandings, the jealousies, and the "socio-sexual" power relations that inspire these incestuous fantasies: Victor Francen as a debonnaire lawyer, tortured for years by a wife (Annie Ducaux) as ravishing as she is "frigid" (the "crazy virgin" of the title), turns to a young woman who is in love with him, but death takes him at the last moment thank to a stray bullet fired by her younger brother, who is jealous of the boss whom he once worshipped.

4. Formulated in the context of a close analysis of the writings of members of the *Freikorps*, the future backbone of the Nazi regime, the following definition has, however, a more general validity: "On can thus see in the concept of nation the most explicit foundation that can be given to the needs of male domination. 'Male chauvinism'—the term chosen by women's liberation movements for masculinity [originally, by the Communist Party of the United States!]—is perfectly appropriate" (Theweleit 1977–1978, 2, 87). As for the "mother country" of the French language, Michelle Perrot reminds us that if "republicans deliberate under Marianne's eye" and if "a delirious statue-mania puts women everywhere," nonetheless "this overinvestment in the imaginary, this frenetic celebration of 'the Muse and the Madonna' are only a way of confronting the duality of public space and private space" (Ariès/Duby 1987, IV, 121).

5. We will see that, in this this great family romance, all pairings are possible. Thus, the confident Father can encounter the Woman with the Tragic Past (Raimu and Michèle Morgan in *Gribouille*), while the self-sacrificing Father can find himself coming to grips with the Bitch (Michel Simon and Janie Marèse in *La Chienne*) or with the Modern Young Woman (Harry Baur and Jacqueline Laurent in *Sarati le Terrible*) or

with the Strong Woman (Eric von Stroheim and Edwige Feuillère in *Marthe Richard au Service de la France*).

6. It is surprising that a French feminist critic, Françoise Jeancolas-Audé, could devote an article to the film entitled "Réévaluation: *La Chienne*" (*Jeune Cinema* 91, December 1974, 22–25) which totally ignores this dimension of the work. (For an anglo-american reading, see E. Ann Kaplan, 1983.)

7. Laughter which François Garçon takes as the expression of the discomfort caused, in prewar French cinema (and society), by illegitimate births. However, the much more conformist *Club des Femmes* suggests the contrary, as does a more precise reading of *Le Crime de Monsieur Lange*. The attitude of tolerance, as we will note with Garçon, will become more general during the Occupation, even including a certain Vichyist Right. But during the 1930s, the libertarian Left could already see the social dimension of illegitimacy, and boulevard theatre found it charming because it defied convention. Perhaps there is a confusion in Garçon's work between the stigmatization of illegitimate births in bourgeois and petty bourgeois society, and the elimination in *Le Crime de Monsieur Lange* of the traces of a worker's rape by her boss. Let us remember that the status of illegitimate children did not pose a problem in working class circles—and *Le Crime de Monsieur Lange* is a film that explicitly finds its inspiration in working-class attitudes.

8. The others are *La Marseillaise* and *La Vie est à Nous*, both made in cooperation with the French Communist Party. To this marginal, utopian current, one can add René Clair's 1932 film, *A Nous la Liberté*.

9. The genre of German-American crime drama is the fruit of the penetration of American capital (Fox) into Weimar cinema during the period of the Dawes Plan (1923–1928). The best-known example, today, is Fritz Lang's *Spione* (1928).

10. "Our society establishes a somewhat anxious distinction between the public world of work and the private world of the family, the world of feelings and of sexuality, because it is felt that the instrumental goals of work (accomplish something, make money, act efficiently) would be undermined by too many emotional or sexual side-issues" (Richard Dyer, in Burch 1993).

11. Furthermore, this at a time when the parties of the Left sought the right of women to vote, and named women, who were ineligible because of their sex, as candidates in various elections, all the while remaining faint-hearted about the inequalities of the *Code civil*. Léon Blum published in 1907 the very feminist *Du Mariage*, but there remained few traces of it in the legislation of the Popular Front, whose deputies even voted in 1939 for the very patriarchal *Code de la famille*.

12. And what of the female social imaginary, absent from movie screens because women are absent from positions of power in the cinema, and more generally in cultural production in France? (See Marcelle Marini, "La place des femmes dans la production culturelle," in *Histoire des femmes*, vol. 5, 1991.)

13. For Mme. Elisabeth Guyon, directrice of the Ecole de Cadres Féminins at Ecully (1941–1942), it was a question of "helping woman to blossom, to understand the role she has to play in the family, in the city, in the country" (unpublished letter to her husband Bernard Guyon, prisoner in Germany, August 9, 1942).

14. See the thoughts on this subject of Catholic intellectuals (Gabriel Marcel) and of the associations for Catholic action, with the appearance in 1945 of the review *L'Anneau Nuptial* ("The Wedding Band").

15. Cf. the opening of *Aurélien*, "Voici le temps enfin qu'il faut que je m'explique. . ." (Paris: Gallimard "Folio," 1966).

16. For example, in *Les J3* by Roger Ferdinand, an ideal woman schoolteacher triumphs over a class of rebellious adolescents; in Marcel Achard's *Mademoiselle Panama* a young woman becomes the inspiration for some discouraged French

engineers; in *Echec à Don Juan* by Claude-André Puget, a beautiful aristocrat decides to avenge the victims of a vile seducer by seducing him and then, disguised as a jealous rival, killing him in a duel.

17. But in France, this period begins to see the beginnings of "american style" crime fiction (Léo Mallet, for example), alongside the older "good Catholic press"— where one finds the same idealized feminine effigies.

BIBLIOGRAPHY

Ariès, Philippe and Georges Duby (eds.). *Histoire de la vie Privée* (Paris: Seuil, 1987).

Bertin-Maghit, Jean-Pierre. *Le Cinéma sous l'Occupation* (Paris: Olivier Orban, 1989).

Bard, C. *Les Filles de Marianne: Feminismes en France* (Paris: Fayard, 1995).

Burch, Noël. *Revoir Hollywood* (Paris: Nathan, 1993).

Chalas, Yves. *Vichy et l'imaginaire totalitaire* (Arles: Actes-Sud, 1985).

Coquillat, Michèle. *La Poétique du mâle* (Paris: Gallimard, 1982).

Corbin, Alain. *Les Filles de Noce* (Paris: Aubier-Montaigne, 1978).

de La Bretèque, François. "Les Belles Histoires du Sam'di Soir: Les Stéréotypes Narratifs," *Cahiers de la Cinémathèque* 23–24 (1977).

Delumeau, Jean and Daniel Roche. *Histoire des pères et de la paternité* (Paris: Larousse, 1990).

Dinnerstein, Dorothy. *The Rocking of the Cradle and the Ruling of the World* (New York: Harper & Row, 1978).

Dufrancatel, Christine. "La Femme imaginaire des hommes." In Dufrancatel, Arlette Farge, and Christine Faure, *L'Histoire sans qualités* (Paris: Galilée, 1979).

Elsaesser, Thomas. "Pathos and Leave-taking," *Sight and Sound* 53:4 (Fall 1984).

Faure, Christian. *Le Projet culturel de Vichy* (Lyon: Presses Universitaires de Lyon, 1989).

Garçon, François. *De Blum à Pétain* (Paris: Le Cerf, 1984).

Huston, Nancy. *Jouer au papa et à l'amant: De l'amour des petites filles* (Paris: Ramsay, 1979).

Kaplan, E. Ann. "Ideology and Cinematic Practice in Lang's *Scarlet Street* and Renoir's *La Chienne*," *Wide Angle* 5:3 (1983): 32–43.

Laborie, Pierre. *L'Opinion publique sous Vichy* (Paris: Seuil, 1990)

———. Contribution in Jean-Pierre Azéma (ed.), *Vichy et les Français* (Paris: Fayard, 1992).

———. "Les symboles sexués dans le système de representation des Français 1940–1944." Unpublished lecture for the Institut de l'Histoire du Temps Présent (Paris), January 1993.

Lagny, Michèle, Marie-Claire Ropars, and Pierre Sorlin. *Générique des années 30* (Paris: Presses Universitaires de Vincennes, 1986).

Le Boterf, Hervé. *Harry Baur* (Paris: Pygmalion, 1995).

Léon, Abraham. *La Conception matérialiste de la question Juive* (1946); trans. as *The Jewish Question: A Marxist Interpretation* (New York: Pathfinder, 1970).

Louis, Marie-Victoire. *Le Droit de cuissage, 1860–1914* (Paris: L'Atelier, 1994).

MacMillan, James. *Housewife or Harlot: The Place of Women in French Society, 1870–1940* (Brighton: Harvester Press, 1981).

Maugue, Anne-Lise. *L'Identité masculine en crise, 1870–1914* (Paris: Rivages, 1987).

Miller, Gérard. *Les Pousse-au-jouir du maréchal Pétain* (Paris: Seuil, 1975).

Schor, Ralph. *L'Opinion française et les étrangers 1919–1939* (Paris: Publications de la Sorbonne, 1985).

Sellier, Geneviève. *Jean Grémillon: Le Cinéma est à vous* (Paris: Méridiens-Klinck-sieck, 1989).

Theweleit, Klaus. *Mannerphantasien* (Frankfurt: Roter Stern, 1977–1978). Published in English as *Male Fantasies* (Minneapolis: Polity Press, 1989).

Vincendeau, Ginette. "Community, Nostalgia, and the Spectacle of Masculinity," *Screen* 26:6 (1985).

———. "Daddy's Girls: Oedipal Narratives in 1930s French Films," *Iris* 5:1 (January 1989).

———. *Jean Gabin: Anatomie d'un mythe* (Paris: Nathan, 1993).

International Relations

Stephen Teo

The Legacy of T. E. Lawrence:
The Forward Policy
of Western Film Critics
in the Far East

Introduction

It is generally accepted that the Hong Kong cinema found its true
identity in the eighties with the rise of a new generation of filmmakers. This was the generation which became active in the late
seventies, forming the core of the Hong Kong New Wave which offi-
cially got off the ground in 1979. But before that there was already a
group of filmmakers—including Michael Hui, Leong Po-chih, and
older generation directors such as Chu Yuan and Liu Jialiang—who
were paving the way. They were doing things with style and technique and, more significantly, once more using Cantonese which
had become a near-defunct language in cinema although everyone
spoke it in the community. Then came New Wave—directors such
as Ann Hui, Allen Fong, Tsui Hark, Yim Ho, Alex Cheung—who consolidated the breakthrough in the use of Cantonese and introduced
a more sophisticated version of Hong Kong cinema. Unlike previous generations of filmmakers, this group owed their allegiance to
Hong Kong in a more comprehensive way, fully cognisant of the fact
that they were existing in a unique society built on a foundation of
laissez-faire capitalism, Western-style government (albeit a colonial
one) and a culture intermixed with Western and Eastern features.

From Retrospective Catalogue of the Fifteenth Hong Kong International Film Festival "Hong Kong Cinema in the Eighties." Reprinted with permission of the author and
the Hong Kong International Film Festival.

The New Wave directors were largely Western-trained; but as their work matures, and as Hong Kong faces the approach of 1997, their work has contributed to a feeling that Hong Kong possesses an identity different from that of other Chinese societies, particularly from the Mainland which is to recover control of the territory. This expression of a "local" identity—perhaps based mainly on the use of Cantonese and its associated patois of street slang and "Chinglish"—distinguishes Hong Kong cinema from the cinemas in the Mainland and Taiwan. The differences are not only in how Hong Kong movies sound but also in how they look. Today, a Hong Kong move is easily recognised. It is fast and furious; its images project a finesse that has a sparkling glint on the surface; there are a lot more special effects; and all the characters love, hate, and kill in such a way that only seeing is believing.

The theme of a "special identity" was incorporated into a kung fu movie directed by Liu Jialiang, *My Young Auntie* (1981). Liu's film is a typically brilliant work in the kung fu genre but it is equally remarkable as a rare example of malapropian comedy in Hong Kong cinema. It paints an amusing picture of what it means to be Hong Kong Chinese and expresses the theme of identity in terms of a spoken dialect which is a unique blend of Chinese and English—"Chinglish," as only Hong Kong people can speak it.

The New Wave directors have done some of their best work dealing with the theme of identity. They have delved deeper into individual psyches, personal conscience and even ethnicity in such films as *Dangerous Encounter—1st Kind* (Tsui Hark, 1980), *Homecoming* (Yim Ho, 1984) and *Song of the Exile* (Ann Hui, 1989). Few directors in the past had explored identity in as personal and sensitive a manner. The New Wave directors came as close as they could to laying bare their souls. This was how Hong Kong people were seeing themselves, in the shape of characters on the silver screen. There is no question now that Hong Kong has an identity unique to its people and place, and that Hong Kong artists are expressing that identity.

However, before one can say there is no turning back, it may be appropriate to recall Liu Jialiang's *My Young Auntie* and the "Chinglish" expressions in the movie. *My Young Auntie* reminds us that Hong Kong is the sum total of an East Asian society having one foot in the West and the other in the East. In addition, the Chinese culture to which Hong Kong has remained faithful is as much a transplanted culture (from the Mainland) as the Western one. It is the feature of transplanted cultures that mark Hong Kong as different. *My Young Auntie* reflects this double-edged sword of Hong Kong identity in a witty fashion, parodying that part of the Hong Konger's two-sided character which has Western culture and manners programmed into it since the start of British colonial adminisration in the last century.

Now that British administration must come to an end in 1997, Hong Kong filmmakers have been trying hard to come to terms with the Chinese side of their identity. As the 1990s roll on, it will be interesting to sea how Hong Kong filmmakers adjust to becoming more Chinese; to transform into a personality and achieve an identity that is not as adulterated as his current one. Both in political and cultural terms, the process may pose a challenge to even the most experienced of social engineers. In the event of that process coming true, Hong Kong would no longer be Hong Kong. It would mark the end of an era.

The "Lawrence Mystique"

As Hong Kong reaches into itself and tries to define what is East and what is West in order to better face the future, others have defined Hong Kong. Western film critics have contributed their fair share in defining the identity of Hong Kong cinema. Some have taken a more active role than others, going as far as possible to immerse themselves in their object of study—the foreign film culture that interests them.

In the colonial era, the term "to go native" has been applied to exotic and eccentric explorer-adventurers such as Will Adams (the character who inspired James Clavell's *Shogun*), the "White Rajah" of Sarawak, James Brooke, and T. E. Lawrence. Today, the term may have gained a certain positive veneer in so far as the promotion of a non-Western culture is concerned. Western critics, writers and scholars who are in the front line of promoting Asian culture to audiences in the West, and even to audiences in the East, gain in status if their work is grounded on native soil, so to speak. There are those who have "gone native" but have retained a basic sense of scholarly objectivity with regard to their culture of interest. There are those, on the other hand, who may have gone too far.

David Lean's *Lawrence of Arabia* (1962) captures the compelling agony of just such a man. Lawrence is adopted by Arab tribes and recognised as a lord and leader. He believes it is possible to work for British and Arab interests and that it is his destiny to unite the Arab tribes. But he cannot completely cross the line into the Arab part of his psyche. His dilemma is presented as romantic irony. In one soul-searching moment, Lawrence (Peter O'Toole) says to Ali (Omar Sharif), "Trust your own people and let me go back to mine."

The exploits of T. E. Lawrence have spawned a body of literature and a film, Lean's masterpiece. These in turn have given rise to a "Lawrence mystique" which places more emphasis on him as a romantic hero than as a man who carried his obsession with native culture to ridiculous lengths. The Lawrence mystique is thus based on the concept of a scholarly but adventurous man whose love for a culture alien to himself drives him into painful, ironic situations as he tries to adopt the customs and way of life of that culture. In the end, both his "home" culture and "host" culture (the culture of his heart) reject him.

The influence of the Lawrence mystique is a powerful one and may have inspired certain Western critics to come to the Far East. While the historical circumstances will have changed, Lawrence lives on in the minds of such critics as a kind of romantic ideal. A Western critic recently likened the Hong Kong cinema to a desert where works of art are like oases which allow cultural life to blossom in the territory. The critic who discovers these "oases" is of course Lawrence riding on a celluloid camel. He collects a band of followers—filmmakers who are naturally gifted and in the front lines of their art—and offers them his leadership and protection.

The Hong Kong environment is conducive to those Western critics who are modern-day Lawrences. Apart from the fact that it is administered by the British government, the territory's population reflects the attributes of East-West irony in social behaviour that

Lawrence himself might have gone through. Once again, *My Young Auntie* may be seen as a kind of sociological pastiche of what Hong Kong has become. Although it is difficult to imagine the real Lawrence accepting the materialistic precepts that rule everyday life in Hong Kong, it is not too far-fetched to imagine that he would appreciate a film like *My Young Auntie* and other films that address the question of identity caught in a web of East-West creation. Today, the irony seems to be commonplace and normal.

Besides cultural irony, I would like to believe that the largely apolitical environment of Hong Kong is another attractive factor for Western critics, writers or experts. It reinforces their status without political obligations. Consequently, they are free to exercise their authority with an air of sublime confidence. In such an environment, locals or natives seldom question their authority; but even if they do, an impassive mentality has been cultivated to deflect any sharp edges of criticism from locals. The difference between modern-day Lawrences and the real Lawrence would lie in the de-politicised atmosphere in which the former operate. T. E. Lawrence was not so lucky. He lived in the heyday of the British Empire, served in the British Army but fought for Arab unity. A genuine believer of the local cause, he was betrayed by his own Western politicians.

Today, the political tables have turned. The fighters of causes will more likely be locals themselves and betrayal—even more swift and brutal—will come from local politicians. It is the rare Western critic or writer who will take up a political cause. Perhaps the reason is that the majority of Western critics have come to terms with the new political equations of a post-colonial world. Yet there are those who will persist in acting like modern-day Lawrences with a sense of manifest destiny, choosing to ignore the fact that Asian critics are now more aware and more confident to assert their own cases. Problems loom ahead as both sides seek to interpret the cultures they study. In the event of disagreement, a dualism of the sort found in political confrontation is provoked. There are those who wield authority on the one hand (the Western experts), and those who question that authority on the other (the Asian critics).

The notion of authority is apposite to this discussion. It is so because we are talking about the Asian environment where authority is felt, not only in the authoritarian nature of most Asian governments but also in the perceived superiority of Western ways and culture. There is the authority of the Western expert on Asia which is exercised even over the way in which Asians view their own culture. The problem centres on those Western critics who may now be described as T. E. Lawrence–inspired critics (henceforth referred to as "Lawrence-critics") who feel it is their manifest destiny to lead Asian filmmakers and unite them, or at the very least offer them their protection. It is against such critics that this essay is targeted; apology is offered beforehand to Western critics in general who may be offended by the thrust of this essay, as it is sometimes necessary to refer to them in critical terms so as to disparage the Lawrences among them. Let me say that the Lawrence-critics are a minority, but they are a very influential minority.

The Importance of Being the Right Sort of Earnest

Why is it important that the Lawrence-critics be challenged? There are two main issues at hand. First, the issue of Western perceptions of Asian culture in general. As much as there is to admire in the crop of work by Western critics applied to Asia, its people and its culture, there is also suspicion of motives and the sense of cultural one-upmanship which such work also conjures, at least in the minds of Asians. There is usually a chance that something does not quite ring true. Let me illustrate with an example. Here is a Lawrence-critic on Stanley Kwan's *Full Moon in New York* (1990): "It is by far the most sophisticated picture yet about the growing Chinese diaspora. It discusses matters that have not yet been raised in any other film, play or novel . . . and it deserves full credit for opening up new ground."

One feels a sense of discomposure with that piece of evaluation although there is nothing fundamentally wrong with what the critic says. It is certain that this critic would have been impressed by Kwan's previous film, *Rouge* (1988) as almost any critic would be, if they had any inkling of style, but *Full Moon in New York* is a picture that does not fully work on style alone. It might be best to point out the somewhat ridiculous nature of the evaluation of *Full Moon* by the Lawrence-critic with the following analogy.

Imagine an Asian critic who is a specialist on British cinema in the eighties. He has been terribly impressed by Hugh Hudson's *Chariots of Fire* (1983) and may conclude that Hudson is the best thing to come along in British cinema for some time. Imagine him writing this about Hudson's *Revolution* (1985) when it first came out: "It is the most remarkable picture ever made by a British director about the American Revolution. Through the performance of Al Pacino, a contemporary look of the 1776 revolution, never before attempted, has been achieved."

I think British—and indeed, American—critics on the whole would agree that there is a problem with that piece of evaluation although there is nothing really wrong with it. If the Asian critic is not quickly dismissed for deliberately going against the grain (for saying that a picture is great when every critic in the West is saying it is a disaster), the issue of how he perceives Western culture would come to the fore. It thus becomes clear that he sees things differently, because he belongs to a different culture. Because his perception is different due to subjective cultural difference, it does not necessarily follow that his perception is right, as in the case of *Revolution*. Nor is it necessarily wrong, of course, it is just problematical. The same principle applies to Western perceptions of Asian works of art.

Where should a reasonable line of interpretation be drawn? I would say that which allows for balanced discussion and a true exchange of views. Part of the problem in Asia is that this line is never drawn. Both sides bear the blame. The other part of the problem is that when the line is drawn, the Lawrence-critics are the ones who set the standards and draw the line according to their subjective interpretations which inevitably overwhelm any discussion. The Lawrence-critics push the boundaries of interpretation too wide off the mark and their level of dominance in any discussion of Asian cinema brings up the question of balance and reciprocity.

If one thinks of the problem in converse, the situation would call for Western critics to question the work that Asian critics apply to Western culture (as in the example of *Revolution* above) and that is addressed to Westerners. But how much of a body of work would that amount to?

Clearly, the question of cultural perception and the idea of balance and reciprocity is an important one. Both the Lawrence-critics and local critics seek the right interpretation of a work of art of a particular culture, but, with cultural matters, there is the factor of "open" interpretation. Just how open may sometimes lead the Lawrence-critics to make perverse conclusions in extreme cases. Here is another example. Who among British critics would take Michael Winner (maker of the *Death Wish* movies) seriously? Yet, there may come a time when British critics will have to put up with the Asian equivalent of a Lawrence-critic who goes to Britain and claims that Winner is a case for serious study. Asian critics have had to put up with Lawrence-critics claiming that the Michael Winners of Asia are worthy of serious study.

In Hong Kong, particularly, Lawrence-critics may confuse their Michael Winners for Jean-Pierre Melvilles or induct the Winners of Asia into the pantheon of "greats" just because they made a few acceptable-to-good films. The distinctiveness of Hong Kong cinema is that it is an extremely malleable beast that offers a mishmash of styles and images. The films of John Woo and Kirk Wong are just some of the examples. The analogy with Winner is not fully applicable in both cases, I will admit, but he comes close. Winner is the sort of director who would fit very well into the environment of Hong Kong and I can imagine that if he were Hong Kong Chinese, he would be making the sort of films John Woo is making.

I can see the Lawrence-critics shaking their heads and saying that Woo makes better films than Winner and that he is a better stylist. But this is the problematical grey area of interpreation of which I speak. It is an area that may involve moral questions but also the aesthetic one of whether style may be wholly divorced from content, an issue that I will not dwell upon here, except to say that it is a common ploy of Lawrence-critics to use style as justification. By the same ploy, one may insist that Winner is a great stylist as well as a socially conscious filmmaker who has exposed the seedier side of American society in the *Death Wish* series.

I have always felt a dreaded sense of disquiet when a Lawrence-critic lays down the line on Woo and Wong and others who are so obviously working with commercial formulae. One good film from these directors is an exception while the rest are repeated exercises in self-parody. But one may not know this from the Lawrence-critics in their boundless enthusiasm for discovering new "auteurs." I submit that Lawrence-critics are more interested in style than in content, and that when they get into the area of interpreting content, they will more likely come up with a bull's head on the body of a horse. The problem is they are as headstrong as the bull.

The second issue concerns the question of fundamental rights and the expression of these rights. In the fifties and sixties, Asian countries had to struggle for political and economic independence. Although political independence was achieved, Asians must continue to fight for economic rights. When the Lawrence-critics ride into Asia from the West, the struggle shifts into the cultural arena. Asian critics must fight for cultural rights in the same way as they fight for economic ones. They must fight for the right of interpretation, the right to criticise, the right to be different in outlook and perception. No treaty protects them against the "protectionist" tendencies of the Lawrence-critics or even of Western critics in general.

The fact of the matter is that the Lawrence-critics would go so far as to deny Asian critics their fundamental right of interpretation. The Asian critic who challenges the Lawrence-critics is thought of by them as impulsive, and worse, ignorant of his own culture and prejudiced against Westerners. In effect, the Lawrence-critics seek to stymie criticism against their own selves and do so by questioning the professional credibility of Asian critics.

To refer once again to the Lawrence-critic writing about *Full Moon* (in response to a critical attack by an Asian critic against that film), he writes: "The overwhelming majority of contemporary Hong Kong films are aimed at the lowest-common-denominator audience. They are chaotic, undisciplined anti-aesthetic and geared to instant gratification. Stanley Kwan is one of the tiny handful of filmmakers in Hong Kong who has refused to succumb to this style of cinema. It's a rash and short-sighted critic who fails to recognise an oasis in a desert, however much he dislikes the 'taste' of the water.

"He [the Asian critic] has a perfect right to loathe any film and criticise it." The Lawrence-critic will support this right to the end, "but the Asian critic must establish a framework for its [*Full Moon*'s] discussion and place it in the context of Hong Kong cinema. It must be rooted in objective analysis and cogent argument." On the surface, the Lawrence-critic has stated his case very reasonably. But if we examine his words carefully, he seems to be saying those artists who are aesthetically ambitious ought to be above criticism, which is to say, above attack. He has possibly put professional standards in greater relief but he seems to link such professionalism to propagating the work of a selective group of artists. The work of these gifted artists may be criticised but only within "a framework of objectrve analysis."

Beyond the bounds of objective analysis, the Asian critic has no right to go. He has no right of attack, apparently not even of fair comment. Can the Asian critic even hope to say that under circumstances where such rights are denied, it is fruitless to talk of "objective analysis"? Reconsidered in the light of fundamental rights, what the Lawrence-critic is saying is very similar to what authoritarian governments in the region have always been saying to dissidents and critics: "You have a right to criticise, but you do so at your peril." We all know the human rights record of such governments.

Once more using the analogy of the Asian expert on British cinema, we may see the picture in its more ludicrous aspects and hopefully understand the situation better. Imagine, once again, the same critic on Hugh Hudson. Imagine him incensed by this insulting attack against Hudson's *Revolution* published in the *Time Out Film Guide* (Penguin Books, 1989): "An almost inconceivable disaster which tries for a worm's eye view of the American Revolution. . . . Maybe the original script had a shape and a grasp of events. If so, it has gone. . . . It's also the first 70mm movie that looks as if it was shot hand-held on 16mm and blown up for the big screen. Director? I didn't catch the credit. Was there one?"

Next, imagine the Asian critic demanding space in *Time Out* to rebut the critic who wrote that irresponsible piece of criticism. How dare he insult Hugh Hudson and readers all over the world concerned about British cinema? Hudson is, after all, one of the few aesthetically ambitious directors working in Britain. In strict "auteurist" terms, *Revolution* is an engrossing extension of his central concerns as an artist. And in strictly cinematic terms, Hudson's film stands in the league of the best Kurosawa and David Lean epics and will not fail to please discriminating audiences in the East. Of course, none of this makes the him immune to criticism. But it's a rash and short-sighted British critic who fails to recognise world-class cinema produced by a British filmmaker.

In the ensuing debate, the Asian British cinema expert then goes on to insist that local reviews must be written within a framework of objective analysis and placed in the context of British cinema and that local critics do not have the right to attack their own filmmakers. By the criteria of the Lawrence-critics, it would appear that the work of aesthetically ambitious British directors such as Derek Jarman, Peter Greenaway and Terence Davies should be above criticism and may not be attacked (any criticism should be placed within a "framework of objective analysis"). What would be the response of British critics in that instance? I would imagine an uproar and cries of "Outrageous!" Should it be any different in Asia? Yet, the influence of the Lawrence-critics in Asia is so great that they are able to ride roughshod over local critics.

That they are able to do so is perhaps because Asians seldom exercise their rights vis-à-vis their Western counterparts. Part of the problem lies in the customary rules of Asian courtesy and manners. The Asian critic will defer to the Western expert out of professional courtesy. This becomes such a custom that when Asian critics assert themselves, there is a shock to the system. Asian critics who insist on their right of interpretation will appear, in the eyes of the Lawrence-critics, to be riding their camels back to front.

There is also the risk that Asians will lapse into a form of cultural recidivism in the belief that the only valid interpretation is the local one. The Lawrence-critics will be quick to condemn such recidivist thinking. However, before Asians fall into that trap, the mere act of expressing their rights will cause no end of outraged reaction from the Lawrence-critics. For starters, they will be labelled with the taint of naiveté and provincialism. It is clear that Asian critics can expect no sympathy from the Lawrence-critics and that now, more than ever, they should be on their toes. As the Western alliance makes war against Saddam Hussein (a twist of historical irony arising from the legacy of T. E. Lawrence's attempt to unite the Arab tribes), critics in the West will be in no mood to be sympathetic to Asian critics wishing to assert local rights.

If Asian critics are not to be outdated and behind the times, they must keep up with the standards set by their Western counterparts. But does this mean total acceptance of the rules and criteria of Western expertise? Does it mean accepting the opinions of Western critics? Although the answer, in both cases, may appear to be a simple "No," the principle that one must fight for one's rights still applies. The aura and status of Western critics offers no guarantee that fundamental rights are automatically granted, applied, or adhered to. It is then a question of human rights. Asian critics must vie for the right to express their own opinions over questions concerning their own culture and their own works of art.

There are other minor and major irritants about Lawrence-critics which I will briefly touch upon. A major irritant is their cliquish approach to cinema. Surrounding themselves with "gifted" artists and obtaining their support confers a kind of legitimacy that allows the Lawrence-critics to deny Asian critics the right of interpretation. It allows them to say, "I have the support of Asian filmmakers," while putting down Asian critics. A minor irritant is that unlike the real Lawrence, the Lawrence-critics do not stay in Asia. They practise their craft behind the safe cover of Western liberal thinking and expect Asian critics to base their interpretations on the same.

Conclusion

To put it plainly, Asian critics seek to become experts themselves. They too wish to be objective analysts of their own cultures, to establish their own "frameworks" whereby Asian works of art may be fully appreciated by all. But they may not be recognised for themselves. They are thought to militate against their own artists; they are also thought to be too local, of interest only to a highly localised home constituency. Hence, it is felt that Asians must still rely on the West for a more "internationalised" view of their culture. They must learn about Asia from the West. But Asians have learned from the West. Today, they may discover that they have nothing else to learn and that they may have become targets of a zero-sum game initiated by Western critics to protect their own interests. Such interests extend to the way in which Asians view Asian culture.

Lacking a strong tradition of film criticism, Asian critics must rely on the findings and theories of the West. But is Asian criticism merely an extension of Western criticism, a rehash of old theories in the form of an appendage to the work of Western experts on Asia? Lacking a professional base for serious film criticism, Asian critics are looked upon as well-meaning amateurs. The impression that they get of Western critics is that they know all there is to know of Asian culture. Possibly. Westerners have perceived that Asians are going through a process of Westernisation and that they have lost sight of their own culture. Are Asian critics, in effect, presenting a "fake Western" view of their own culture, and that the only genuine interpretations of Asian culture come from Western critics?

As both sides come close to a zero-sum outcome, it is appropriate to ask at what point Asian critics should review what they have learned from the West and make their own conclusions. There will come a point when Asian critics must defend their own interests too. Perhaps it is the point when Asian critics ask, "Has Western film criticism reached a dead end?" It is a question worth asking.

Western film criticism, based on the idea of pushing the frontiers of cinema, passed through several phases of discovery As the twentieth century draws to a close, cinema has become more than a mature medium. Its great artists have now passed into history and theories regarding realism and non-realism, authorship and structure have become an integral part of the paradigm. Existing artists must adapt themselves to changing patterns of the medium as wall as new patterns of consumption. Pushing its frontiers into the East the Lawrence-critics assume a pioneering role in assimilating the cinemas of Asia into the historic mainstream. But the notion of discovery is not as it was. There can be no new "auteur" theory to discover. No new structuralist or semiotic theory. There may be one discovery: that a new generation of Asian artists has come of age, and also, a new generation of Asian critics. While recognition is rendered to the former, there is contention with the latter. Since the medium itself has matured, what can Western critics say about the work of Asian filmmakers that Asian critics themselves cannot say? The answer lies in the level of interpretation and understanding of Asian culture as expressed in Asian cinema.

The eighties may have marked the end of the frontier of Western film criticism, a frontier pushed into Asia where cinemas other than that of Japan and India have been "opened up." The discovery mentality of Western film criticism may now work against its own progress. It has settled questions of the art of cinema but it cannot settle questions of cultural interpretation. Even if other frontiers are left to be discovered, those emerging cinemas will be presenting further variations of culture as forms already integrated into the universal paradigm of the cinema. So long as Western critics refuse to recognise the existence of local critics and their right of interpretation, progress will be inimical to proper understanding.

The ball is in the court of Western critics. They must choose whether to continue playing a zero-sum game with our Asian counterparts or to recognise the existence of Asian critics on the principle that they are equal but different.

Ana M. López

Are All Latins from Manhattan?
Hollywood, Ethnography,
and Cultural Colonialism

She's a Latin from Manhattan
I can tell by her mañana
She's a Latin from Manhattan
And not Havana.
　　—Al Jolson in *Go Into Your Dance* (1935)

The commonplace of ethnic studies of the Hollywood cinema is to begin with the obvious: the classic Hollywood cinema was never kind to ethnic or minority groups. The standard claim is that, be they Indian, black, Hispanic, or Jewish, Hollywood represented ethnics and minorities as stereotypes that circulated easily and repeatedly from film to film. More significantly, minorities and ethnics were most noticeable by their absence in classic Hollywood films. Rarely protagonists, ethnics merely provided local color, comic relief, or easily recognizable villains and dramatic foils. When coupled with the pervasiveness of stereotypes, this marginalization or negation completes the usual "pattern" of Hollywood's ethnic representation and its standard assessment as damaging, insulting, and negative.

But Hollywood's relationship to each ethnic and minority group is far more nuanced than this simple narrative at first seems to allow. And, in fact, each of these relationships is unique; each has its own complex history with a specificity derived from Hollywood's position as a socioculturally bound ethnographer.

What does it mean to say that Hollywood has served as an ethnographer of American culture? First, it means to conceive of ethnography not as a scientific methodology that through detailed description and analysis unearths holistic truths about "other" cultures,[1] but as a historically determined practice of cultural interpretation and representation from the standpoint of participant observation.[2] And it also means to think of Hollywood not as a simple reproducer of fixed and homogenous cultures or ideologies, but as a producer of some of the multiple discourses that intervene in, affirm, and contest the socioideological struggles of a given moment. To think of a classic Hollywood film as ethnographic discourse is to affirm its status as an authored, yet collaborative, enterprise, akin in practice to the way contemporary ethnographers have redefined their discipline. James Clifford, for example, has analyzed the discursive nature of ethnography "not as the experience and interpretation of a circumscribed 'other' reality, but rather as a constructive negotiation involving . . . conscious politically significant subjects."[3]

When ethnographers posit their work as "the mutual, dialogical production of a discourse" about culture that "in its ideal form would result in a polyphonic text," we also approach a descrirtion of the operations of an ideal, albeit not of Hollywood's cinema.[4] The difference lies in the deployment of power relations, what Edward Said calls the "effect of domination," or the ethnographic, cinematic, and colonial process of designing an identity for the other and, for the observer, a standpoint from which to see without being seen.[5] Obviously, neither ethnography nor the cinema have achieved that ideal state of perfect polyphony or perspectival relativity where the observer-observed dichotomy can be transcended and no participant has "the final word in the form of a framing story or encompassing synthesis."[6] Power relations always interfere. However, both ethnographic and cinematic texts, as discourses, carry the traces of this dialogic-polyphonic process and of the power relations that structure it.

Thinking of Hollywood as ethnographer—as co-producer in power of cultural texts—allows us to reformulate its relationship to ethnicity. Hollywood does not represent ethnics and minorities; it creates them and provides its audience with an experience of them. It evokes them, as the postmodern ethnographer Stephen Tyler might say. Rather than an investigation of mimetic relationships, then, what a critical reading of Hollywood's ethnographic discourse (a meta-ethnography) requires is the analysis of the historical-political construction of self-other relations—the articulation of forms of difference—sexual and ethnic—as an inscription of, among other factors, Hollywood's power as ethnographer, as creator, and translator of otherness.

One characteristic of standard "Hollywood's image of ———" studies is that, no matter how bleakly the overall mimetic accuracy of Hollywood's representations of a particular group is evaluated, the analyst always manages to pinpoint a golden, or near-golden, moment when Hollywood, for complex conjunctural reasons, sees the light and becomes temporarily more sensitive to an ethnic or minority group. In the history of Hollywood's treatment of the American Indian, for example, that moment arrives in the 1960s and 1970s. For other ethnic and minority groups—Jews and Latin Americans, for example—usually there is a significant improvement noticed in the post–World War II period of "social consciousness."[7] What interests me are not the historical specifics of each of these moments, but the fact that such moments of the "discovery" and inscription of ethnic otherness play a critical role in the structure of texts about Hollywood and ethnicity, serving as the linchpin of teleological historical arguments decrying Hollywood's stereotypical, unrealistic, and biased representations of ethnics.

My project is to question precisely this historical-narrative *topos* in the history of Hollywood's representation of Latin Americans. I will focus upon what is perceived as the "golden moment" or "break" in that history—the Good Neighbor Policy years (roughly 1939–47)—in order to analyze the moment's historical coherence and its function for Hollywood as an ethnographic institution, that is as creator, integrator, and translator of otherness. What happens when Hollywood self-consciously and intentionally assumes the role of cultural ethnographer?

My emphasis is on three stars whose ethnic otherness was articulated according to parameters that shifted as Hollywood's ethnographic imperative became clear: Dolores del Rio, Lupe Vélez, and Carmen Miranda. That these three figures are Latin American and female is much more than a simple coincidence, for the Latin American woman poses a double threat—sexual and racial—to Hollywood's ethnographic and colonial authority.

The Good Neighbor Policy:
Hollywood Zeroes in on Latin America

After decades of portraying Latin Americans lackadaisically and sporadically as lazy peasants and wily señoritas who inhabited an undifferentiated backward land, Hollywood films between 1939 and 1947, featuring Latin American stars, music, locations, and stories flooded United States and international markets. By February 1943, for example, thirty films with Latin American themes or locales had been released and twenty-five more were in the works. By April 1945, eighty-four films dealing with Latin American themes had been produced.[8] These films seemed to evidence a newfound sensibility, most notably, a sudden respect for national and geographical boundaries. At the simplest level, for example, it seemed that Hollywood was exercising some care to differentiate between the cultural and geographic characteristics of different Latin American countries by incorporating general location shots, specific citations of iconographic sites (for example, Rio de Janeiro's Corcovado Mountain), and some explanations of the cultural characteristics of the inhabitants.

Why did Hollywood suddenly become interested in Latin America? In economic terms, Latin America was the only foreign market available for exploitation during World War II. Before the war, the industry had derived a large percentage of its gross revenues from foreign markets, and upon the closing of the European and Japanese markets, it set out, in Bosley Crowther's words, on "a campaign to woo Latin America" with films of "Pan-American" interest.[9]

Pan-Americanism was also, however, an important key word for the Roosevelt administration, the Rockefeller Foundation, and the newly created (1940) State Department Office of the Coordinator for Inter-American Affairs (CIAA) headed by Nelson Rockefeller. Concerns about our Southern neighbors' dubious political allegiances and the safety of United States investments in Latin America led to the resurrection of the long-dormant Good Neighbor Policy and to the official promotion of hemispheric unity, cooperation, and nonaggression (in part, to erase the memories of the not-so-distant military interventions in Cuba and Nicaragua). Charged with the responsibility of coordinating all efforts to promote inter-American understanding, the CIAA set up a Motion Picture Section and appointed John Hay Whitney, vice president and director of the film library of the Museum of Modern Art (MOMA) in New York, as its director.[10]

The CIAA sponsored the production of newsreels and documentaries for Latin American distribution that showed "the truth about the American way," contracted with Walt Disney in 1941 to produce a series of twenty-four shorts with Latin American themes that would "carry the message of democracy and friendship below the Rio Grande," sponsored screenings of films that celebrated the "democratic way" in what became known as the South American embassy circuit, and, together with the Hays Office's newly appointed Latin American expert, began to pressure the studios to become more sensitive to Latin issues and portrayals.[11] This impetus, when coupled with the incentive of Latin America's imminently exploitable 4,240 movie theaters, was sufficient to stimulate Hollywood to take on the project of educating Latin America about the democratic way of life and its North American audience about its Latin American neighbors.

This self-appointed mission, however, needs to be questioned more closely. How does Hollywood position itself *and* North Americans in relation to the Southern "neighbors"? How is its friendliness constituted? How does it differ from Hollywood's prior circulation of so-called stereotypes and its negligent undifferentiation of the continent?

From an industrial perspective, Hollywood's policies in the Good Neighbor period were directed by the assumption that Latin Americans would flock to see themselves created by Hollywood in glorious TechniColor and with an unexpected linguistic fluency. The pre–Good Neighbor films of the 1930s dealing with Latin Americans (primarily dramatic stories) were notorious for linguistic blunders and regional undifferentiation. They also directly promoted the development of proto-industrial filmmaking in Argentina, Mexico, and Brazil, which had already begun to compete for the Latin American market. Furthermore, several Latin American nations had regularly begun to ban or censor Hollywood films deemed offensive to the national character, most notoriously, RKO's *Girl of the Rio* (1932), a film banned by a number of Latin American countries because its lecherous and treacherous central character, Sr. Tostado (Mr. "Toast," "Toasted," or "Crazed"), was considered "the most vile Mexican" ever to appear on the screen.[12] To forestall censorship and protests and to decrease the competitive edge of national productions, Hollywood began to feature more Latin American actors, songs and dances, and to differentiate among different cultures.

Three basic kinds of Good Neighbor Policy films were produced. First, there were a number of standard, classic Hollywood genre films, with North American protagonists, set in Latin America and with some location shooting, for example, Irving Rapper's *Now Voyager* (1942), with extensive footage shot in Rio de Janeiro; Edward Dmytryk's *Cornered* (1945), shot totally on location in Buenos Aires; and Alfred Hitchcock's *Notorious* (1946), with second-unit location shots of Rio de Janeiro. Then there were B– productions set and often shot in Latin America and that featured mediocre United States actors and Latin entertainers in either musicals or pseudo-musical formats, for example, *Mexicana* (1945) starring Tito Guizar, Mexico's version of Frank Sinatra, and the sixteen-year-old Cuban torch singer Estelita; Gregory Ratoff's *Carnival in Costa Rica* (1947) starring Dick Haymes, Vera Ellen, and Cesar Romero; and Edgar G. Ulmer's remake of *Grand Hotel, Club Havana* (1945), starring the starlet Isabelita, Tom Neil, and Margaret Lindsay. Finally, the most successful and most self-consciously "good-neighborly" films were the mid-to-big budget musical comedies set either in Latin America or in the United States but featuring, in addition to recognizable United States stars, fairly well-known Latin American actors and entertainers.

Almost every studio produced its share of these films between 1939 and 1947, but Twentieth Century–Fox, RKO, and Republic specialized in "good neighborliness" of the musical variety. Fox had Carmen Miranda under contract and produced films that featured her between 1940 and 1946; RKO followed the Rockefeller interest in Latin America by sending Orson Welles on a Good Neighbor tour of Brazil to make a film about Carnival,[13] and with films such as *Panamericana* (1945); Republic exploited contract players Tito Guizar and Estelita in a number of low-budget musicals such as *The Thrill of Brazil* (1946).

Notwithstanding the number of films produced, and the number of Latin American actors contracted by the studios in this period, it is difficult to describe Hollywood's position with regard to these suddenly welcomed "others" as respectful or reverent.[14] Hollywood (and the United States) needed to posit a complex otherness as the flip side of wartime patriotism and nationalism and in order to assert and protect its colonial-imperialist economic interests. A special kind of other was needed to reinforce the wartime national self, one that—unlike the German or Japanese other—was nonthreatening, potentially but not practically assimilable (that is, nonpolluting to the purity of the race), friendly, fun-loving, and not deemed insulting to Latin American eyes and ears. Ultimately, Hollywood succeeded in all except, perhaps, the last category.

The Transition: From Indifference to "Difference" Across the Bodies of Women

Before the Good Neighbor Policy period, few Latin Americans had achieved star status in Hollywood. In fact, most of the "vile" Latin Americans of the early Hollywood cinema were played by United States actors. In the silent period, the Mexican actor Ramón

Novarro, one of the few Latin American men to have had a consistent career in Hollywood, succeeded as a sensual yet feminized "Latin Lover" modeled on the Valentino icon,[15] but the appellation "Latin" always connoted Mediterranean rather than Latin American. Ostensibly less threatening than men, Latin American women fared differently, particularly Dolores del Rio and Lupe Vélez.

Del Rio's Hollywood career spanned the silent and early sound eras. Although considered exotic, del Rio appeared in a variety of films, working with directors as diverse as Raoul Walsh, King Vidor, and Orson Welles.[16] After a successful transition to talkies in Edwin Carewe's *Evangeline* (1929), her place in the Hollywood system was unquestionable and further legitimized by her marriage to the respected MGM art director Cedric Gibbons. Undeniably Latin American, del Rio was not, however, identified exclusively with Latin roles. Hers was a vague upper-class exoticism articulated within a general category of "foreign/other" tragic sensuality. This sensual other, an object of sexual fascination, transgression, fear, and capitulation not unlike Garbo or Dietrich, did not have a specific national or ethnic provenance, simply an aura of foreignness that accommodated her disruptive potential. Her otherness was located and defined on a sexual rather than an ethnic register, and she portrayed, above all, ethnically vague characters with a weakness for North American "white/blond" men: Indian maidens, South Seas princesses, Latin American señoritas, and other aristocratic beauties. Although she often functioned as a repeatable stereotype (in her role in *Girl of the Rio*, for example), her undifferentiated sexuality was not easily tamed by the proto-colonial ethnographic imperatives of Hollywood's Good Neighbor period. In a precursor of the Good Neighbor films like *Flying Down to Rio* (1933), the explicit and irresistible sensuality of her aristocratic Carioca character (all she has to do is look at a man across a crowded nightclub and he is smitten forever) could be articulated because it would be tamed by marriage to the North American hero. However in the films of the Good Neighbor cycle, that resolution/partial appeasement of the ethnically undifferentiated sexual threat of otherness she unleashed was no longer available. Likewise, in another pre–Good Neighbor policy film in which she portrays a Latin American, Lloyd Bacon's *In Caliente* (1935), del Rio is not identified as a *Mexican* beauty, but as the *world's* greatest dancer. As Carlos Fuentes has remarked, del Rio was "a goddess threatening to become woman,"[17] and neither category—goddess or woman—was appropriate to Hollywood's self-appointed mission as goodwill imperialist ethnographer of the Americas. Del Rio's persona and her articulation in Hollywood films, in fact, comprise a perfect cinematic example of what Homi K. Bhabha has described as the phenomenon of the colonial hybrid, a disavowed cultural differentiation necessary for the existence of colonial-imperialist authority, where "what is disavowed [difference] is not repressed but repeated as something different—a mutation, a hybrid."[18]

Del Rio chose to return to Mexico in 1943 and dedicated herself—with a few "returns" to Hollywood, most notably to appear in John Ford's *The Fugitive* (1947) and *Cheyenne Autumn* (1964)—to the Mexican cinema and stage, where she assumed a legendary fame inconceivable in Hollywood. The impossibility of her status for Hollywood in 1939–1947 was, however, literally worked through the body of another Mexican actress, Lupe Vélez.

Like del Rio's, Vélez's career began in the silent period, where she showed promise working with D. W. Griffith in *Lady of the Pavements* (1929) and other directors. But Vélez's position in Hollywood was defined not by her acting versatility, but by her smoldering ethnic identifiability. Although as striking as del Rio's, Vélez's beauty and sexual appeal were aggressive, flamboyant, and stridently ethnic. Throughout the 1930s, she personified the hot-blooded, thickly accented, Latin temptress with insatiable sexual appetites, on screen—in films such as *Hot Pepper* (1933), *Strictly Dynamite* (1934), and *La Zandunga* (1938)—and with her star persona—by engaging in much-publicized simultaneous affairs with Gary Cooper, Ronald Colman, and Ricardo Cortez, and marrying Johnny Weismuller in 1933.[19] (Impossible to imagine a better match between screen and star biographies: Tarzan meets the beast of the Tropics.) Vélez was, in other words, outrageous, but her sexual excessiveness, although clearly identified as specifically ethnic, was articulated as potentially subsumable. On and off screen, she, like del Rio, was mated with and married North American men.

The dangers of such explicit on-screen ethnic miscegenation became apparent in RKO's *Mexican Spitfire* six-film series (1939–1943), simultaneously Vélez's most successful films and an index of the inevitability of her failure. Vélez portrayed a Mexican entertainer, Carmelita, who falls in love and marries—after seducing him away from his legitimate Anglo fiancee—Dennis Lindsay, a nice New England man. Much to the dismay of his proper Puritan family, Dennis chooses to remain with Carmelita against all obstacles, including, as the series progressed, specific references to Carmelita's mixed blood, lack of breeding and social unacceptability, her refusal to put the entertainment business completely behind her to become a proper wife, her inability to promote his (floundering) advertising career, and her apparent lack of desire for offspring. Although the first couple of installments were very successful, the series was described as increasingly redundant, contrived, and patently "absurd" by the press and was cancelled in 1943. Not only had it begun to lose money for RKO, but it also connoted a kind of Latin American otherness anathema to the Good Neighbor mission. Summarily stated, the questions posed by the series could no longer be tolerated because there were no "good neighborly" answers. The ethnic problematic of the series—intermarriage, miscegenation, and integration—could not be explicitly addressed within the new, friendly climate. Ironically highlighting this fictional and ideological question, Vélez, unmarried and five months pregnant, committed suicide in 1944.

Neither del Rio nor Vélez could be re-created as Good Neighbor ethnics, for their ethnic and sexual power and danger were not assimilable within Hollywood's new, ostensibly friendly, and temperate regime. Del Rio was not ethnic enough and too much of an actress; Vélez was too "Latin" and untamable. Hollywood's new position was defined by its double-imperative as "ethnographer" of the Americas; that is, by its self-appointed mission as translator of the ethnic and sexual threat of Latin American otherness into peaceful good neighborliness *and* by its desire to use that translation to attempt to make further inroads into the resistant Latin American movie market without damaging its national box office. It, therefore, could not advantageously promote either a mythic, goddess-like actress with considerable institutional clout (del Rio) or an ethnic volcano (Vélez) that was not even subdued by that most sacred of institutions, marriage to a North American. What Hollywood's Good Neighbor regime demanded was the articulation of a different female star persona that could be readily identifiable as Latin American (with the sexual suggestiveness necessary to fit the prevailing stereotype) but whose sexuality was neither too attractive (to dispel the fear-attraction of miscegenation) nor so powerful as to demand its submission to a conquering North American male.

The Perfect "Good Neighbor": Fetishism, Self, and Others

Hollywood's lust for Latin America as ally and market—and its self-conscious attempt to translate and tame the potentially disturbing radical (sexual and ethnic) otherness that the recognition of difference (or lack) entails—are clearest within the constraints of the musical comedy genre. Incorporated into the genre as exotic entertainers, Latin Americans were simultaneously marginalized and privileged. Although they were denied valid narrative functions, entertainment, rather than narrative coherence or complexity, is the locus of pleasure of the genre. Mapped onto the musical comedy form in both deprivative (the denial of a valid narrative function) and supplemental (the location of an excess pleasure) terms, this Hollywood version of "Latin American-ness" participates in the operations of fetishism and disavowal typical of the stereotype in colonial-imperialist discourses.[20] This exercise of colonial-imperialist authority would peak, with a significant twist, in the Carmen Miranda films at Twentieth Century–Fox, a cycle which produced a public figure, Miranda, that lays bare, with surreal clarity, the scenario of Hollywood's own colonial fantasy and the problematics of ethnic representation in a colonial-imperialist context.[21]

In these films, Carmen Miranda functions, above all, as a fantastic or uncanny fetish. Everything about her is surreal, off-center, displaced onto a different regime: from her extravagant hats, midriff-baring multicolored costumes, and five-inch platform shoes to her linguistic malapropisms, farcical sexuality, and high-pitched voice, she is an other, everyone's other. Although not even Brazilian-born (she was born in Portugal to parents who immigrated to Brazil and named her Maria do Carmo Miranda da Cunha), she became synonymous with cinematic "Latin American-ness," with an essence, defined and mobilized by herself and Hollywood throughout the continent. As the emcee announces at the end of her first number in Busby Berkeley's *The Gang's All Here*, "Well, there's your Good Neighbor Policy. Come on honey, let's Good Neighbor it."

Miranda was "discovered" by Hollywood "as is," that is, after her status as a top entertainer in Brazil (with more than three hundred records, five films—including the first Brazilian sound feature—and nine Latin American tours) brought her to the New York stage, where her six-minute performance in *The Streets of Paris* (1939) transformed her into "an overnight sensation."[22] Her explicit Brazilian-ness—samba song and dance repertoire, Carnival-type costumes—was transformed into the epitome of *latinidad* by a series of films that "placed" her in locales as varied as Lake Louise in the Canadian Rockies, Havana, or Buenos Aires.

Her validity as "Latin American" was based on a rhetoric of visual excess—of costume, performance, sexuality, and musicality—that carried over into the mode of address of the films themselves. Of course, since they were produced at Fox, a studio that depended on its superior TechniColor process to differentiate its product in the marketplace,[23] these films are also almost painfully colorful, exploiting the technology to further inscribe Latin Americanness as tropicality. For example, although none of the Fox films was shot on location, all include markedly luscious "travelogue-like" sections justifying the authenticity of their locales. Even more significantly, they also include the visual representation of travel, whether to the country in question or "inland," as further proof of the validity of their ethno-presentation within a regime that privileges the visual as the only possible site of knowledge.

Weekend in Havana is a prototypical example. The film begins by introducing the lure of the exotic in a post-credit, narrative-establishment montage sequence that situates travel to Latin America as a desirable sightseeing adventure: snow on the Brooklyn bridge dissolves to a brochure of leisure cruises to Havana, to a tourist guide to "Cuba: The Holiday Isle of the Tropics," to a window display promoting "Sail to Romance" cruises featuring life-size cardboard cutouts of Carmen Miranda and a Latin band that come to life and sing the title song (which begins, "How would you like to spend the weekend in Havana . . ."). Immediately after, the romantic plot of the musical is set up: Alice Faye plays a Macy's salesgirl whose much-scrimped-for Caribbean cruise is ruined when her ship runs aground. She refuses to sign the shipping company's release and is appeased only with the promise of "romance" in an all-expenses-paid tour of Havana with shipping-company executive John Payne.

The trip from the marooned cruise ship to Havana is again represented by an exuberantly colorful montage of the typical tourist sights of Havana—el Morro Castle, the Malecon, the Hotel Nacional, Sloppy Joe's Bar—with a voiceover medley of "Weekend in Havana" and typical Cuban songs. Finally, once ensconced in the most luxurious hotel in the city, Faye is taken to see the sights by Payne. They travel by taxi to a sugar plantation, where Payne's lecture from a tourist book, although it bores Faye to yawns, does serve as a voiceover narration for the visual presentation of "Cubans at work": "Hundreds of thousands of Cubans are involved with the production of this important commodity. . . ." These three sequences serve both important narrative and legitimizing functions, testifying to the authenticity of the film's ethnographic and documentary work and eliding the fact that the featured native entertainer, Rosita Rivas (Miranda), is neither Cuban nor speaks Spanish.

More complexly, all the Fox films depend upon Miranda's performative excess to validate their authority as "good neighborly" ethnographic discourses. The films' simple plots—often remakes of prior musical successes and most commonly involving some kind of mistaken identity or similar snafu—further highlight the importance of the Miranda-identified visual and musical regime rather than the legitimizing narrative order. The beginning of *The Gang's All Here*, for example, clearly underlines this operation by presenting a narrativized re-presentation of travel, commerce, and ethnic identity. After the credits, a half-lit floating head singing Ary Barroso's "Brasil" in Portuguese suddenly shifts (in a classic Busby

Berkeley syntactical move) to the hull of a ship emblazoned with the name *SS Brazil*, docking in New York and unloading typical Brazilian products: sugar, coffee, bananas, strawberries, and Carmen Miranda. Wearing a hat featuring her native fruits, Miranda finishes the song, triumphantly strides into New York, switches to an English tune, and is handed the keys to the city by the mayor as the camera tracks back to reveal the stage of a nightclub, an Anglo audience to whom she is introduced *as* the Good Neighbor Policy and whom she instructs to dance the "Uncle Sam-ba."

The Fox films' most amazing characteristic is Miranda's immutability and the substitutability of the narratives. Miranda travels and is inserted into different landscapes, but she remains the same from film to film, purely Latin American. Whether the action of the film is set in Buenos Aires, Havana, the Canadian Rockies, Manhattan, or a Connecticut mansion, the on-screen Miranda character—most often named Carmen or Rosita—is remarkably coherent: above all, and against all odds, an entertainer and the most entertaining element in all the films.[24] While the North American characters work out the inevitable romance plot of the musical comedy, Miranda—always a thorn to the budding romance—puts on a show and dallies outrageously with the leading men. Normally not permanently mated with a North American protagonist (with the notable exception of *That Night in Rio*, where she gets to keep Don Ameche, but only because his identical double gets the white girl played by Alice Faye), Miranda, nevertheless, gets to have her fun along the way and always entices and almost seduces with aggressive kisses and embraces at least one, but most often several, of the North American men.

Miranda's sexuality is so aggressive, however, that it is diffused, spent in gesture, innuendo, and salacious commentary. Unlike Vélez, who can seduce and marry a nice WASP man, Miranda remains either contentedly single, attached to a Latin American Lothario (for example, the womanizing manager-cum-gigolo played by Cesar Romero in *Weekend in Havana*), or in the permanent never-never land of prolonged and unconsummated engagements to unlikely North American types. For example, in *Copacabana* she has been engaged for ten years to Groucho Marx and, at the end of the film, they still have separate hotel rooms and no shared marriage vows.

Miranda, not unlike other on-screen female performers (Dietrich in the Von Sternberg films, for example), functions narratively and discursively as a sexual fetish, freezing the narrative and the pleasures of the voyeuristic gaze and provoking a regime of spectacle and specularity. She acknowledges and openly participates in her fetishization, staring back at the camera, implicating the audience in her sexual display. But she is also an ethnic fetish. The look she returns is also that of the ethnographer and its colonial spectator stand-in. Her Latin Americanness is displaced in all its visual splendor for simultaneous colonial appropriation and denial.

Although Miranda is visually fetishized within filmic systems that locate her metaphorically as the emblem of knowledge of Latin American-ness, Miranda's voice, rife with cultural impurities and disturbing syncretisms, slips through the webs of Hollywood's colonial and ethnographic authority over the constitution and definition of otherness. It is in fact within the aural register, constantly set against the legitimacy of the visual, that Hollywood's ethnographic good neighborliness breaks down in the Fox-Miranda films. In addition to the psychosexual impact of her voice, Miranda's excessive manipulation of accents—the obviously shifting registers of tone and pitch between her spoken and sung English and between her English and Portuguese—inflates the fetish, cracking its surface while simultaneously aggrandizing it. Most obvious in the films where she sings consecutive numbers in each language (*Weekend in Havana* and *The Gang's All Here* are two examples), the tonal differences between her sung and spoken Portuguese and her English indicate that her excessive accent and her linguistic malapropisms are no more than a pretense, a nod to the requirements of a conception of foreignness and otherness necessary to maintain the validity of the text in question as well as her persona as an ethnographic good neighborly gesture. That the press and studio machinery constantly remarked upon her accent and problems with English further highlight their ambiguous status.[25] At once a sign of her otherness as well as of the artificiality of all otherness, her accent ultimately became an efficient marketing device, exploited in advertisements and publicity campaigns: "I tell everyone I know to DREENK Piel's."26

Throughout the Good Neighbor films, Miranda remains a fetish, but a surreal one, a fetish that self-consciously underlines the difficult balance between knowledge and belief that sustains it and that lets us hear the edges of an unclassifiable otherness, product of an almost undescribable bricolage, that rejects the totalizing search for truth of the good neighborly Hollywood ethnographer while simultaneously submitting to its designs.

"Are All Latins from Manhattan?"

Miranda's Hollywood career was cut short both by the demise of Hollywood's good neighborliness in the postwar era as well as by her untimely death in 1955.27 However, Hollywood's circulation and use of her persona as the emblem of the Good Neighbor clearly demonstrates the fissures of Hollywood's work as Latin American ethnographer in this period. With Miranda's acquiescence and active participation, Hollywood ensconced her as the essence of Latin American otherness in terms that, on the surface, were both nonderogatory and simultaneously nonthreatening. First, as a female emblem, her position was always already that of a less-threatening other. In this context, the potential threat of her sexuality—that which was troubling in Vélez, for example—was dissipated by its sheer visual and narrative excess. Furthermore, her legitimizing ethnicity, exacerbated by an aura of the carnivalesque and the absurd, could be narratively relegated to the stage, to the illusory (and tameable) world of performance, theater, and movies. This is perhaps most conclusively illustrated by the frequency with which her persona is used as the emblem of Latin American otherness and exoticism in Hollywood films of the period: in *House Across the Bay* (Archie Mayo, 1940) Joan Bennett appears in a Miranda-inspired *baiana* costume; in *Babes on Broadway* (Busby Berkeley, 1941) Mickey Rooney does a number while dressed like her. In *In This Our Life* (John Huston, 1942) Bette Davis plays a Miranda record and hums along to "Chica Chica Boom Chic," and in *Mildred*

Pierce (Michael Curtiz, 1945) Jo Ann Marlow does a fully costumed Miranda imitation.

At the same time, however, Miranda's textual persona escapes the narrow parameters of the Good Neighbor. As a willing participant in the production of these self-conscious ethnographic texts, Miranda literally asserted her own voice in the textual operations that defined her as *the* other. Transforming, mixing, ridiculing, and redefining her own difference against the expected standards, Miranda's speaking voice, songs, and accents create an other text that is in counterpoint to the principal textual operations. She does not burst the illusory bubble of the Good Neighbor, but by inflating it beyond recognition, she highlights its status as a discursive construct—as myth.

When we recognize that Hollywood's relationship to ethnic and minority groups is primarily ethnographic—that is, one that involves the co-production in power of cultural texts—rather than merely mimetic, it becomes possible to understand the supposed break in Hollywood's misrepresentation of Latin Americans during the Good Neighbor Policy years textually as well as in instrumental and ideological terms. It is particularly important to recognize that Hollywood (and, by extension, television) fulfills this ethnographic function, because we are in an era that, not unlike the Good Neighbor years, is praised for its "Hispanization." While the media crows about the 1987–1988 successes of *La Bamba* and *Salsa: The Motion Picture* and a special issue of *Time* proclaims "Magnifico! Hispanic Culture Breaks Out of the Barrio,"[28] it might prove enlightening to look at this particular translation, presentation, and assimilation of Latin American otherness as yet another ethnographic textual creation that must be analyzed as a political co-production of representations of difference and not as a mimetic narrative challenge.

NOTES

1. This is, for example, how Karl G. Heider describes it in *Ethnographic Film* (Austin: University of Texas Press, 1976), one of the few texts to express the relationship between ethnography and the cinema directly (see, especially, 5–12).

2. James Clifford, *The Predicament of Culture: Twentieth-Century Ethnography, Literature, and Art* (Cambridge: Harvard University Press, 1988).

3. James Clifford, "On Ethnographic Authority," in *The Predicament of Culture,* 41.

4. Stephen A. Tyler, "Post-Modern Ethnography: From Document of the Occult to Occult Document," in *Writing Culture: The Poetics and Politics of Ethnography,* ed. James Clifford and George Marcus (Berkeley: University of California Press, 1986), 126.

5. Edward Said, *Orientalism* (New York: Random House, 1979).

6. Tyler, "Post-Modern Ethnography," 126.

7. For an interesting and useful survey of the literature on the cinematic representation of ethnics and minorities, see Allen L. Woll and Randall M. Miller, eds., *Ethnic and Racial Images in American Film and Television: Historical Essays and Bibliography* (New York: Garland, 1987).

8. Donald W. Rowland, *History of the Office of the Coordinator of Inter-American Affairs* (Washington: Government Printing Office, 1947), 74, 68.

9. Bosley Crowther, *"That Night in Rio," New York Times,* March 10, 1949, 21.

10. For a popular assessment of the power of the cinema as democratic propaganda for the American way of life in South America, see, from the many possible examples, Florence Horn, *"Formidavel, Fabulosissimo," Harper's Magazine* 184 (December 1941): 59–64. Horn glowingly describes how well a young Brazilian and her housewife "friends" understand and recognize "America" because of their constant exposure to U.S. films. After reading the following sentence, one wonders whether Orson Welles might have also read this piece before setting off on his CIAA-sponsored Brazilian project in 1942: "He [the Brazilian boy] returns home, almost without exception, to tell his friends that it's all true—and even more so" (60). For self-assessments of the power and efficacy of the Good Neighbor Policy, see, in particular, Nelson Rockefeller, "Fruits of the Good Neighbor Policy," *New York Times Magazine,* May 14, 1944, 15, and "Will We Remain Good Neighbors After the War? Are We Killing Our Own Markets by Promoting Industrialization in Latin America?" *Saturday Evening Post,* November 6, 1943, 16–17.

11. See Allen L. Woll, *The Latin Image in American Film* (Los Angeles: UCLA Latin American Center Publication, 1977) and Gaizka S. de Usabel, *The High Noon of American Films in Latin America* (Ann Arbor: UMI Research Press, 1982).

12. Woll, *The Latin Image in American Film,* p. 33.

13. See Lester D. Friedman, ed., *Unspeakable Images: Ethnicity and the American Cinema* (Urbana & Chicago: University of Illinois Press, 1991), pp. 274–76.

14. As does Allen Woll's analysis of this period in *The Latin Image in American Film* (and a number of other texts). In particular, Woll praises the "unheard of" cultural sensitivity of RKO's *Flying Down to Rio* (1933), a film that featured Dolores del Rio as a Carioca enchantress and Rio de Janeiro as a city defined by its infinite romantic possibilities and as the South American meeting place of new United States communication technologies and capital: airplanes for Southern travel, telegraphs for speedy communication, records and movies for music and romance. See Sergio Augusto, "Hollywood Looks at Brazil: From Carmen Miranda to *Moonraker,*" in *Brazilian Cinema,* ed. Randall Johnson and Robert Stam (Austin: University of Texas Press, 1988), 352–61.

15. See Miriam Hansen on the Valentino legend in "Pleasure, Ambivalence, Identification: Valentino and Female Spectatorship," *Cinema Journal* 25 (Summer 1986): 6–32.

16. Del Rio's Hollywood filmography includes, among other titles, *What Price Glory?* (1926, d. Walsh); *The Loves of Carmen* (1927, d. Walsh); *Ramona* (1928, d. Carewe); *The Red Dance* (1928, d. Walsh); *The Trail of '98* (1929, d. Brown); *Evangeline* (1929, d. Carewe); *The Bird of Paradise* (1932, d. Vidor), *Flying Down to Rio*

(1933, d. Freeland); *Wonder Bar* (1934, d. Bacon); *Madame DuBarry* (1934, d. Dieterle); *In Caliente* (1935, d. Bacon); *The Lancer Spy* (1937, d. Ratoff); and *Journey into Fear* (1941, d. Foster). In *Journey into Fear,* del Rio worked closely with Orson Welles (the first director of the film), with whom she had previously collaborated in the Mercury Theater production *Father Hidalgo* (1940) and during the production of *Citizen Kane* (1941).

17. Carlos Fuentes, "El Rostro de la Escondida," in *Dolores del Rio,* ed. Luis Gasca (San Sebastian, Spain: 24th Festival Internacional de Cine, 1976), 10; my translation.

18. Homi K. Bhabha, "Signs Taken for Wonders: Questions of Ambivalence and Authority under a Tree Outside Delhi, May 1917," in *Race, Writing, and Difference,* ed. Henry Louis Gates, Jr. (Chicago: University of Chicago Press, 1986), 172.

19. For the best summary and analysis of Vélez's career, see Gabriel Ramirez, *Lupe Vélez: la mexicana gue escupía fuego* (Mexico City: Cineteca Nacional, 1986).

20. See Homi K. Bhabha's discussion of this process in "The Other Question . . . ," *Screen* 24:6 (1983): 18–36.

21. Between 1940 and her death in 1955, Miranda made fourteen films: ten for Twentieth Century–Fox, one for United Artists, two for MGM, and one for Paramount. The Fox "cycle," between 1940–1946, consisted of *Down Argentine Way* (1940, d. Cummings); *That Night in Rio* (1941, d. Cummings); *Weekend in Havana* (1941, d. Lang); *Springtime in the Rockies* (1942, d. Cummings); *The Gang's All Here* (1943, d. Berkeley); *Four Jills in a Jeep* (1944, d. Seiter); *Greenwich Village* (1944, d. Lang); *Something for the Boys* (1944, d. Seiter); *Doll Face* (1946, d. Seiter); and *If I'm Lucky* (1946, d. Seiter).

22. See Rodolfo Konder, "The Carmen Miranda Museum: The Brazilian Bombshell Is Still Box Office in Rio," *Americas* 34:5 (1982): 17–21. In a review of *The Streets of Paris,* Harry C. Pringle wrote in 1939 that "[the opening] was a pleasant but not an exciting evening until, at approximately 10 o'clock, six young men appeared on the stage and were followed by a vibrant young woman wearing an exotic dress and a turban hat with bananas, peaches, pears and other fruitstand wares on it. . . . But the magic of her appeal lay in the degree to which she seemed to be having an enormously good time: that, and in the implication that she loved everybody in general and all men in particular"; cited by Cassio Emmanuel Barsante, *Carmen Miranda* (Rio de Janeiro: Ed. Europa, 1985), 12.

23. See Douglas Gomery, *The Hollywood Studio System* (New York: St. Martin's Press, 1986), 76–100.

24. Among others, see, for example, the *Variety* reviews of her Fox films—especially of *Down Argentine Way* (October 9, 1940), *Springtime in the Rockies* (November 24, 1937), and *That Night in Rio* (March 12, 1941)—which specifically comment upon the weakness of the romance narratives and the strength of her musical comedic performances.

25. See the *New York Post,* November 30, 1955; cited by Allen L. Woll, *The Hollywood Musical Goes to War* (Chicago: Nelson Hall, 1983), 114–15. According to Woll, Fox encouraged Miranda to learn English on a "fiscal" basis: a 50 cent raise for each word she added to her vocabulary. Miranda's quoted response again subverts the intended effect of Fox's integrationist efforts: "I know p'raps one hondred words— preety good for Sous American girl, no? Best I know ten English words: men, men, men, men, and monee, monee, monee, monee, monee, monee." According to Cassio Emmanuel Barsante, one of Miranda's most assiduous biographers and fans, "after living less than a year in the United States, Carmen had learned to speak English correctly, but started to take advantage of her accent for comic effect," *Carmen Miranda,* p. 188.

26. Full-page advertisement for Piel's Light Beer in the New York *Daily Mirror,* July 25, 1947: "A lighting flash along Broadway means Carmen Miranda! That Luscious, well-peppered dish! She glitters like a sequin, with her droll accent and spirited dances. And Carmen goes for Piel's—with all its sparkle and tang! 'I tell everyone I know to DREENK Piel's' she exclaims."

27. Miranda died at the age of forty-four, of a heart attack, on August 5, 1955, after taping a television program with Jimmy Durante. By this time—after a series of less than memorable screen appearances, alcohol and drug abuse, and a nervous breakdown in 1954—Miranda's presence had waned considerably. Although she was still a recognizable star, she had begun to work far more for television than for the cinema.

28. Special issue of *Time,* July 11, 1988.

A "Global" (Postnational) Future?

Jonathan Rosenbaum

Multinational Pest Control: Does American Cinema Still Exist?

Independence Day, *the first election-year motion picture to receive the endorsement of both major party Presidential candidates, opened to national acclaim on 2 July 1996, the day that alien spacecraft were first sighted. "I recommend it," President Bill Clinton told a crowd the next morning. Hillary, Bill and Chelsea Clinton watched the incineration of the White House on 2 July from the scene of the crime. They were joined by Dean Devlin and Roland Emmerich, who produced, directed and wrote the film, and by the film Chief Executive, Bill Pullman, who sat next to his real-life counterpart. President Clinton comforted his daughter when she took fright at the obliteration of her home; soon after, the on-screen President would comfort his daughter when her mother, who had been away from the White House on business, died from the effects of the blast that levelled Los Angeles.*

Hollywood and Washington, twin capitals of the American empire and seats of its international political. economy, collaborated to promote the movie that filmed their destruction.
—Michael Rogin, *Independence Day* (1998)[1]

Motion pictures are the most conspicuous of all American exports. They do not lose their identity. They betray their nationality and country of origin. . . . They are demonstrably the single greatest factors in the Americanization of the world and as such fairly may be called the most important and significant of America's exported products.
—The Motion Picture Producers and Distributors Association (1928)[2]

When did American action blockbusters stop being American? It's hard to define a precise point when this happened in the two decades separating the genocidal adventures in George Lucas's *Star Wars* from those in Paul Verhoeven's *Starship Troopers* (a much more interesting and provocative film), but the differences in national pedigree are palpable, even when it comes to an ostensible and ratified flag-waver like *Independence Day*. Despite the facts that the latter film all but busts a gut in declaring its national credentials and that *Starship Troopers* is a creative adaptation of an all-American novel (by Robert A. Heinlein), was consciously modeled on Hollywood World War II features (as was much of *Star Wars*), and even boasts a hyperbolically all-American cast that could have sprung full blown out of a camp classic of Aryan physiognomy like Howard Hawks's *Red Line 7000*, the only state that either can be said to honor or reflect is one of drifting statelessness.

What I mean is that if the alien bugs from Verhoeven's movie wanted to learn what American life and culture was like in 1977, *Star Wars* would serve as a useful and appropriate object of study. It would tell them, among other things, something about the video games children played, the voyeuristic distance of most of the population towards warfare, some of the puritannical attitudes in 1977 America regarding sex, a certain amount about the attitudes of middle-class American children towards both pets and servants, and a good deal about the economic power of teen and preteen culture and the sense of entitlement that went with it. But if they wanted to know what American life was like in 1997, *Starship Troopers* wouldn't have nearly as much to tell them, and *Independence Day* would arguably tell them even less about American life in 1996—except, perhaps, for how little life in the remainder of the world is allowed to penetrate our national borders. (Sigificantly, every time another country needs to be represented in abbreviated form in *Independence Day*, a stereotypical image dating back to the fifties is reverted to.) The confidence of the Motion Picture Producers and Distributors Association seventy years ago is hard to imagine in the multinational globalized money markets of the nineties—in contradistinction to the hooplah reported by Michael Rogin, all of which seems contrived to convince us that an anonymous piece of nostalgic uplift like *Independence Day* is as American as apple pie.

Maybe it is in some way, but whether or not the apple pie served in McDonald's strictly qualifies as "American"—at least for an everyday customer in Beijing—is quite another matter; and whether it's as quintessentially and as exclusively American as we habitually think it is also warrants a certain amount of healthy skepticism. Back in the late sixties, when my youngest brother was living in Nairobi, Kenya, he spent part of his time conversing with members of the Red Guard who were stationed there, and one of the topics of their conversation was the nationality of Coca-Cola. The Red Guard soldiers, who liked Coca-Cola, were convinced that it was a product of Kenya; they refused to believe that a corrupt capitalist and imperialist nation such as the United States could have produced it.

My point here is that what we—and the Motion Picture Producers and Distributors Association in 1928—tend to assume automatically is American may not necessarily signify the same thing in the same way to other inhabitants of the planet, especially now that the capital controlling the flow of so-called American products is just as likely to come from somewhere else. The question of a film's national identity, which could be posed with a lot more simplicity in 1928, is often not so simple nowadays when the same patterns of life created by capitalism in different corners of the world may wind up mattering a great deal more than the particular distinguishing features of nationality. A few years back, a Peruvian film critic in Chicago told me that the contemporary film that had the most to say to him about life in contemporary Peru was Hou Hsiao-hsien's *Goodbye South, Goodbye,* and the fact that he was telling me this in Chicago rather than in Lima or Tapei seemed significant as well—along with the fact that the film is best known under its English title outside the Chinese-speaking world. It's equally pertinent that Wong Kar-wai's *Happy Together*—a film about Hong Kong with an American title derived from a Frank Zappa song—is set almost entirely in Buenos Aires.

Manoel De Oliveira's Portuguese-French *Voyage to the Beginning of the World,* a meditation on the various differences between being Portuguese and being French, uses an Italian actor (Marcello Mastroianni in his last performance) playing De Oliveira to preside over these reflections. Manuel Poirier's French road movie *Western* focuses on a Catalan Spaniard and a Russian immigrant of Italian origins in a small section of Brittany. Even more typical of art movies of the mid-nineties is *The End of Violence,* a French-German-American coproduction with an American subject, setting, and writer, a German director (Wim Wenders), and an Anglo-American cast. For even more recent films, one may well ask which is more modern and contemporary in feeling: Pedro Almodóvar's *All About My Mother,* which is all in Spanish (although it deals with a stage production of Tennessee Williams's *A Streetcar Named Desire,* and borrows separate portions of its plot from Mankiewicz's *All About Eve* and Cassavetes's *Opening Night*), or Luís Galvão Teles's *Women (Elles)*—a Portugese film that has only French dialogue to accommodate its international cast of Carmen Maura, Miou-Miou, Marisa Berenson, Kathe Keller, Guesh Patti, and Joaquim De Alminda? For all the Europudding limitations of *Elles,* I would still be inclined to argue that it's the Almodóvar film that's relatively out of date.

All these movies help to show not only how much the world is shrinking and interfacing, but also how much the idea of national cinema that we've been carrying around for so long is beginning to seem shopworn and inadequate to the films actually being made. And if we except big-budget American movies from this trend we're not being entirely candid with ourselves either about how these movies are being financed and made or how they're being received in other parts of the world. *Star Wars, Independence Day,* and *Starship Troopers* may, to varying degrees, be regarded as American products in most places, but how much these respective movies reflect contemporary and everyday American life is another matter entirely. The fact that they're shown dubbed in many non–English-speaking countries already removes one substantial layer of what we automatically and in many cases unconsciously perceive as their Americanness. And if we factor in the sort of ideological alterations and abridgements that frequently come with subtitling,[3] some of which likely carry over into dubbing as well, it starts to become obvious that some of the traits in these movies that we routinely regard as American may not necessarily be regarded in the same fashion in other corners of the globe. (Western visitors to Asia often observe uses of printed English as decor rather than as concrete messages in such places as shop signs and taxicab upholstery, much as Chinese and Japanese characters are often used decoratively in western countries. In keeping with this practice, it appears that in some cases what most westerners perceive as English might be perceived as simply "western" by some Asians.)

All three movies might be loosely perceived as odes to American values set in the fanciful future mixed with the half-remembered, mid-century past, but this similarity is only skin deep, and not only because Verhoeven hails from the Netherlands and Roland Emmerich, the director and co-writer of *Independence Day*, hails from Germany. (*Starship Troopers* and *Independence Day* are probably even less Dutch and German than they are American.) The earlier space opera was made at a time when American pop cinema still mainly belonged to Americans; now it belongs mainly to global markets and overseas investors, and because so-called "American cinema" is the brand name that sells best in those markets and for those investors, that's what it says on the label. But what's inside the package is something else, and properly speaking, its existential identity is multinational, not national—which in thematic terms involves subtraction more than addition. Maybe that's why loss of identity was the very theme of *Face/Off*—another recent multinational action special, and one that perhaps marked the end of John Woo's career as a director of Hong Kong action films.

Directors who hail from countries deemed marginal in relation to the international film marketplace probably know this better than anyone. Especially for someone as talented, as singular, and as prescient as Verhoeven, being considered a Dutch filmmaker immediately becomes a commercial liability. There isn't even the consolation of the "one director per country" principle that seems to rule the discourse of most American film critics writing about foreign films, which appears to constitute part of what keeps Almodóvar, Begnini, the Kaurismaki brothers, Kitano, and Von Trier afloat as cult figures in American culture. Yet the moment Verhoeven becomes a Hollywood director, he doesn't so much exchange one nationality for another; rather, he hides, dilutes, and/or dissolves his Dutchness into something that calls itself American only because that makes it easier to sell. Where he differs from someone like Emmerich as an essentially stateless director is his more satirical and sardonic edge that he shares with the late Stanley Kubrick, an attitude that on occasion profitably confuses gloating with jeering, celebration with ridicule, and, most importantly, Americanism with anti-Americanism, meanwhile sustaining an elegant clarity of line. And the anti-Americanism he's selling becomes less a portrait of a country than a portrait of whoever buys his product—a look, maybe a sense of entitlement, conceivably even a style, but not exactly a way of life.

This has only a superficial resemblance to the process by which directors ranging from Chaplin to Hitchcock, Maurice Tourneur to Rene Clair, Stroheim to Lang or Preminger, and Lubitsch to Wilder transformed themselves into American filmmakers, because in each of these cases it was by superimposing a view of the United States from the outside over a view from the inside. In Verhoeven and Emmerich, among others, there's no longer a view from the inside— perhaps because Americans are by now as dependent on external views of America as everyone else; and even the view from the outside, as I've already suggested, is more of an idea of America that has international currency than anything else, a form of promotion more than a form of observation. Like the lingua franca English the currently circles the globe via the Internet, Verhoeven's style functions less like the front line of a particular invading army than like a streamlined highway others can travel down, and maybe even a destroyer of nationality for that reason rather than a purveyor of it.

Can we relate this style, in fact, to the protest that disrupted the World Trade Organization's Seattle summit during the last month of the millennium, and to the impromptu coalition that made it possible? The progressive shrinking of the planet and the growing irrelevancy of nationality to common interests and even common experiences (compared with those of class, race, and ethnicity, for instance) certainly suggest that Verhoeven's evocation of the future may have more to do with global trends than with Heinlein's original cold war vision.

———————

It's difficult to make hasty judgements about paradigmatic shifts of the kind that I'm trying to describe because many of the results are likely to be extremely varied as well as unforeseeable. I know someone who happened to be with the experimental filmmaker, critic, and programmer Jonas Mekas in 1970 when the word came that Nasser had just died, and according to her, his first response to this news was to ask himself, "Is this a good thing or a bad thing for cinema?" Similarly, I don't know if the fading and blurring of national cinema as a viable concept is good or bad for cinema, but I strongly suspect it's both, which makes things especially confusing.

In some circumstances it may be bad for art and good for commerce, but in other circumstances it might be the reverse, because surely there are times when highways are more desirable for art than invading armies. When the British Film Institute decided to commission a series of videos about film history a few years ago, the decision to get certain filmmakers to recount the stories of national cinemas played havoc with my own training as a devotee of Henri Langlois's Cinémathèque programming, where cinema itself was often the only true nationality and the Tower of Babel somehow provided a more worthy model than those bureaucratic inventions called national cinemas that came afterwards. My ambivalence about *Starship Troopers* as entertainment and as art is a direct function of this uncertainty.

I'm also entering somewhat treacherous waters by discussing the overall impressions of audiences in both the United States and abroad—a subject that no one knows very much about, least of all the so-called experts. (Once one starts considering the self-fulfilling prophecies and voodoo science that rule test marketing and the routinely doctored figures offered by studios regarding weekend grosses and the relative rankings of new movies, most of the "expertise" offered by film industry analysts is little more than an extension of studio propaganda.) But it's the even vaguer impressions fostered by commentators about what "American" means that I feel need to be questioned and challenged. Just as many of the would-be prophets who proclaim that video is replacing film across the globe aren't even factoring in most of the countries that have found ways of eluding the domination of Hollywood through quota systems and other means, we tend to conclude that what we and foreigners mean by "American" is invariably the same thing when in practice this often isn't the case. Typically, the habit of western media to call the 1989 demonstrations of Chinese students in Beijing "pro-democracy" seemed to stem from the Cold War reflex of assuming that everything that wasn't communist necessarily had to be pro-democracy when in fact it appears that part of what the students had in mind was protesting government corruption. By the same token, when Americans discuss the paradigm of television in relation to movies across the globe, they often forget how much of television elsewhere tends to be state-run, with positive as well as negative consequences that are rarely considered in the United States.

By national cinema, I mean a cinema that expresses something of the soul of the nation that it comes from: the lifestyle, the consciousness, the attitudes. By virtue of coming more from an American individual than either *Starship Troopers* or *Independence Day*, *Star Wars I—The Phantom Menace* surely qualifies as being more American in this respect, if only because its auteur has more power and independence—a fact that in this case may partially serve as a commercial disadvantage. (Even more alarmingly, it may serve in this instance as an artistic disadvantage as well: Lucas becomes freer than either Verhoeven or Emmerich to become obsessed with digital effects at the expense of his story, and to consciously or inadvertently recreate the wooden performances of westerns and SF serials that he saw on TV as a boy.) Lucas may depend on multinational markets for much of his merchandising, but in the realm of SF blockbusters he still has an autonomy denied to his competitors. And outside the realm of SF blockbusters, it might be argued that Clint Eastwood has a comparable creative freedom; the fact that he isn't obliged to test-market his movies with preview audiences already places him outside the multinational trends I've been discussing, and insofar as he's relatively free to express his own tastes and inclinations, his movies could be called every bit as American as those of some of his predecessors, like John Ford and Howard Hawks.

For that matter, I wouldn't want to quibble with anyone who argues that *Starship Troopers* or *Independence Day* are American in the same way—or to the same degree—that French fries are French. What I mean is something more delicate and complex—a matter of

substance more than packaging, yielded to us by most national cinemas over the past century, but no longer available to us in most
multinational blockbusters. For a movie to belong to a particular
national cinema often means that it's likelier to have a stronger
impact on its home turf, as the recent American art movie *In the
Company of Men* did: in France, the same film was cursorily dismissed by the two leading-critical monthly film magazines, *Positif*
and *Cahiers du Cinema*, while at the Viennale in Austria its impact
seemed minimal alongside other current American films the same
year, including even Joe Dante's made-for-cable *The Second Civil
War*. I suspect this is because taboos against discussing capitalism
critically, which gives *In the Company of Men* much of its subversive
impact in the United States, don't exist in the same fashion in
Europe. But a pseudo-American farrago like *Starship Troopers* was
likely appreciated (and avoided) for the same reasons by outsiders
across the planet: spiffy special effects, severed limbs, and lots of
nonstop action.

Superficial enjoyment isn't really the issue. I like bug-crunching
as well as the next fellow—although this movie dishes out more of
it than I could possibly want—and there are undeniable kicks to be
had from Verhoeven's sneering use of recruitment ads, his handsome styling of interstellar navigation, and his abbreviated glimpses
of future cityscapes. The point is that calling this and other expensive action-explosion specials "American" only confuses us that
much more about our already alienated and scattered self-images.
And to assume so cavalierly that this is exactly what teenage boys
everywhere are itching for is to overlook the heaps of contempt for
that demographic constituency that this movie dispenses every
chance it gets. A lot of grownup reviewers wondered whether the
jeering satire directed at this crowd would sail right past them, but
if the Sunday crowd I saw *Starship Troopers* with at Chicago's 600
North Michigan was any indication, the laughter and applause were
both sporadic and laced with hints of self-contempt, and the overall enthusiasm seemed to wane towards the end. It seems to me
that we were all too eager to share the movie's disdain for its target
audience ("A new kind of enemy, a new kind of war," said some of the
ads—as if alien insects and fifty-year-old weaponry were nineties

innovations), just as we're much too docile about accepting the bloodlust as strictly or specifically American.

Consider what Verhoeven says about *Starship Troopers* in the movie's press book: "When I came to the United States I felt that initially I wouldn't know enough about American culture to make movies that accurately reflected American society. I felt that I would make lot of mistakes because I would not be aware of things such as expressions and social behavior.

"I felt I could make science fiction movies because I wouldn't have to worry about breaking any rules of American society. Science fiction reflects those rules but does not represent them." From this point of view, both *RoboCop* and *Total Recall* present successive steps toward *Starship Troopers,* not to mention wacko fantasies like *Basic Instinct* and *Showgirls* (which are science fiction in spirit if not in substance). All five films project different versions of the same dark irony, the same hyperbolic comic-strip iconography, and the same partially comic and satirical conception of overblown characters without depth. And arguably it was the awkward yet provocative attempt of *Showgirls* to say something about America—Hollywood in particular—that spelled its commercial doom: it's a film that fundamentally said, "We're all whores, aren't we?" and the American public answered, in effect, "Speak for yourself."[4] *Starship Troopers* modified that statement to read, "We're all stupid apes and cannon fodder, aren't we?" and this time audiences all over the world, more accustomed to receiving such epithets as natural and everyday parts of their action kicks, were somewhat more prone to agree (or disagree, depending mainly on gender and age group).

But whether this movie conveys the desired euphoria to potential warmongers, American and otherwise—at least to anything like the same degree that *Star Wars* and its sequels do—is another matter. Wiping out entire planets in the Lucas scheme of things is clean, bloodless, fun that never threatens the camaraderie between fuzzy creatures and humans who trade affectionate wisecracks while zapping enemies from afar, even when it gets ennobled by mythical conceits derived from Joseph Campbell. (In *The Phantom Menace,* wisecracks were reduced to an absolute minimum and humor was mainly restricted to a digitally generated overgrown lizard with a

Jamaican accent named Jar Jar Binks whose principal function was to tell the audience when it was okay to laugh; most of the warfare, moreover, was restricted to earlier forms of combat stretching back to medieval weaponry. But the overall bloodlessness of the warfare remained a constant.) Verhoevian genocide, by contrast, assumes no such pretensions; it's a messy affair involving extensive dismemberment on both sides, loads of blood and goo, loss of privacy and comfort, and only a modicum of emotional satisfaction—in short, none of the media pleasures offered by demolishing Bagdad. Most of us Americans probably know as little about Iraqis as the starship troopers do about the alien bugs they fight, and the topography of the bug planet, as Dave Kehr pointed out in the *New York Daily News*, "suggests the scene of the Gulf War," but there the similarities end—especially after one factors in the anachronistic weaponry and forms of combat in Verhoeven's movie, most of it derived from forties and fifties war films, and the power of the enemy to retaliate.

The issues that are being fought over are hardly the same either, however rudimentary they appear in both cases. When Luke Skywalker loses his relatives to alien villains, we're invited to spend at least a few seconds of commiseration with him to validate his desire for payback. When the parents of Johnny Rico (Casper Van Dien) get nuked, on the other hand—as part of twelve million earth casualties, no less—what we've already seen of this pair makes them only slightly less repellent than the bugs who wipe them out, so the tragedy and outrage are strictly rhetorical. If this is the life on earth worth protecting and risking one's neck and limbs for—and just about the only glimpses of private life that we see are restricted to that yammering couple in their home—then the coed showers and twenty minutes allotted for sex between battles, two rare perks of committed army service, are made to seem nominally more attractive. (The lead characters' home base is "Buenos Aires"—a dimly defined setting with no Latino traces whose loss is about as wrenching in this movie's scheme of things as stubbing one's toe.)

The militarized fascist utopia, presented mainly in the form of interactive recruiting commercials, is presented so sketchily that its main virtue ironically seems to be a leveling of class difference for the volunteer soldiers, the only citizens allowed to vote—though who or what any of them might vote for is anyone's guess.

Paradoxically, the genuine Americanism of Heinlein's tiresome 1959 novel is a good deal more international than the ersatz Americanism of Verhoeven's movie, but that's because thirty-eight years of American history—including the cold war and its aftermath and the passage from both nationalism and internationalism to multinationalism—separate these two versions of The Good Fight. In the novel, the fighting youth of Earth's galactic empire seen in boot camp includes the son of a Japanese colonel working on his Black Belt and two Germans with duelling scars; Johnnie Rico himself, also known as Juan, is the son of a Filipino tycoon, and turns out in one of the novel's delayed revelations to be black. The movie's boot camp, by contrast, is basically American white bread with a few multicultural trimmings—a reflection of neither the fifties nor the nineties but an incoherent mishmash of the two—and it's also coed, which is presumably supposed to reflect the future. (The novel also featured women pilots, but not unisexual showers and sleeping quarters.)

As critic H. Bruce Franklin rightly points out in his 1980 book *Robert A. Heinlein: America as Science Fiction*, Heinlein's "right-wing" militarism actually corresponds to the liberal ideology of John F. Kennedy, elected president the year after the novel was published, in anticipating the creation of an elite corps like the Green Berets; Kennedy's signature "Ask not what your country can do for you" speech also seems to come straight out of the novel. (Written as Heinlein's thirteenth juvenile novel for Scribner's—a series celebrating the conquest of space whose first filmic incarnation was the 1950 *Destination Moon*, adapted from *Rocket Ship Galileo*—the book was rejected for its unapologetic and extreme militarism, then published as an "adult" novel by Putnam. The quaint 1959 notion of shielding teenage boys from this sort of thing—minus most of the graphic gore in the movie, which is now aimed at them—is another indication of how much we changed in thirty-eight years.)

Franklin also points out that Heinlein's novel, as steeped in cold war ideology as his 1951 *The Puppet Masters*—and in striking contrast to his neo-hippie and neo-communist *Stranger in a Strange Land* (1961)—posits the alien bugs as Chinese communists and another humanoid race that's omitted in the movie, the "Skinnies," as Russian communists. (The novel is in fact crammed with pompous, didactic lectures about the communist menace and the errors of Karl Marx, most of them linked to the "hive" mentality of the bugs—which makes it all the more ironic that the classless military utopia proffered as an ideal alternative seems no less socialist and totalitarian. The movie only intensifies this paradox by showing how impossible it is for Johnnie to speak to his girlfriend or parents on the video phone without all his coed bunkmates being present.)

Pictorially speaking, the bugs in the movie on their home planet recall the giant ants of *Them!* (another cold war allegory, 1954) and the attacking natives in *Zulu* (1964). But ideologically speaking, they're boring cyphers without any discernible language, culture, architecture, or technology (apart from their capacities to bomb Earth and suck out individual brains)—creatures of action storyboards rather than anyone's notion of a society. And, this being a Paul Verhoeven film, humanity doesn't fare much better, either onscreen or off.

NOTES

1. London: British Film Institute, 9.
2. Ibid., 73.
3. For an excellent introduction to this subject, see Mark Nornes, "For an Abusive Subtitling," *Film Quarterly* 52:3 (Spring 1999): 17–34.
4. Not quite all American viewers—or western viewers, for that matter—responded to *Showgirls* in quite this fashion. Two of the film's biggest defenders and champions are Jim Jarmusch and Jacques Rivette. In an interview in *Les Inrockuptibles* (no. 144, 1997), Rivette avowed that he'd seen *Starship Troopers* twice: "I like it very much, but I prefer *Showgirls*. *Showgirls* is one of the great American films of the past few years; it's Verhoeven's best American film and his most personal. It's also the one that's closest to his Dutch films" (my translation).

Janet Staiger

A Neo-Marxist Approach:
World Film Trade
and Global Culture Flows

The opening of Jean Renoir's *Grand Illusion* contrasts two great nation-states at war, but it also subtly undermines that struggle. As Charles Altman has pointed out in a valuable analysis of the film, the opposition between France and Germany, and their particular cultures of drink, music, and ideal women, is eliminated in the second scene of the movie. There the bourgeois and proletariat of each nation find common friendship, interests, and support in the middle of the strife. Marechal (Jean Gabin) is helped to cut his food; Captain de Boeldieu (Pierre Fresnay) and Captain von Rauffenstein (Erich von Stroheim) choose a neutral third language, English, in which to chat about mutual friends and relatives.[1]

As a participant in the 1930s French left politics, Renoir analyzes "the grand illusion" consistently with theorizing from the Communist Party of the era: the nation-state is not a progressive imagined community.[2] Rather its ideology is in the service of capitalism. The fundamental alliances are class, not nation. In fact, contemporary Marxist theory is not at odds with the general thrust of his thesis. Thus, the purpose of my essay is to reiterate Renoir's argument, but also to describe several important sophistications that Neo-Marxism offers to the understanding of world film trade and global culture flows. I shall be asking two questions:

1) How might we understand what causes what in what in world trade? and world production practices?

2) What are the consequent effects of that (and other causal factors) for global culture flows?

This latter question is of particular concern because the products flowing have both content and service characteristics. I shall need, thus, to address the concerns of "domination" of a so-called "national culture" and the "homogenization" of world culture as a consequence of world film trade. I shall also argue that since the early 1980s and certainly after the end of the cold war, it does not make sense to think about world trade on the basis of nation-state identities.

Three Models of the Flow of Products

Although world trade patterns have existed for centuries, in the last two hundred years capitalism has intensified its global activities.[3] Simultaneously, economic theories have been employed to explain and, often, to exploit the observations of the theories. I will briefly consider three current economic theories of product flow: 1) the international relations/neo-classical economics theory; 2) the traditional marxist theory; and 3) one neo-marxist theory known as "world-systems" theory.[4] This third position, I believe, provides a profound and useful rethinking of what is going on globally.

International relations/neo-classical economics assumes that international trade operates as a consequence of exchange between firms as buyers and sellers in nation-states in a situation of natural supply-and-demand equations. For the most efficient economics, this supply-and-demand equation should be left to operate without state interference since it should produce the most competitive consequences which should have the most beneficial results world wide. Eventually, the most efficient producers will secure competitive advantage. Trade restrictions are only justifiable on the short-term to reduce local unemployment; to create diversification and self-sufficiency, again on the short-term; and to protect a "infant industry" until it "grows up." It was just that sort of rationale that was used to justify trade restrictions for some European film industries during the 1920s and then again after World War II.

The *traditional marxist* criticism of the international relations/ neo-classical theory is that neo-classical economics assumes a static world and does not recognize already-existing economic inequities. Moreover, unlike neo-classical economics, traditional marxist theory does not assume efficiency is the ultimate goal of nation-states. It presumes politics and power are embedded in the actions of nation-states as economic agents. Traditional marxist economics finds central to its analysis the activities of multinational corporations which seek to extract surplus value where they may. Traditional marxist economics understands the creation of trade restrictions as methods by which nation-states, acting on behalf of the dominant class, attempt to secure advantages in the world market. Traditional marxist economics argues that it is not sensible to understand world trade after World War I as a world in which corporations produce products within and for a nation-state; advanced capitalists operate in a world market dominated by multinational corporations.

World-systems theory, most notably formulated by Immanuel Wallerstein in the mid 1970s, is a neo-marxist economic theory that reconsiders the facts of world trade. World-systems theory sees the world "as developed and underdeveloped states, or zones, the interaction of which, through unequal exchange processes, produces a global core-periphery division of labor."[5] As Albert Bergesen argues, it is important, however, to recognize the initial exploitation of power in creating the inequalities between the core and peripheries. The European–U.S. colonial expansion subjugated other nations which then made possible the unequal exchanges that have organized world trade: "In short, trade, unequal exchange, or long commodity chains do not construct the core-periphery structure of power and domination, but the core-periphery domination relation makes possible the surplus extraction and the directionality of its flow—that is, makes unequal exchange possible and reproduces it over the centuries."[6] Part of the original power relation is also the ideologies that informed, promoted, and justified those nation-states' behaviors. Thus, culture as well as power is bound up in creating and maintaining these relations.

This version of neo-marxism hopes to replace the individualism implicit in both international relations/neo-classical economics and traditional marxism which tend to represent events in terms of nation-states or multinational corporations as intentional agents. World-systems theory advocates an analysis that emphasizes advanced capitalism as a global structure enacting a power arrangement producing and reproducing the core-periphery arrangement, the unequal distribution of divisions of labor, and the asymmetrical flow of capital, commodities, and cultural products.

Intriguingly, of course—if one is even something of a dialectician—this theoretical representation helps to explain an important change developing since the early 1970s: the so-called *deterritorialization* of capitalism. Although multinational corporations have existed for at least one hundred years, the 24-hour stock market exchange and electronic transfer of funds has moved capitalism into the supra-national realm.

I would suggest that if one starts to rethink the history of global capitalism, it becomes obvious that the nation-state has been a useful imaginary community only *for a while* for capitalism. As capitalism now has less need of the nation-state as an agent for its goals (the dynamics of the core-periphery are well entrenched for maximum exploitation), and is perhaps even being hindered by the older ideology of nationalism in its process of extracting surplus value, global capitalism is discarding the nation-state as a significant conceptual entity and replacing it with other imaginary communities. I shall discuss below the importance of identity-theory to this neo-marxist analysis. What *is* known is that a Post-Fordist mode of production is also arriving to facilitate capitalism's advancement to its post-nation-state stage.

Post-Fordism and Neo-Marxism

Post-Fordism is described in opposition to Fordism, a term used to detail the mode of production operating in Euro–U.S. economies the past couple centuries. Fordism is a system of mass production eventually permitting mass consumption. As Kevin Robins describes Fordism, certain problems have lead to a crisis: rising wages and declining productivity, overcapacity and market saturation, competition from low-wage countries, increasing costs for public services. Post-Fordism, or Neo-Fordism as Robins prefers, is a mode of production promoting "flexible specialization." Features of it include: "decentralized and disseminated production," "design and product mix aimed at niche markets," "demassified enterprises [that] abandon economies of scale for economies of scope," and "workers [who] supposedly assume new skills and responsibilities and a new sense of autonomy."[7] This Neo-Fordism appears to be played out in space—or at least new spaces. Neo-Fordist capitalism appears to be "decentralized" and "disseminated." Zones of production exist, and they are controlled by "nerve centres in the cybernetic grids" (148) of financial information systems.

Thus, Robins is able to explain the seeming contradiction that world economies are becoming both global *and* local at the same time. Capitalism as an economic structure and mode of production transcends traditional [e.g., nation-state] notions of location to become "deterritorialized and delocalized," "hypermobile and hyper-flexible" (149). "These new forms of spatial deployment very much reflect the changing organizational structure of accumulation, and, particularly, new patterns of combined corporate integration and disintegration" (149). Meanwhile, physical production and consumption increasingly take on local, or more individualized, flavors. This hyperflexibility is driven by and permits specialization. Niche marketing can exploit more particularized life-styles, linking together, for example, Euro–U.S. classes along taste culture lines, rather than by national-identity configurations. Selling is not to a mass but to many subgroups with particular lifestyles and tastes.

In terms of the global film business, world-systems theory and neo-Fordism are particularly powerful theories to explain what has been occurring. Anyone attempting to figure out to what "nation" any major film conglomerate "belongs" is really attempting the impossible—*and the unnecessary*. But it is possible to locate local zones of media production financed by international capital: Hollywood being the most obvious but also Hong Kong, Bombay, Egypt, Brazil, and Japan. The fact that in the past ten years several movie firms in the United States have had significant portions of their stock purchased by firms seemingly from other nation-states such as Australia, Japan, and Italy proves this point. None of the "U.S." firms appealed to the United States government to protect them from the acquisitions. Why? Because the firms recognized that international capitalism provides excellent profit-making opportunities. Capital has been world-capital for many years now. Moreover, the stock acquisitions and infusions of capital backing did not effect the zones of production. Hollywood remains a dominant conceptual nerve center for producing the sorts of entertainment labeled "Hollywood" before and after the acquisitions. As I shall expand upon below, trying to figure out what constitutes "American" cinema—either by locating the ownership of the firms or by describing the features of a national cultural product—is no longer a worthwhile project (and may not have been for some time). Knowing what constitutes Hollywood or Hong Kong cinema is, however, meaningful.

As a way of organizing thinking and behavior, nation-states are not going to go away for some while. However, some neo-marxists have asserted new ways to imagine the world in the face of these changes in capitalism. One model that I have found particularly stimulating is proposed by Arjun Appardurai. Appardurai proposes thinking about these issues on the basis of five "scapes."[8] The first three are reconfigurations of the traditional "base" of classical marxism; the second two replace the "superstructure." Scape #1 is the *ethnoscape:* "the landscapes of persons who constitute the shifting world," the people who are the work force of the world. Appardurai emphasizes that the world labor force is now mobile, partially from necessity. Immigrants, exiles, tourists, and refugees are a fact of the modern work force—witness the changing demographics in France, the United States, and many other Euro–U.S. nations. Scape #2 is the *technoscape:* "the flow of information and mechanical equipment" across former boundaries. Scape #3 is the *finanscape:* the flows of money. Beyond these three are two more scapes, both in the realm of ideology. The *mediascape* is scape #4: the dispersion of abilities to produce information and images; scape #5 is the *ideoscape:* also images but those images directly related to political agendas.

Appardurai's model is especially handy since it permits him to point out that due to the speed of various flows, disjunction among the five scapes is increasingly non-isomorphic. One example he dwells on, which is important for media historians, is the deterritorialization not only of capital but of peoples from "original homes." This movement creates new problems as individuals of various ethnicities, races, religions, and cultures are increasingly uprooted and placed into communication with other ethnicities, races, religions, and cultures. However, this deterritorialization also creates, he points out, new markets for "invented homelands," for "imagined communities" of "primordia," based on language or skin color or neighborhood or kinship (300–308) for both the "native" and the newcomer.

Moreover, unlike earlier waves of migration, these newcomers do not face the older problems of memory loss; the technoscapes and mediascapes of telephones, television, video recorders, and the internet provide means for continual communication and community reinforcement with the original family and neighbors, and even new contacts with other hitherto unknown members of those who might constitute the new imagined community of the migrant. One important area of study in communication history is how new technologies have permitted the subcultural dissemination of nondominant images—i.e, minority views within a nation-state but also nazi propaganda, apocalyptic theory, erotic materials—across nation-state boundaries, often in overt resistance to the national regulations. Where the flow is progressive materials into non-democratic countries, liberals and marxists alike applaud the event; when the flow helps terrorists or right-wing groups, we express deep concern. These facts of the technoscape and the mediascape and ideoscape cut both ways.

These facts of the ideoscape flows are also pertinent to the creation and maintenance of identities of people. Neo-marxist theory has been particularly recognized that it needs to understand how and which identities are created and reproduced. Through heritages from the work of Louis Althusser, Pierre Bourdieu, Michel de Certeau, Raymond Williams, E. P. Thompson, Stuart Hall, and many others, the scholarly movement labeled "cultural studies" in the United States and Britain has explored the ideological and cultural implications of how people think themselves. These identities and their implications for economic and political behavior constitute the philosophical sources for identity politics.[9]

The thrust of neo-marxist approaches to the question of what causes what in world trade and modes of production has been to take into account capitalism as an economic process affecting the construction and deconstruction of entities such as nation-states, multinational corporations, and identities, but also to recognize that a theory that does not account for contradictions in the process of history is fundamentally flawed. Moreover, neo-marxism has attempted to foreground an initial premise of marxism, and that is the potential for resistance by subordinated groups to identifying with the dominant. Power, ideology, and desire require being incorporated within the explanations of events. These premises are particularly important in understanding how a neo-marxism approach would respond to the second question that I am posing: What are the consequent effects of deterritorialized capitalism and neo-Fordism for global cultural flows?[10]

Global Culture Flows

I am not so sure that any one would be much concerned about global cultural flows if it were assumed that neo-classical economic theory is accurate. Then, one could simply say, well, people get want they want. It is simply democratic laws of supply and demand. However, the observation of an apparent "homogenization" of culture, usually also coupled with the belief that the homogenization is really an "Americanization" of culture, *and* the belief that the United States has used particular trade restrictions internally and trade behaviors externally to secure its world domination, is perceived as a threat.

Although the traditional marxist position aligns with such representations of oppression, hegemony, and imperialism, neo-marxist theory predicts and observes a more complex, contradictory situation. Yes, at one level a global flow moving from core to periphery exists, but so do significant countervening regional and local flows to which we must pay attention. Yes, Hollywood culture dominates some nation-state exhibition outlets, but that does not insure that individual audiences take up the materials in the same ways that peoples do in the United States. Yes, Hollywood culture is widely enjoyed, but it is not enjoyed in uniform ways even in the United States. The negotiation, appropriation, and resistance to any cultural product must be considered, according to neo-marxists, to understand, as Appardurai would phrase it, the ethnoscapes, mediascapes, and ideoscapes of global culture flows.

What I have been discussing so far has been fairly abstract. Here I would like to make four observations about contemporary global culture flows and analyze them from the neo-marxist approach that I have been describing.

1) *New technologies have altered the realities of consumer choices.*

In television studies, one hypothesis about consumer behavior during the network era in the United States has been the so-called "least objectionable programming" thesis. This proposition suggests that people do not so much actively choose to watch a particular program as they desire to watch television and turn on the least objectionable program out of the choices available. During periods of mass production and mass media, this might be said to be how many people behave. Media scholars think that in the United States during the 1920s through about 1950, moviegoing behavior functioned like that. People enjoyed movies as a medium, and while some theaters might attract them, basically, people went to whatever was playing. Of course movies had to be fundamentally satisfying at a general level, and audiences certainly had preferences, but exhibitors tried to cater to those various tastes by showing a *variety* of materials—news, cartoons, shorts, and one or two features from different genres. When broadcast television became a mass-media competitor with film after 1950, the three commercial networks in the United States and their audiences operated much the same way as the older film exhibition system. If one wanted to watch television, a choice was made among three programs. Analysis of audience ratings suggests that only occasionally do people go out of their way to schedule their lives so they do not miss a program.[11]

This mass-media situation has changed with the advent of video cassette recorders, satellite transmission, cable, and the internet. The available range of materials at a low (or competitive) price has exploded so that since the middle 1980s, the notion of "choice" really makes sense. "Narrow-casting" and "niche markets" are now realities. Moreover, several of the new technologies (VCRs, satellite transmissions, the internet) easily elude government restrictions, particularly in attempts to prevent nation-state boundaries from being breached. A major cause for the concerns in Europe regarding non-European produced materials is the real inability to enforce trade barriers even if they are legislated. Neo-marxism would note the potential by oppressed groups for both conservative and progressive effects as a consequence of these possibilities in the technoscape.

This issue of choice may have some bearing on the recent general decline in box office attendance in France. According to a January 1996 article in *The New York Times*, attendance for French-produced cinema has fallen in the last five years from 94 million people to 35 million. However, the culprit in this story is not any direct invasion by United States product. Admissions to films produced in the United States have remained consistent during these five years, at around 75 million.[12] Where has the audience gone? Perhaps to their VCRs.

2) The desire to extract surplus value from the heterogenity of identities in any nation-state has altered the selling process from a mass-market strategy to a target-market one.

The new technologies that cater to specialized choices were not innovated in a vacuum but created out of manufacturers' desire to exploit discretionary access to preferred materials. Attempts to analyze audiences existed in ad hoc form in the United States from the 1910s. In the 1920s, Paramount studios even hired social scientists to use psychological theory to advise how best to address consumers. By the late 1930s, George Gallup was trying to sell scientific polling to the major movie firms.

Every audience study, no matter how flawed, indicates distinctions in tastes in relation to demographic variables. As market research has become more complicated, demographics have given way to psychographics, lifestyles, taste cultures. An outstanding example of such research is the work of Bourdieu on correlations between education and consumption preferences.

As market research has tried to penetrate the human psyche and motivate it to consume, market research has also been interested in reaching most efficiently and effectively those individuals most able to afford to buy the product and most likely to do so. A major turn-around in programming strategies for network television in the United States occurred in the early 1970s when network executives began to sell specific audiences to advertisers, rather than just num-bers of people. Although recognized theoretically since the turn of the century, targeting women (who are thought to be the major pur-chasers for a household) has become increasingly significant for net-work prime-time programming in the United States.

Advertisers on television are not the only groups interested in target markets. So are individuals with particular messages such as religious and political groups, and cable channels give them an out-let for their addresses. Movie firms know that specific age groups are much more likely to go to movies, and that prime spenders of movie dollars are young men who are influential in determining the chances for a movie to become a blockbuster. This altered way to consider selling—"hyperflexible," "demassified"—is so deeply embedded in how deterritorialized capitalism is thinking about consumer behav-ior that Hollywood and United States media firms now think of tar-get groups first, and then seek "cross-over" effects: stars, movies, or recording artists that appeal to more than one category of consumer.

As a neo-marxist I would point out here that thinking of an audi-ence by terms such as "American" or "French"—terms which seem not particularly pertinent to most consumers as "self-identity labels"—is likely a losing procedure in the face of this enhanced pen-etration of personal identity-spaces by advanced capitalism. I never go to a movie because I am an American; I do go because I take plea-sure in the genre, or I'm part of the intelligentsia and colleagues will be talking about the film, and so on. Service and content affect me greatly in terms of the identities and pleasures to which I can be appealed as a consumer.

The use of co-productions in Europe to increase capital, spread risks, and permit access to each partner's nation-state market may have some competitive economic advantages. However, I also believe it would be a mistake for the co-production to employ a mass-market strategy such as soliciting some hypothetical "European" identity, particularly when, as I noted above, nation-state identities seem less relevant nowadays to individuals while other identities are surfacing as more significant on the mediascape and ideoscape. Another way to look at this is to say that what is now "French" is not a single national identity but instead a set of preferences knowable in other vocabularies of taste and address than in terminology constructed on the basis of a nation-state identity. This loss of "national" identity is, I am suggesting, to the advantage of deterritorialized, neo-Fordist capitalism, but as a neo-marxist (and like Jean Renoir), I am likewise not disappointed by its disappearance as a pertinent imaginary community.

3) The study of identity construction and reinforcement will be important for global culture studies and analysis of global cultural flows.

I have suggested consistently above that assessing how individuals think of themselves will be pertinent to analysis of global culture flows. In a study of the global syndication of television programming, Yahia Mahamdi discusses the development of "consumer convergences." He points out that the elite in New York City and in Paris may be closer to each other in taste preferences than are the elite and poor in either city.[13] A pertinent example of this is the success of the "art" movie in the United States after World War II. I have argued elsewhere that that type of film appealed to particular group of educated spectators who preferred cinema that they believed had serious messages and who were trained to mobilize aesthetic intertexts and literary behaviors to read the films as examples of modernism.[14] The "art" movie is a good example of a historically specific consumer convergence that reached a class of people across nation-state borders and which companies in the United States have been willing to exploit as long as it has been profitable. This educated class as a niche market has been profitable for awhile, but this market now seems dominated by other consumer convergences.

What "Hollywood-as-a-zone" produces is a set of products and services that appeals to a number of niche market psychographics that coincides well with the peoples of the core nations, the Euro–U.S. set of individuals who have the discretionary funds and desires to go to movies, rent video tapes, or watch television. Much space in trade papers in the United States is allocated to statistics observing these global trends in preferences. Among the observations that distributors and scholars have determined are the following:

1) Certain genres relying on visual materials sell better worldwide. These genres are action pictures, but also comedies that emphasize visual humor.[15] The language issue seems important, and I shall return to that below.

2) Stars connected to these preferred genres do particularly well as global culture stars: Sean Connery, Arnold Schwarzenegger, Eddie Murphy.[16] There are also the so-called "Mega-Stars" of the music scene: Michael Jackson and Madonna, figures that seem to reach either the right consumers or groups of right consumers.

3) In the world television trade, the high end of the products that are most profitable are series and serials, children's programs, and feature movies—in large part duplicating the characteristics for the global film market. For series and serials, ten of the fourteen firms that do the best business are English-language–based: from the United States, Britain, or Canada. However, Brazil's telenovelas do particularly well in the Latin American region and Spanish-speaking markets.[17] Indeed, the success of the telenovela brings me to my fourth observation.

4) The Hollywood zone may be dominant in many markets, but it is not dominant in every market and that dominance may have its limits because of the ideoscape.

What is bought of Hollywood is not everything, and this buying of Hollywood is not by everyone. Scholars have noted that "counter-flows" to the Hollywood zone and flow also exist. Or rather, particular consumer identities that circulate around language, ethnicity, and beliefs can sustain periphery and regional zones and flows.

To begin with, while Hollywood does well, it relies on core markets for most of its profitmaking. That is, periphery nations are not very economically significant to Hollywood. This may be because periphery nations are not worth exploiting because the profit potentials are too meager to justify the exploitation. Much as the Hollywood movie business abandoned its own rural market after the 1940s and television in the United States deserted the older, poorer, rural, and male[18] consumer after the 1970s, Hollywood has not, despite all sorts of opportunities, tried hard to penetrate poor regions. The United States exports to eighty nation-state markets but only fifteen of these account for 75 percent of its income. These fifteen (in descending percentages of business in 1991) are Japan (15%), Canada (11.3%), France (9.5%), West Germany (8.7%), United Kingdom/Ireland (8.6%), Spain (7.0%), Italy (6.3%), Australia (5.5%), Sweden (2.9%), Brazil (2.5%), Netherlands (1.7%), Switzerland (1.6%), Taiwan (1.6%), Mexico (1.6%), and Belgium (1.5%).[19] The opening of the East European nation-states are seen as the next best market to exploit, but not the poor nations of the Southern-hemisphere periphery. What concerns the United States about the peripheries is piracy through VCRs and satellites, but not direct access to the weak markets.[20]

This is not to say, however, that a small nation from the point of view of the United States has the same view of the impact of the trade flow. Even if the United States gains only 9.5 percent of its foreign film box office revenues from France, from France's position that accounts for 57 percent of its box office.[21] This is the so-called unidirectional feature to the flow. The flow goes: United States (as a core nation) to Europe (as a core) to the periphery. A hierarchy of penetration occurs in which Hollywood product can get into either region, but Europe or other groups of nations have difficulty moving against the tide. One reason scholars give for this is that English has become the global lingua franca (excuse the irony here), which helps maintain the dominance of the Hollywood zone.[22] The other major reason, developed above, is that Hollywood has learned to sell to the range of core consumers.

While this Hollywood flow is strong, it is not the only current operating. Other flows exist for reasons neo-marxists have indicated. Certain personally-significant identities attracted by particular ideoscapes are not reached (and even ignored) by the Hollywood zone and may, in fact, find other products of more service. Subcenters in the periphery nations are becoming culturally important metropoles in their own right. What even counts as a domestic preference is extremely more complicated as a consequence of the ethnoscape discussed above. Because of their colonialism, U.S.–European nations are no longer culturally homogenous, but themselves are a "rich diversity of cultures and identities."[23]

Thus, regional and domestic subcultural blocs and flows exist because of audience preferences in terms of language, genre or star familiarity, nostalgia for the homeland, or suitability for religious or moral reasons. When the regional markets of television products are explored, buyers often find themselves unable to afford United States product but also uninterested because of local preferences.[24] For instance, Mahamdi notes that "European audiences seem to prefer domestic [television] channels, then foreign channels in the same language, and lastly foreign language channels."[25] Egypt has a strong position in the Arab region through its popular stars and its dialect which now dominates media channels. The VCR-revolution permits consumers to exercise preferences based on language. Chinese in Singapore prefer Chinese-language video tapes of Hong Kong to the nation-state Bahasa Malaysia mass media.[26]

Subcenters also exist by exploiting genres underdeveloped by Hollywood. Examples beyond the Latin American telenovela (Brazil's TV Globo exports to 128 countries[27]) include Japanese animation, Chinese martial arts, and Indian romances. These products do replace Hollywood imports when they are shown competitively. Also competitive are local adaptations of Hollywood genres.[28]

Countercurrents exist not only in other cultural products but also in the way that local audiences understand imported materials. Research on the reception of the extremely popular United States television program *Dallas* indicates significant variations in interpreting that serial. The variations include viewing it as a good example of the *corruption* of American life by consumerism—

probably just about the reverse that a traditional marxist might theorize would be its reception if the homogenization thesis were to hold perfectly true.[29]

While potentially important as counterflows to the Hollywood zone, these localisms in production and reception should not be assumed to be pure or progressive resistances. As Annabelle Sreberny-Mohammadi reminds neo-marxists, much of what is local is still produced by capitalist firms with consumerist values. What is local may duplicate dominant ideological views, and is not necessarily sub-ideological or grassroots based or pure of contamination from dominant ideologies. The local product may well represent a class elite of the region that can afford its own niche-market preferences. As Mahamdi notes, buyers of television product for periphery nations are often torn between their sense of their cultural identities and a desire to participate in the "international business class." Hence, "class interests seem almost always to win over national interests, and in this way, the reproduction of the national and international system remains assured."[30] Localisms may also be politically reactionary. They may attempt to recuperate the history of an imaginary community, an ideoscape that may not promote democracy.[31]

Despite these countercurrents, the unidirectionality of the flow deserves recognition. I *might* want to argue that the Hollywood zone is actually becoming *dependent* on its exploitation of other core and periphery markets. Where once foreign revenues were considered frosting on the cake, now they are part of the initial calculations in anticipating income for making movie budgets. Statistics indicate that in 1984 33 percent of United States film revenues came from foreign film markets; that figure in 1989 was 43 percent. A recent prediction is that by the year 2000 the figure will be 80 percent— and every Hollywood producer and distributor knows this.[32] After about 1989 Hollywood ceased releasing its foreign prints some six months after the opening in the United States.[33] Now films may even debut abroad as deterritorialized capital takes advantage of global television to exploit publicity, advertising, and promotional tie-ins. World box-office figures in *Variety* track these performances. Recently the domestic "flop" *Waterworld* had recouped its production and distribution costs by doubling abroad its United States revenue figures. *Die Hard With a Vengeance,* which did great box office in the United States at $100 million in domestic gross, pulled in $254 million in foreign funds.[34]

I *might* want to argue this growing dependency of the United States on the markets it exploits *but* as a neo-marxist what I see happening is the deterritorialization of capital away from nation-states and into global financscapes. As I indicated above, to think of capital in traditional nation-state ways is to potentially misunderstand its current global characteristics. It is also to misunderstand that the nation no longer really matters to capitalism. It was a temporarily useful imaginary community, currently being discarded in favor of other imaginary communities more suitable for deeper penetration. It is a deterritorialized, hyperflexible capitalism, employed on a global scale.

This is a time of profound global relignments of geopolitical identities away from "capitalist" versus "communist" and for many diasporatic groups away from "nation-state" identities and movement toward (or reaffirming as more primary) identities based on language, ethnicity, home-region, religion, lifestyle, and class. These reimagined communities have implications for global marketing and consuming. As Jean Renoir pointed out some sixty years ago, those with whom we identify may cross former boundaries. As the film *Grand Illusion* continued, of course, de Boeldieu eventually chose his identity as French captain to sacrifice himself for his nation-state compatriots and as a gesture of alliance with the future proletariat rather than the dying aristocracy. In today's global market, capitalism seems less devoted to nation-states and more to taste cultures and niche marketing. Today a capitalist version of the dilemma might have de Boeldieu choosing the international popular cultures of the Euro–U.S. core instead of his national identity.

NOTES

Special thanks to Karin Wilkins for her comments on a draft of this paper.

1. Charles F. Altman, "Classical Narrative Revisited: *Grand Illusion*," in *1976 Film Studies Annual,* ed. Ben Lawton and Janet Staiger (West Lafayette, Ind.: Purdue University, 1976), 87–98.

2. Here and elsewhere I am referring to the seminal work by Benedict Anderson, *Imagined Communities: Reflections on the Origin and Spread of Nationalism* (London: Verso, 1983).

3. On "globalization" as thinking about the world as united, see Roland Robertson, "Mapping the Global Condition: Globalization as the Central Concept," in *Global Culture: Nationalism, Globalization and Modernity,* ed. Mike Featherstone (London: Sage, 1990), 15–30.

4. The following material is particularly indebted to Albert Bergesen, "Turning World-System Theory on Its Head," in *Global Culture,* ed. Featherstone, 67–81. Also see Janet Staiger and Douglas Gomery, "The History of World Cinema: Models for Economic Analysis," *Film Reader* 4 (1979): 35–44.

5. Bergesen, "Turning World-System Theory on Its Head," 67.

6. Bergesen, "Turning World-System Theory on Its Head," 74.

7. Kevin Robins, "Reimagined Communities? European Image Spaces, Beyond Fordism," *Cultural Studies* 3:2 (May 1989): 145–46.

8. Arjun Appardurai, "Disjuncture and Difference in the Global Cultural Economy," in *Global Culture,* ed. Featherstone, 296–301.

9. For an example directly on the issue of global culture, see Jonathan Friedman, "Being in the World: Globalization and Localization" [1990], in *Global Culture,* ed. Featherstone, 310–28.

10. It is important to recognize that theories are produced by history. It may well be that neo-marxist theory is a response to a particular historical moment as much as a better theory than traditional marxism. That is, traditional marxist explains the pre-1980s world; neo-marxist explains pre-1980s and the present.

11. This occurs for some people for their afternoon soap operas. It also has occurred for certain episodes of a program, such as the "Who Shot J. R." episode of *Dallas.* Finally, during the history of prime-time television, several shows have had ratings sufficiently in excess of other competing programs to suggest a behavior other than "least objectionable programming" behavior.

12. Alan Riding, "Sacré Bleu! French Film à la Hollywood," *New York Times* January 8, 1996, C1.

13. Yahia Mahamdi, Television, Globalization, and Cultural Hegemony: The Evolution and Structure of International Television. Unpublished PhD dissertation, University of Texas at Austin, 1992, 162.

14. See Janet Staiger, *Interpreting Films: Studies in the Historical Reception of American Cinema* (Princeton, N.J.: Princeton University Press), 178–95.

15. "The Year in Review," *1991 International Motion Picture Almanac* (New York, N.Y.: Quigley Publishing, 1991), 19A–20A.

16. Ibid.

17. Mahamdi, Television, Globalization, and Cultural Hegemony, 234.

18. Except for Sunday sports shows.

19. "The Year in Review," 19A. Also see "The Entertainment Industry," *The Economist* December 23, 1989, 16, which substantiates this ranking.

20. Annabelle Sreberny-Mohammadi, "The Global and the Local in International Communications," in *Mass Media and Society,* ed. James Curran and Michael Gurevitch (London: Edward Arnold, 1991), 127–28.

21. Figures from 1991 *Variety* cited in Mahamdi, Television, Globalization, and Cultural Hegemony, 187. Also see p. 133 on the percentage of National Origin of Television Programming in fifteen European countries where France's domestic production accounts for 78% of its programming; the other 22% comes entirely from the United States.

22. Mahamdi, Television, Globalization, and Cultural Hegemony, 279–80.

23. Robins, "Reimagined Communities?" 161.

24. Ibid., 243.

25. Mahamdi, Television, Globalization, and Cultural Hegemony, 132.

26. Michael Tracey, "Popular Culture and the Economics of Global Television," *Intermedia* 16:2 (March 1988): 10–14.

27. Sreberny-Mohammadi, "The Global and the Local," 119–122.

28. Connie McNeely and Yasemin Muhoglu Soysal, "International Flows of Television Programming: A Revisionist Research Orientation," *Public Culture* 2:1 (Fall 1989): 136–45.

29. Ien Ang, *Watching Dallas: Soap Opera and the Melodramatic Imagination* [1982] (London: Methuen, 1985), trans. Della Couling. For another case study, see Jostein Gripsrud, *The Dynasty Years: Hollywood Television and Critical Media Studies* (London: Routledge, 1995). An extended critique of the homogenization thesis from a Latin American perspective is in Jesus Martin-Barbero, *Communication, Culture and Hegemony* (London: Sage Publications, 1993). Also see McNeely and Soysal, "International Flows of Television Programming," 137, and Tracey, "Popular Culture and the Economics of Global Television," 9–10.

30. Mahamdi, Television, Globalization, and Cultural Hegemony, 35.

31. Robins, "Reimagined Communities?" p. 153. Also see Hamid Naficy, "The Poetics and Practice of Iranian Nostalgia in Exile," *Diaspora* 1:3 (1991): 289–91.

32. "The Year in Review," 19A; "Week in Review," *The Hollywood Reporter* January 16, 1996. For actual billions of dollars, see Jack Egan, "Hollywood's numbers game," *U.S. News & World Report* 108:13 (April 2, 1990). Specifically, 1989 Hollywood domestic box-office revenues were $22 billion, foreign box office was $15.5 billion, and domestic and foreign video and television releases accounted for an additional $7.5 billion plus.

33. "The Year in Review," 20A.

34. "World B.O. Clicks," *Variety* December 4–10, 1995.

Selected Bibliography

This list is, obviously, highly selective. The field is vast. References are restricted to works in English, with preference given to works that exemplify a wide variety of different approaches to the various questions and problems of cinema and nation. It is often difficult to place a text in one category; for example, the Mead and Métraux collection on French culture includes a major piece by Métraux on film analysis. Multiple works by the same author(s) are included only sparingly. Most of these authors have published more than one work in their areas, but the wide availability of electronic data bases via the internet makes searching for such other works fairly easy. What is not as easy to get, and what this bibliography attempts to provide, is some sense of the shape of the field, and the various possible approaches to its multiple, related problems and questions.

Nationalism and "National Character"

Altman, Rick. "What can genres teach us about nations?" In Altman, *Film/Genre* (London: British Film Institute, 1999), 195–206.

Anderson, Benedict. *Imagined Communities: Reflections on the Origin and Spread of Nationalism*, rev.ed. (London & New York: Verso, 1991).

Bellah, Robert N., Richard Madsen, William M. Sullivan, Ann Swindler, and Steven M. Tipton. *Habits of the Heart: Individualism and Commitment in American Life* (Berkeley & Los Angeles: University of California Press, 1985).

Bhabha, Homi, ed. *Nation and Narration* (London & New York: Routledge, 1990).

Breuilly, John. *Nationalism and the State* (Chicago: University of Chicago Press, 1994).

Hobsbawm, Eric. *Nations and Nationalism since 1788*, 2d ed. (Cambridge: Cambridge University Press, 1993).

Hobsbawm, Eric and Terence Ranger, eds. *The Invention of Tradition* (Cambridge: Cambridge University Press, 1983).

Métraux, Rhoda, and Margaret Mead (eds). *Themes in French Culture: Preface to a Study of French Community* (Stanford: Stanford University Press [Hoover Institute], 1954).

Schudson, Michael. "Culture and the Integration of National Societies." In *The Sociology of Culture*, ed. Diane Crane (Oxford: Blackwell, 1994), 21–43.

Smith, Anthony D. *Nationalism and Modernism: A Critical Survey of Recent Theories of Nations and Nationalism* (London and New York: Routledge, 1998).

General and Theoretical Works on Cinema and Nation

Hall, Stuart. "Cultural Identity and Cinematic Representation," *Framework* 36 (1989): 68–81.
Hayward, Susan. "Defining the 'National' of a Country's Cinematographic Production." In *French National Cinema* (London: Routledge, 1993), 1–17.
Hjort, Mette and Scott MacKenzie (eds.). *Cinema and Nation* (London and New York: Routledge, 2000).
Huaco, George A. *The Sociology of Film Art* (New York and London: Basic Books, 1965).
Jameson, Fredric. *The Geopolitical Aesthetic: Cinema and Space in the World* (Bloomington: Indiana University Press, 1992).
Nowell-Smith, Geoffrey and Steven Ricci, eds. *Hollywood & Europe: Economics, Culture, National Identity 1945–1995* (London: British Film Institute, 1998).
Pines, Jim and Paul Willemen, eds. *Questions of Third Cinema* (London: British Film Institute, 1989).
Shohat, Ella and Robert Stam. *Unthinking Eurocentrism: Multiculturalism and the Media* (London and New York: Routledge, 1994).
Walsh, Michael. "National Cinema, National Imaginary," *Film History* 8:1 (1996): 5–17.
Willemen, Paul. *Looks and Frictions: Essays in Cultural Studies and Film Theory* (Bloomington: Indiana University Press, 1994).

National Cinemas

Bateson, Gregory. "An Analysis of the Nazi Film *Hitlerjunge Quex*." In *The Study of Culture at a Distance*, ed. Margaret Mead and Rhoda Métraux (Chicago and London: University of Chicago Press, 1953), 302–14.
Bordwell, David. *Planet Hong Kong: Popular Cinema and the Art of Entertainment* (Cambridge, Mass. and London: Harvard University Press, 2000).
Burch, Noël. *To The Distant Observer: Form and Meaning in the Japanese Cinema* (Berkeley and Los Angeles: University of California Press, 1979).
Buss, Robin. *The French Through Their Films* (New York: Ungar, 1988).
Burgoyne, Robert. *Film Nation: Hollywood Looks at U.S. History* (Minneapolis: University of Minnesota Press, 1997).
Dalle Vacche, Angela. *The Body In the Mirror: Shapes of History in Italian Cinema* (Princeton: Princeton University Press, 1992).
Davis, Darrell William. *Picturing Japaneseness: Monumental Style, National Identity, Japanese Film* (New York: Columbia University Press, 1995).
Doherty, Thomas. *Projections of War: Hollywood, American Culture, and World War II* (New York: Columbia University Press, 1993).
Kenez, Peter. *Cinema and Soviet Society, 1917–1953* (Cambridge and New York: Cambridge University Press, 1992).

Kracauer, Siegfried. *From Caligari to Hitler: A Psychological History of the German Film* (Princeton, N.J.: Princeton University Press, 1947).

Mayer, J. P. *British Cinemas and Their Audiences: Sociological Studies* (London: Dobson, 1948).

Nandy, Ashis. *The Secret Politics of Our Desires: Nation, Bulture and Gender in Popular Indian Cinema* (New York: St. Martin's, 1998).

Petrie, Duncan. *Creativity and Constraint in the British Film Industry* (Basingstoke: Macmillan, 1991).

Rentschler, Eric. *The Ministry of Illusion: Nazi Cinema and its Afterlife* (Cambridge, Mass.: Harvard University Press, 1996).

Turner, Graeme. *Making It National: Nationalism and Australian Popular Culture* (Sydney: Allen & Unwin, 1994).

Vasey, Ruth. *The World According to Hollywood 1918–1939* (Madison: University of Wisconsin Press, 1997).

Von Papen, Manuela. "Keeping the Home Fires Burning?—Women and the German Homefront Film 1940–1943," *Film History* 8:1 (1996): 44–63.

Wolfenstein, Martha and Nathan Leites. *Movies: A Psychological Study* 2d (paper) ed. (New York: Atheneum, 1970).

Wood, Michael. *America in the Movies, or "Santa Maria, It Had Slipped My Mind"* (New York: Basic Books, 1975).

International Relations

Armes, Roy. *Third World Film Making and the West* (Berkeley and Los Angeles: University of California Press, 1987).

Bernstein, Matthew and Gaylyn Studlar, eds. *Visions of the East: Orientalism in Film* (New Brunswick: Rutgers University Press, 1997).

Diawara, Manthia. *African Cinema: Politics and Culture* (Bloomington: Indiana University Press, 1992).

Durham, Carolyn. *Double Takes: Culture and Gender in French Films and Their American Remakes* (Hanover, Conn.: University Press of America, 1998).

Ehrlich, Evelyn. *Cinema of Paradox: French Filmmaking Under the German Occupation* (New York: Columbia University Press, 1985).

Fu, Poshek. "The Ambiguity of Entertainment: Chinese Cinema in Japanese-Occupied Shanghai, 1941 to 1945," *Cinema Journal* 37:1 (Fall 1997): 66–84.

Higashi, Sumiko. "Melodrama, Realism, and Race: World War II Newsreels and Propaganda Film." *Cinema Journal* 37, 3 (Spring 1998): 38–61.

Hirano, Kyoko. *Mr. Smith Goes to Tokyo: Japanese Cinema under the American Occupation, 1945–1952* (Washington, D.C.: Smithsonian Institution Press, 1992).

Mukherjee, Bharati. "Love Me or Leave Me." In *The Movie That Changed My Life*, ed. David Rosenberg (New York: Viking Penguin, 1991).

Mulvey, Laura. "Americanitis: European Intellectuals and Hollywood Melodrama." In Mulvey, *Fetishism and Curiosity* (Bloomington: Indiana University Press, 1996).

Nornes, Abé Mark. "For an Abusive Subtitling," *Film Quarterly* 52:3 (Spring 1999): 17–34.

———. "Paul Rotha and the Politics of Translation," *Cinema Journal* 38:3 (Spring 1999): 91–108.

Slavin, David. "French Cinema's Other First Wave: Political and Racial Economies of Cinéma colonial, 1918 to 1934," *Cinema Journal* 37:1 (Fall 1997): 23–46.

Thompson, Kristin. "National or International Films? The European Debate during the 1920s," *Film History* 8:3 (1996): 281–96.

———. *Exporting Entertainment: America in the World Film Market 1907–34* (London: British Film Institute, 1985).

Tsivian, Yuri. "The Wise and Wicked Game: Re-editing and Soviet Film Culture of the 1920s," *Film History* 8:1 (1996): 327–43.

Ulff-Moller, Jens. The "Film Wars" Between France and the United States: Film-Trade Diplomacy and the Emergence of the Film Quota System in France, 1920–1939. Ph.D. dissertation, Brandeis University, 1998.

Willemen, Paul. "The Making of an African Cinema," *Transition* 58 (1992): 138–50.

Williams, Alan. "The Raven and the Nanny: Politics and Narrative Structure in Two International Remakes." In *Dead Ringers: The Remake in Theory and Practice*, ed. Jennifer Forrest (Albany and New York: SUNY University Press, 2001).

Global Cinema and World Culture

Appardurai, Arjun. *Modernity at Large: Cultural Dimensions of Globalization* (Minneapolis: University of Minnesota Press, 1996).

Danan, Martine. "From a 'Prenational' to a 'Postnational' French Cinema," *Film History* 8:1 (1996): 72–84.

Jameson, Fredric and Masao Miyoshi, eds. *The Cultures of Globalization* (Durham: Duke University Press, 1998).

Morley, David and Kevin Robins. *Spaces of Identity: Global Media, Electronic Landscapes and Cultural Boundaries* (New York and London: Routledge, 1995).

Mattelart, Armand. *Transnationals and the Third World: The Struggle for Culture* (S. Hadley, Mass.: Bergin & Garvey, 1983).

Nichols, Bill. "Global Image Consumption in the Age of Late Capitalism," *East-West Film Journal* 8:1 (1994): 68–85.

Schiller, Herbert I. "Transnational Media: Creating Consumers Worldwide," *Journal of International Affairs* 47:3 (1993): 47–58.

Contributors

NOËL BURCH is Professor of Cinema History at the University of Lille and the author of *Theory of Film Practice, To A Distant Observer,* and other books. He has also made films such as *Correction, Please, or How We Got Into Movies,* and *What Do These Old Films Mean?*

STEPHEN CROFTS teaches at the University of Auckland. He has published extensively in film history, theory, and television studies, including monographs on Australian cinema, Godard, and Australian television.

ANDREW HIGSON is Senior Lecturer in Film Studies at the University of East Anglia. He is the author of *Waving the Flag: Constructing a National Cinema in Britain* and the coeditor of *"Film Europe" and "Film America: Cinema, Commerce and Cultural Excange 1920–1939.*

ANA M. LÓPEZ is an Associate Professor of communication at Tulane University. She has published widely on Latin American film and media and is currently writing a book on Latin American Film Genres.

TOM O'REGAN teaches Communication Studies at Murdoch University, Western Australia. He is the author of *Australian Television Culture* and is co-editor of *Australian Screen* and *An Australian Film Reader.*

ERIC RENTSCHLER is Chair and Professor of German at Harvard University and the author of *The Ministry of Illusion: Nazi Cinema and its Afterlife,* and *West German Cinema in the Course of Time.*

JONATHAN ROSENBAUM is lead film critic for the *Chicago Reader* and the author of *Moving Places: A Life in the Movies, Movies as Politics,* as well as other books, articles, reviews, and edited anthologies.

GENEVIÈVE SELLIER teaches at the University of Paris and at the Ecole Supérieure d'Arts Appliqués Duperré and is the author of *Jean Grémillon: Le Cinéma est à vous* and *Les Enfants du paradis.*

JANET STAIGER is the William P. Hobby Centennial Professor in Communication at the University of Texas at Austin. Her most recent books are *Perverse Spectators: The Practices of Film Reception* and *Blockbuster TV: Must-See Sitcoms in the Network Era.*

STEPHEN TEO is a writer, critic, and former film programmer currently teaching cinema studies at the Royal Melbourne Institute of Technology. He is the author of *Hong Kong Cinema: The Extra Dimension.*

ALAN WILLIAMS is Professor of French and Cinema Studies at Rutgers University and the author of *Max Ophuls and the Cinema of Desire* and *Republic of Images: A History of French Filmmaking.*

MARTHA WOLFENSTEIN was a close collaborator of Margaret Mead and the author (with Nathan Leites) of *Movies: A Psychological Study* and other works in the anthropological analysis of film and culture.

Index

Film and Nationalism

Rutgers Depth of Field Series

Charles Affron, Mirella Jona Affron, Robert Lyons, Series Editors

Richard Abel, ed., *Silent Film*

John Belton, ed., *Movies and Mass Culture*

Matthew Bernstein, ed., *Controlling Hollywood: Censorship and Regulation in the Studio Era*

John Thornton Caldwell, ed., *Electronic Media and Technoculture*

Peter X Feng, ed., *Screening Asian Americans*

Marcia Landy, ed., *The Historical Film: History and Memory in Media*

Peter Lehman, ed., *Defining Cinema*

James Naremore, ed., *Film Adaptation*

Stephen Prince, ed., *Screening Violence*

Valerie Smith, ed., *Representing Blackness: Issues in Film and Video*

Janet Staiger, ed., *The Studio System*

Alan Williams, ed., *Film and Nationalism*

Linda Willams, ed., *Viewing Positions: Ways of Seeing Film*

Barbie Zelizer, ed., *Visual Culture and the Holocaust*